New Directions in Irish and Irish American Literature

Contemporary Irish Republican Prison Writing: Writing and Resistance
By Lachlan Whalen

Contemporary Irish Republican Prison Writing

Writing and Resistance

Lachlan Whalen

palgrave
macmillan

CONTEMPORARY IRISH REPUBLICAN PRISON WRITING

First published in 2007 by
PALGRAVE MACMILLAN™
175 Fifth Avenue, New York, N.Y. 10010 and
Houndmills, Basingstoke, Hampshire, England RG21 6XS
Companies and representatives throughout the world.

PALGRAVE MACMILLAN is the global academic imprint of the Palgrave Macmillan division of St. Martin's Press, LLC and of Palgrave Macmillan Ltd. Macmillan® is a registered trademark in the United States, United Kingdom and other countries. Palgrave is a registered trademark in the European Union and other countries.

ISBN-13: 978–1–4039–8193–6
ISBN-10: 1–4039–8193–0

Library of Congress Cataloging-in-Publication Data

Contemporary Irish Republican prison writing : writing and resistance / by Lachlan Whalen.
p. cm. — (New directions in Irish and Irish American literature)
Includes bibliographical references.
ISBN 1–4039–8193–0
1. Political prisoners' writings, Irish. 2. Republicanism—Northern Ireland—History–20th century. 3. Political prisoners—Northern Ireland—History—20th century. I. Whalen, Lachlan, 1969–

DA990.U46C674 2007
820.9'206927—dc22 2007010216

A catalogue record for this book is available from the British Library.

Design by Newgen Imaging Systems (P) Ltd., Chennai, India.

First edition: December 2007

10 9 8 7 6 5 4 3 2 1

Printed in the United States of America.

An té nach bhfuil láidir, ní foláir dhó bheith glic.
Seanfhocal

Contents

Acknowledgments

This book would not have been possible without the help of many individuals and organizations. First and foremost, *go raibh míle maith agaibh* to all of the Republican ex-POWs who shared their stories and writings with me and who assisted in innumerable ways. This is especially true of Dr. Laurence McKeown, who provided invaluable aid throughout. For allowing me to include three of her poems and for her other insights into Armagh Gaol, Roseleen Walsh was more generous than I can say. I am extremely grateful to Martin Gough for the use of his art for the book cover, an image drawn while incarcerated in the H Blocks. Rosena Brown, Brian Campbell, Síle Darragh, Eileen Hillen, Gerry Kelly, Chrissy McAuley, and several poets who will remain anonymous also contributed much by sharing their time, experiences, and texts. As author, interviewee, and secretary of the Bobby Sands Trust, Danny Morrison provided crucial assistance. I owe a deep debt of gratitude to everyone at Coiste na n-Iarchimí for their work in coordinating interviews, especially Mike Ritchie. Thanks also to Dominic Adams and Irene Sherry for helping me get permissions for some of the women's writing included in this book. Whatever errors or mischaracterizations that may be contained in this book are mine alone, not any of the people mentioned above.

Others in Ireland also aided this project in important ways as well. Thanks to those in the permissions department at Mercier Press and Brandon Books. The staff at the Northern Ireland Political Collection of Linenhall Library were always helpful, and I am particularly thankful to Alastair Gordon and Yvonne Murphy for going above and beyond the call of duty on a number of occasions. A very belated thanks to the Gunning family for putting up with me for a summer in the earliest stages of this project, and to E. Gillespie and family for their hospitality. The McCaul family also took in this foundling on a number of occasions, for which I remain indebted. Art Hughes's patience with a struggling learner of Irish many years ago earns him a place in these acknowledgments, as have Pat Beag and Noel Lenaghan for the seisiúns. Buzz Ó Briain deserved a better pupil on the uilleann pipes, but he could not find one more thankful.

Archival research was assisted by funding from a West Virginia Humanities Council Fellowship. The Marshall University Research

Committee provided additional resources through Summer Research Awards, as did the Marshall University College of Liberal Arts Faculty Development Award and the Marshall University Graduate School Faculty Development Award. Dr. Christina Murphy provided much appreciated funding at critical points in the manuscript's composition.

I am blessed with a wonderful and supportive family both biological and adopted, who helped me in more ways than I can count, including by having patience with my excesses of silence: Frank and June Vesterman, Bill, Linda, and Kate Hunter, and E.J. Whelan (who despite it all I still must number in this song). Amongst the North Dakota/ Minnesota *tiyospaye,* Wm. Ambrose and Aileen Anna Littleghost, Ron and Loretta Leith, Anne Graham and family, and everyone at Red Lake (including Chris Leith and family, the Donnell family, and the Johnson family), all taught me more things of real importance than I ever learned in graduate school: *wopila tanka mitakuyapi/ migwitch.* Rex Bluestone, Blaise Mybeck, and especially Dave Villarreal contributed to my survival with music and friendship while studying and writing on the prairie. Michael Beard, Michael Berthold, Ursula Hovet, and Hugh Ormsby-Lennon provided much-appreciated mentoring and assistance in my years in graduate school.

In West Virginia, thanks to Marshall University English Department chair David Hatfield who scheduled a heavy teaching load as best as possible to accommodate my research. Kellie Bean, Mary Moore, Katharine Rodier, Sherri Smith, and John Young all offered valuable critical insights on what eventually would become the second chapter in this book. Much gratitude to Jason, Amber, and all the folks at Java Joint for offering a place of refuge and creating a center of culture that Huntington cannot do without. Janet Badia would deserve praise simply for putting up with me throughout the process of composition but did much more, something I always recognized and for which I continue to be appreciative even if I have failed to express it adequately—in particular I am thankful for her periodic reminders that there is more to life than the writing of books. And finally, I am grateful to Emma and MK for just being bad every day of their lives.

Permissions

I am very grateful to acknowledge permission to reprint copyright material from the following:

The Bobby Sands Trust (in addition to the overlapping permissions for work by Bobby Sands published by Mercier Press): unpublished poetry by Bobby Sands quoted in Denis O'Hearn, *Nothing but an Unfinished Song* (New York: Nation, 2006) 333–334; pamphlet version of the hunger strike diary *The Diary of Bobby Sands* (Dublin: Sinn Féin Publicity Department, June 1981) 19, 42; the poem "An Mhaidin" from *Faoi Ghlas ag Gaill* (Belfast: Gaeil Bheal Feirste in Eadan H-Bloc agus Ard Mhacha, 1981); excerpts from Danny Morrison's introduction to *Prison Poems* (Dublin: Sinn Féin Publicity Department, October 1981) 10; Editorial commentary introducing "The Writings of Bobby Sands" *An Phoblacht/Republican News* 21 March 1981: 6–7; 2 passages from Gerry Adams's introduction to the first version of the pamphlet *The Writings of Bobby Sands* (Belfast?: Sinn Féin, March? 1981) no pagination; Gerry Adams's introduction to the pamphlet *The Writings of Bobby Sands* (Dublin: Sinn Féin POW Department, April 1981) 5–6; portion of "The Battle for Survival" 83.

Brandon Books: From Gerry Adams's *Cage Eleven* (Dingle: Brandon, 1990): passage from "Only Joking,"141; passage from "Frank Stagg,"117, 119–120, 124; passage from "An Árd [*sic*] Fheis," 76; two passages from "Christians for Freedom," 100, 102; passage from "Screws" 27; two passages from "The Fire" 37, 46.

Martin Gough for use of his artwork as the cover illustration.

Laurence McKeown, permissions to photograph and use text of *teachtaireachtaí*.

Mercier Press: From *Skylark Sing Your Lonely Song* (Cork and Dublin: Mercier, 1982): eight lines from "Trilogy," 57–58; excerpts from "I Once Had a Life," *Skylark Sing Your Lonely Song* 19–20; the final three lines from "Christmas Eve," 99; four passages from "The Harvest Britain Has Sown," 26–27; three lines from "Teach Your Children," 113; brief passage from "A Thought in the Night," 23; three brief passages from "The Lark and the Freedom Fighter," 15;

the final three paragraphs of the hunger strike diary, 172; the editor's translation of these three paragraphs, 172–173; two sentences from the second diary entry, 154; A portion of one sentence from the first entry of the hunger strike diary, 153; One word from Sands's final diary entry and its English translation, 171 & 172; two lines from "Nuair a thigeann ar [*sic*] lá," 167–8.

Mercier Press: From *One Day in My Life* (Cork and Dublin: Mercier, 1983): the first paragraph in its entirety, 25; the final 187 words, 117–118.

New Hibernia Review/ Iris Éireannach Nua for the reprint of portions of my article "'Our Barbed Wire Ivory Tower': The Prison Writings of Gerry Adams," published in New Hibernia Review/ Iris Éireannach Nua 10.2 (Summer 2006) 123–139.

Nua: Studies in Contemporary Irish Writing "'You Look Like Jesus Christ': The Troubled Cinematic Iconography of Irish Republican Prisoners," forthcoming in *Nua* 6.2 (Spring 2007).

An Phoblacht/Republican News: From "Inside Story," *Republican News* 16 August 1975: 6; excerpts from "Out There on the Motorway," *Republican News* 23 August 1975: 7; excerpts from "Screws," *Republican News* 10 April 1976: 7–8; passage from Gerry Adams's review of *Prison Poems*: "Real poetry," *An Phoblacht/Republican News* 17 December 1981: 9; editorial commentary introducing "The Writings of Bobby Sands," *An Phoblacht/Republican News* 21 March 1981: 6–7.

Irene Sherry/ Sinn Féin's Women's Department: the full text of "Alone" and "From Eve," in *Voices Against Oppression*, (Dublin: Sinn Féin's Women's Department, 1991) 5, 11.

Roseleen Walsh: the full text of "To Aine," "Imprisoned Lovers," and "To My Silent Church," in *Aiming Higher* (Belfast: Glandore, 1999) 32, 33, 37.

Teachtaireacht by Laurence McKeown on toilet paper, 1980 (a letter to the *Irish Press*). Photo by L. Whalen.

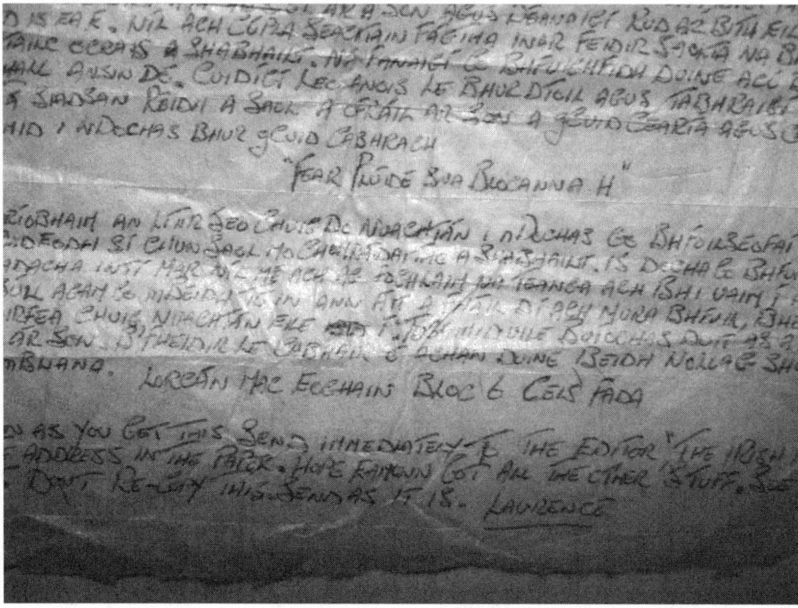

"FEAR PLÚIDE SNA BLOCANNA H"

LORCÁN MAC EOGHAIN BLOC 6 CEIS FADA

...N AS YOU GET THIS SEND IMMEDIATELY TO THE EDITOR "THE IRISH ...
...E ADDRESS IN THE PAPER. HOPE EAMONN GOT ALL THE OTHER STUFF. ...
... DON'T RE-COPY THIS SEND AS IT IS. LAURENCE

Close-up of *teachtaireacht* (a letter to the *Irish Press*). McKeown signs it in three different ways: *"Fear Plúide Sna Blocanna H"* (A Blanket Man in the H Blocks); *"Lorcán Mac Eoghain Bloc 6 Ceis Fada"* (Laurence McKeown Block 6 Long Kesh); and "Laurence." Photo by L. Whalen.

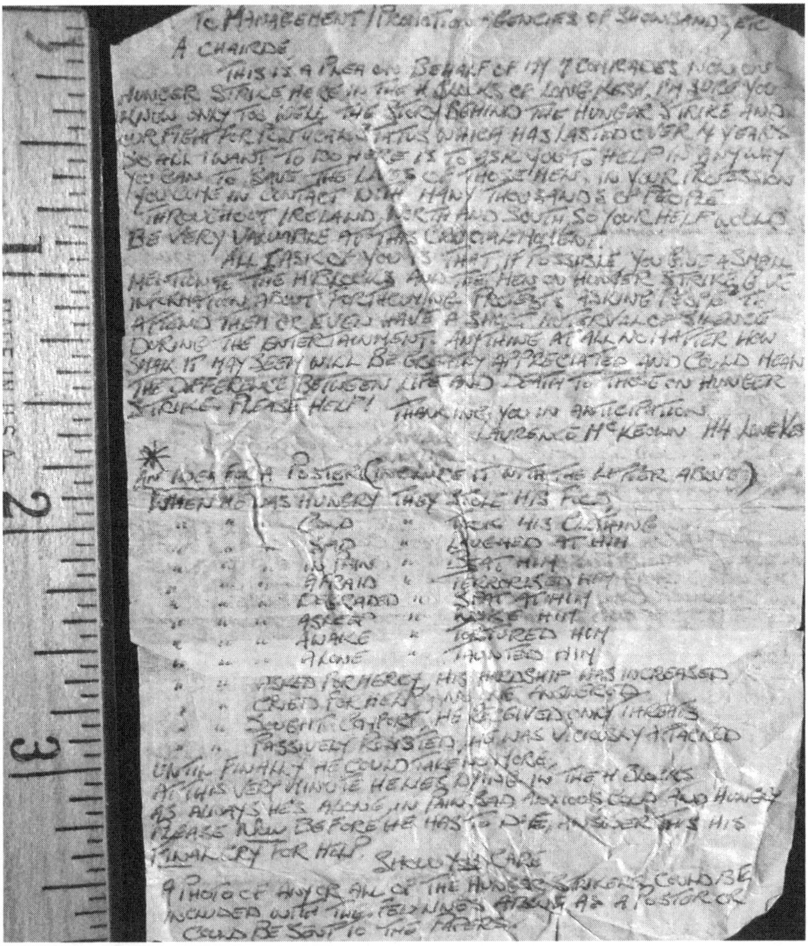

TO MANAGEMENT / PROMOTION AGENCIES OF SHOWBANDS, ETC
A CHAIRDE,
THIS IS A PLEA ON BEHALF OF MY 7 COMRADES NOW ON HUNGER STRIKE HERE IN THE H BLOCKS OF LONG KESH. I'M SURE YOU KNOW ONLY TOO WELL THE STORY BEHIND THE HUNGER STRIKE AND OUR FIGHT FOR POLITICAL STATUS WHICH HAS LASTED OVER 4 YEARS. SO ALL I WANT TO DO HERE IS TO ASK YOU TO HELP IN ANY WAY YOU CAN TO SAVE THE LIVES OF THOSE MEN. IN YOUR PROFESSION YOU COME IN CONTACT WITH MANY THOUSANDS OF PEOPLE THROUGHOUT IRELAND, NORTH AND SOUTH, SO YOUR HELP WOULD BE VERY VALUABLE AT THIS CRUCIAL MOMENT.
ALL I ASK OF YOU IS THAT, IF POSSIBLE, YOU GIVE A SMALL MENTION TO THE H BLOCKS AND THE MEN ON HUNGER STRIKE, GIVE INFORMATION ABOUT FORTHCOMING PROTESTS ASKING PEOPLE TO ATTEND THEM OR EVEN HAVE A SHORT INTERVAL OF SILENCE DURING THE ENTERTAINMENT. ANYTHING AT ALL NO MATTER HOW SMALL IT MAY SEEM WILL BE GREATLY APPRECIATED AND COULD MEAN THE DIFFERENCE BETWEEN LIFE AND DEATH TO THOSE ON HUNGER STRIKE. PLEASE HELP!
THANKING YOU IN ANTICIPATION
LAURENCE McKEOWN H4 LONG KESH

* AN IDEA FOR A POSTER (ENCLOSE IT WITH THE LETTER ABOVE)
WHEN HE WAS HUNGRY THEY STOLE HIS FOOD
" " " COLD " TOOK HIS CLOTHING
" " " SAD " LAUGHED AT HIM
" " " IN PAIN " BEAT HIM
" " " AFRAID " TERRORISED HIM
" " " DEGRADED " SPAT AT HIM
" " " ASLEEP " WOKE HIM
" " " AWAKE " TORTURED HIM
" " " ALONE " TAUNTED HIM
" " ASKED FOR MERCY, HIS HARDSHIP WAS INCREASED
" " CRIED FOR HELP, NO ONE ANSWERED
" " SOUGHT COMFORT, HE RECEIVED ONLY THREATS
" " PASSIVELY RESISTED, HE WAS VICIOUSLY ATTACKED
UNTIL FINALLY HE COULD TAKE NO MORE.
AT THIS VERY MINUTE HE LIES DYING IN THE H BLOCKS
AS ALWAYS HE'S ALONE, IN PAIN, SAD, ANXIOUS, COLD AND HUNGRY
PLEASE NOW BEFORE HE HAS TO DIE, ANSWER THIS HIS FINAL CRY FOR HELP. SHOW YOU CARE
A PHOTO OF ANY OR ALL OF THE HUNGER STRIKERS COULD BE INCLUDED WITH THE [illegible] AS A POSTER OR COULD BE SENT TO THE PAPERS.

Teachtaireacht on cigarette paper by Laurence McKeown, 1980. Photo by L. Whalen.

Chapter One

Introduction: Taoibh Amuigh agus Faoi Ghlas: *The Counter-aesthetics of Republican Prison Writing*

Gerry Adams's short story "The Fire" begins with several Long Kesh internees discussing their memories of the conflagration that destroyed a fair portion of the prison compound. When two characters disagree about some of the particulars, another Republican POW named Cedric announces that he possesses a text whose contents might settle the argument. That text is a diary he kept in the days prior to the fire, one he continued writing even during the subsequent battles between the Security Forces and the prisoners. Cedric was forced to conceal his clandestine account when the British Army finally overran the POWs; though he secretly passed a copy of his diary to his comrades on the outside, he kept the original inside the Cages with him. If his fellow POWs would like, he offers, he will get it for them. Cedric's comrades enthusiastically request that he do so; however, their excitement at the prospect of viewing such a text turns to horror when the diary is retrieved from its hiding place. Adams describes the scene that unfolds:

> [Cedric] returned a few minutes later with a small packet wrapped in polythene. He unfolded his bundle carefully and passed a handful of soiled and creased pages to Egbert.
>
> "They're stinking!" Egbert protested, "I thought you said it was a diary!"
>
> "I hid them in a sewer. That's why I still have them. They were too smelly to send out. And they *are* a diary..."[1] (emphasis mine)

Curiosity proves stronger than the scent, and the POWs pore over the account of nine violent days in the life inside the Long Kesh prison compound, written by one of its residents. When the reading of the diary is complete, the prisoners comment on the text:

> "It's a pity it doesn't include the solidarity actions by the women in Armagh, or the lads in the Crum who got beaten up, or the fire in

> Magilligan, but of course you wouldn't have known that," Egbert mused.
>
> "It's a pity it's stinking," Your Man said. "The Public Records Office or the National Library Archives would never accept it in that condition..."[2]

Your Man's last comments reveal precisely the tensions one encounters when attempting to reconcile Republican prison writing with the traditional literary canon: jail literature often is excluded from public view in archives, anthologies, or university curricula precisely because it is frequently untidy. The soiling is literal in the case of Cedric's diary and, later, the *teachtaireachtaí* (communiqués) that had to be smuggled out of H Block cells concealed in the body orifices of POWs; moreover, in the eyes of many critics—particularly the so-called revisionists within Irish studies—this uncleanness often extends metaphorically to the shape and content of such writings. To these theorists, the writings themselves are tainted not only because of perceived formal weaknesses, but also simply because they are authored by Republicans. Another hobby-horse among earlier conceptions of literature is evoked in Egbert's recognition in the passage above of the isolation that Long Kesh seeks to impose on the POWs. This moment asks us to reconsider the claim that "Literature" somehow has no connection to the space or historical moment in which it was composed, and in a related fashion that "great writings" are not judged to be "great" by culturally and historically specific aesthetics, but rather by some apolitical, universal standard.

As Chinua Achebe and others contend, such claims ignore the manner in which this supposedly self-evident, "universal" standard has been historically used to reify specifically Western—especially Anglo-American—literary tastes, often in the service of a wider colonial appropriation of land and culture. As critic and Republican ex-prisoner Pat Magee wittily puns, mainstream literature often proves to be the "paraliterary wing" of the status quo, whether the writings in question are trashy thrillers or "the classics."[3] The insidiousness of conservative literary aesthetics evinces itself in the fact that at times the prisoners themselves have so internalized elitist perceptions of literary production and consumption that they hesitate to conceive of themselves as authors. The reactions of figures such as Your Man to the secret diary in Adams's story cited above are intriguing because they not only illuminate some of the complexities of composition in a prison but they also reveal the POWs' conception of text. We should note that the prisoners all view the written word as authoritative: the diary, after all is retrieved in order to evaluate competing memories; however, the Republicans disagree—at least initially—with regard to what form an authoritative text must take. Egbert's initial dismissal of Cedric's text is evident in his reaction to the soiled pages: "I thought you said it was a diary!" he exclaims. In this moment Egbert demonstrates that form is as important to him as it is to both revisionist critics and the archives that the POWs reference at the story's conclusion. Simply put, the crumpled and dirty stack of paper produced by Cedric does not match Egbert's preconception of a text. In contrast, Cedric maintains that the integrity and authority of a text derive from its content rather than its form. He remains firm in his conviction that the diary is an important document worthy of their study, despite its disheveled appearance, a form dictated by the necessities of their particular conditions of incarceration.

The chapters that follow will explore precisely this intersection of politics and literary form, of physical space and historical moment, of center and margin. But perhaps the place we must first begin is a definition of precisely what this book defines as "prison writing." The term seems self-evident enough and yet, like the term "postcolonial," in recent years the genre boundaries of "prison literature" have been so blurred as to become nearly meaningless. To illustrate, *Irish Writing in the Twentieth Century*'s introduction foregrounds the anthology's commendable interest in subaltern voices, insisting that "Prison writings occupy a site of special interest in this *Reader*."[4] Eight entries are then defined as prison writing. Unfortunately, two of these works are by authors who never spent any time in jail, at least as inmates: a poem by Vincent Buckley about Bobby Sands, and Seamus Heaney's poem "From the Republic of Conscience," which the editor describes as "written for all political prisoners."[5] In point of fact, only one of *Irish Writing in the Twentieth Century*'s selections was composed during actual incarceration. Though its intentions are noble, by obscuring the difficulties peculiar to composition in a carceral space this anthology's extension of the genre to include texts *about* prisoners does a great disservice to writers actually struggling within confinement.

Variants of this elision are evident even in the work of scholars who specialize in prison literature. Regrettably, at times there has been a tendency to oversimplify the cultural, historical, and political differences that shape incarcerated authors' experiences. Sheila Roberts goes so far as to claim that the

> homogeneity of substance, tone, and mood of prison writing—no matter the form—comes from the physical conditions out of which prison

> literature springs being always similar. It makes little difference whether the author or protagonist be a felon, political dissenter or Joseph K.: a prison is a prison.[6]

This approach is mistaken on many levels: first and foremost, it assumes that a uniform state of discipline within prison walls is possible and achievable, each prisoner experiencing incarceration both physically and mentally in the same fashion. Secondly, such a model conceives of the writer-prisoners as helpless victims of the panoptic eye, victims who—consciously or not—behave and write in entirely predictable ways due to unvarying institutional influences and practices.

Roberts's perspective is common among some of the poststructuralist heirs of Michel Foucault, and some critics even fault Foucault himself for not emphasizing strongly enough the possibility of resistance in works such as *Discipline and Punish.* While I agree with the critique of poststructuralists' tendency to dismiss the possibility of real agency, Foucault's work must be differentiated from that of his successors in this regard. Because of the force with which he theorizes the disciplinary space, it perhaps is easy to miss the allowances Foucault makes for human agency. By way of example, in "Power and Strategies," Foucault emphasizes (albeit somewhat defensively) "That to say that one can never be 'outside' power does not mean that one is trapped and condemned to defeat no matter what."[7] Indeed, as Foucault himself recognized,[8] although carceral spaces strive to sustain a monolithic field of discipline in both temporal and spatial terms, in reality prisons are not static, unvaried enclosures, but ones that are in constant flux, subject to internal and external stresses alike. Even in one historical moment, there actually may be several disparate prisons within one institution, each with different levels and foci of discipline and unique physical layout. Time brings institutional change as well, and the same prison may see multiple prison administrations within brief periods, often heralding alterations in the conditions experienced by one, some, or all of these "prisons within prisons."

We also must take into account—as Roberts's statement above does not—the specificity of the *individual* experiencing prison: his/her race, gender, political affiliations, and socioeconomic background disappear in the model that Roberts suggests. To ignore such categories is to ignore the very method by which prisons frequently classify, segregate, and discipline prisoners. To illustrate, as Breyten Breytenbach reveals in *The True Confessions of an Albino Terrorist,* Apartheid-era South African prisons mirrored the political system that created them, for they separated prisoners by race and even fed them different meals according to the inmates' officially designated color: Once a week "Whites" were allotted one piece of fruit, which the "Black" and "Brown" prisoners did not receive, while according to Breytenbach, "Blacks and Browns get more 'pap' than Whites do."[9] Ioan Davies addresses these disparities in prison experience by conceiving of three categories of prison writing: that produced by incarcerated intellectuals (generally defined as politicized before incarceration), that produced by "the writer who operates directly out of a prison experience" (i.e., a nonpolitical prisoner, one whom the British penal system would term an "Ordinary Decent Criminal"), and finally, a third grouping in which "the writings merge in a collectivity of epic and self-critical ur-epic where oral stories and songs become part of a folk history of incarceration, exile and slavery."[10] We cannot ignore that political "offenders" are often arrested, detained, questioned, and charged under special legislation of a sort not utilized in dealing with the nonpolitical "felon" mentioned in the passage above, as has been the case in the North of Ireland for over eight decades. In this manner, even before political prisoners are actually incarcerated, their experience differs from the average inmate. When critics ignore these disparities in treatment and experience, they actually assist state campaigns to deny the existence of political incarceration within their borders, the British government's abolition of Special Category Status in 1976 being only one exemplar. Certainly in the North of Ireland judicial structures have been co-opted as a tool of counterinsurgency, largely at the expense of the pursuit of justice.

Yet, although all of Davies's categories merit consideration, they lack specificity in important respects. Although he does at times briefly consider disparities in prison regimes endured by prisoners, acknowledging, for instance, that Constance Markievicz faced "less comfortable" conditions than Rosa Luxemburg,[11] the carceral space itself fades into the background in his model. Similarly, under the regime that Breytenbach endured, an intellectual whom the state defined as "Black" would have faced very different circumstances than a "White" intellectual. I insist that we must also take into account material and institutional incongruities among prisons, for they often affect the form and subject of the writings produced. For instance, as chapter four will outline in detail, carceral discipline is intentionally gendered. Prison work generally replicates patriarchal expectations regarding behavior and occupation and it attempts to force female inmates in particular to internalize and obey sexist norms. Privileging the individual her/himself—even as a collective category—over the larger context in which that person must move has the potential to entrench further in literary studies the notion of the autonomous hero somehow untouched by ideology, historical moment, or advantage of class, race, or gender.

In fact, precisely because they are produced within a special matrix—at once removed from the bounds of everyday society, yet also within the undiluted heart of that society as replicated in its disciplinary structure—prison texts are able to cast light upon subjects quite external to the physical prison cell, subjects that may in fact be invisible to those outside. Jail literature reverses the panopticon, fragmenting the state's attempts to appear unassailably unified. The carceral regime gazes into the cell, but in the case of the Republican POWs whose work this book examines, the cell gazes back, defiant. In effect, when prison writing exits the carceral space and is published outside, the cell becomes the observation tower in which the world outside scrutinizes the disciplinary regime.

A more nuanced definition of prison literature must take into consideration the *conditions surrounding* textual composition rather than issues of subject matter alone. In so doing, not only do we explore the diversity of carceral spaces, we also very swiftly encounter a number of uninterrogated assumptions central to traditional literary aesthetics. As a starting point, I will make a distinction between texts written *faoi ghlas* (locked up) and memoirs about the experience of incarceration produced *taoibh amuigh* (outside), and I make this distinction for a reason. In the first place, texts by imprisoned political offenders frequently have to be produced in secret, often at great peril to the authors' safety, though this varies according to historical moment and individual prison regime. For instance, during the later years of Special Category Status in the Cages of Long Kesh there were fewer restrictions on writing than during the Blanket Protest and the Hunger Strikes, when writing was completely forbidden in the cells of the H Blocks. In turn, by the late 1990s the H Blocks would regain—and in some respects surpass—the access to the raw materials of discourse once available in the Cages. In all of these prison regimes, however, danger was involved in the production of texts, not infrequently a *physical* peril that historically has been dismissed or overlooked by literary critics.

Writings produced in an atmosphere such as that of Long Kesh—be it the communal incarceration of the Cages or the cellular confinement of the H Blocks—can never truly follow the old Wordsworthian paradigm of composition and literary value: the production of works exemplifying "emotion recollected in tranquility"[12] that in only somewhat altered form retains its influence today. In "Inside Story," the first article Adams wrote in Long Kesh, we see that prisoners in the Cages were apparently allowed typewriters under the terms of Special Category Status;[13] however, this did not exempt what POWs wrote from censorship or worse. Prisons remain prisons despite any privileges granted to inmates. The necessity of concealing political works in progress during composition—as well as the necessity of smuggling out the finished product—complicates the writing process and makes it a far more nerve-wracking experience than it is for those *taoibh amuigh*. Adams reminds us in *Cage Eleven* that the prisoners "are forced to endure British military raids" executed by several regiments of soldiers "at an unearthly hour in the morning and entirely without notice."[14] It is hopefully a statement of the obvious that despite the presence of typewriters, such an environment is not conducive to the sort of creative process favored by Wordsworth.

However, in making this observation, I do not seek to argue that formalist models of literature are inherently repressive; rather, the danger is in the mystification of formalism. Indeed, I recognize the potentially emancipatory aspects of Romantic aesthetics. For example, to quote the preface to *Lyrical Ballads*—Wordsworth sought a language that does not "differ in any material degree from that of all other men who feel vividly and see clearly,"[15] a "language closely resembling that of real life."[16] On the surface, this sounds democratic enough: if followed through to their logical end, these sentiments would permit even those of the humblest backgrounds to become poets. Yet, even the most liberal of the Romantics assumed that this "language of real life" could only produce "a complex feeling of delight"[17] via metrical forms that today seem fairly rigid. Wordsworth thus conflates strict formalism and this "language of real life," a conflation so subtle that one might miss it. It would be dangerous to ignore this blurring, for as Terry Eagleton correctly argues,

> It is never easy to distinguish an appeal to taste and sentiment which offers an alternative to autocracy from one which allows such power to ground itself all the more securely in the living sensibilities of its subjects. There is a world of political difference between a law which the subject really does give to itself, in radical democratic style, and a decree which descends from on high but which the subject now "authenticates."[18]

By creating a model that sees formalism as organic and not as an artificial imposition, the Romantics do not put poetic composition within the reach of the masses, but rather they mystify a potentially coercive and elitist aesthetics.

Like Byron himself, arbiters of Irish literary taste in the succeeding centuries renounced even the facade of such a "language of real life," much to the detriment of Irish prison writers. Yeats, for example, as both poet and anthologist, championed composition principles difficult at best for an incarcerated author to emulate, abandoning any aspect of Romantic aesthetics that could potentially lend itself to prison writing. In a late essay entitled "A General Introduction for My Work," Yeats reveals he seeks

> not as Wordsworth thought, words in common use, but a powerful and passionate syntax, and a complete coincidence between period and stanza. Because I need passionate syntax for passionate subject matter I compel myself to accept those traditional metres [sic] that have developed with the language.[19]

Such a "complete coincidence" undoubtedly requires multiple drafts, and Yeats's emphasis on such intricate formal aesthetics betrays his privileged position. That, for example, redrafting literary productions might be a *luxury* does not seem to concern many writers and critics who adhere to the Yeatsean model. Such luxury, only imperfectly attainable by inmates of the Cages, is quite absent from the lives of POWs imprisoned in the H Blocks between 1976 and 1981 after the removal of Special Category Status. In the early years of the H Blocks, pragmatic brands of formalism took precedence regarding document length: determining what words could fit on the last remaining sheet of toilet paper or what could be smuggled out to visiting areas concealed in a POW's foreskin were concerns frequently more relevant to imprisoned Republican authors.

Indeed, because of the excesses of the regime in which they were produced, such writings merit a subcategory beneath the larger heading of *faoi ghlas* composition. In this book, I will term them *téacs pluide* or *téacsanna pluide* (blanket text/ texts), for these writings might be likened to the Blanket Protest in which they were born. Like the Republican POWs, these are writings stripped naked by the prison regime, texts that must struggle to resist the fragmentation imposed on them by the material conditions of the cell. Composed on whatever scraps of paper the prisoners could smuggle into their cells, the *téacsanna pluide* bear the marks of the H Blocks of that specific moment in time, even on a physical level in their manuscript form.

When considered in Yeatsean aesthetic terms for inclusion in an anthology, the works of someone such as Bobby Sands, who in his own words had to secretly share "one miserly pencil and a pen refill" with his entire prison wing, are at a distinct disadvantage.[20] By reinscribing complex formalism as an essential component of serious literature, Yeats blocks Republican prison writers from participating in all-party literary talks. Indeed, one might at times search in vain for a "well-wrought urn" among the shards of prison writing, for at the best of times composition *faoi ghlas* is fraught with difficulties proceeding directly from the writer's material conditions. And, of course, in the case of writers such as Bobby Sands, there sometimes is no possibility of prison authors revising their own work after release.[21]

Turning again to Yeats's comments in his "General Introduction," it is also worth noting his apparent drive to contain emotion. Like the Romantics, Yeats disapproves of *unfiltered* emotion: his "passionate syntax" and "passionate subject matter" must be reined in by the limiting force of "traditional metres." Such internment extends to the world of political subject matter as well. For example, as editor of *The Oxford Book of Modern Verse,* Yeats defends his choice not to anthologize certain poems centering on World War I by arguing the often-quoted sentiment that "passive suffering is not a theme for poetry."[22] On the surface, such a remark might be viewed as commendable, for it refers specifically to poems that Yeats describes as "written by officers" who "plead for the suffering of their men," poems "written in the first person [that] made that suffering their own."[23]

Certainly in today's age of multiculturalism, we are more aware than ever of the deleterious effects of writers appropriating the lives and experiences of subaltern populations (and it is indeed something I consciously attempt to avoid in this book). However, given Yeats's exclusion of war poets such as Wilfred Owen as well as any war poems by Sassoon—both of whom saw active duty and active suffering, Owen killed in a matter of days before the Armistice—it is easy to recognize that there is more to Yeats's decision than he initially allows. One paragraph later in his introduction, Yeats more openly reveals his position, insisting that "If war is necessary, or necessary in our time and place, it is best to forget its suffering as we do the discomfort of fever, remembering our comfort at midnight when our temperature fell, or as we forget the worst moments of more painful disease."[24] To use the Wordsworthian phrasing, Yeats here reemphasizes the supposed necessity of "selection": he follows to the letter Wordsworth's admonition in the preface to *Lyrical Ballads*, that poets are responsible for "removing what would otherwise be painful or disgusting" from their poetry.[25] But, to ask Irish POWs to bracket the experience of war is to ask them to forget both the prison that confines them and the wider historical forces that caused such places as the H Blocks to be built in the first place. One cannot reasonably expect POWs on the No-Wash Protest, their walls covered with their own excreta—and in the case of the women in Armagh Gaol, their own menstrual blood—to delete the painful and the disgusting from their writings, for it literally surrounds them and intrudes upon their consciousness at every moment.

Yet, many later writers, critics, and anthologists follow Yeats's lead, in some cases going further, positing the possibility of completely severing the aesthetic from the political. For instance, in her 1987 book *Poetry in the Wars*, leading Irish critic Edna Longley implies that such a peace wall is not only desirable but also possible when she writes that "Poetry and politics, like church and state, should be separated."[26] Perhaps realizing that such a statement is itself a political one, four years later Longley engages in some revisionism of her own position, specifying in her book *The Living Stream* that "By politics I meant predatory ideologies, fixed agendas and fixed expectations."[27]

At the risk of being deemed one of the "[m]isty-eyed Americans"[28] that Longley so abhors, I argue that in either case Longley's use of the term "politics" would benefit from some deconstruction. Returning to *Poetry in the Wars*, one can wonder how possible a completely apolitical poetry might be, particularly if one agrees at all with the old feminist maxim that "the personal is the political." Even more interesting is Longley's partial retraction in *The Living Stream*: embedded in her redefinition is the notion that politics are apparently something that *other* people have. Undoubtedly, Longley is aware that she occupies a particular place in the political spectrum; however, her specific attachment of the term "politics" to a viewpoint in opposition to her own speaks volumes. It is another elision redolent of the Romantics' conflation of a fairly rigid formalism and "the language of real life." In addition, when Longley asserts that nationalism "breeds bad literature...which in a vicious cycle breeds—or inbreeds—bad politics," she is certainly guilty of the essentialist "fixed expectations" she condemns in others.[29]

Despite revisionists' attempts to deny such charges, Terry Eagleton's description of "the aesthetic as 'disinterested' mythic solution to real contradictions" is indeed apropos in this instance. Eagleton asserts,

> the poetic is still being counterposed to the political—which is only to say that the "poetic" as we have it today was, among other things, historically constructed to carry out just that business of suppressing political conflict. Imagination and enlightened liberal reason are still being offered to us in Ireland today as the antithesis of sectarianism;

> and like all such idealized values they forget their own roots in a social class and history not unnoted for its own virulent sectarianism, then and now...The liberal humanist notion of Culture was constituted, among other things, to marginalize such peoples as the Irish...[30]

Tellingly enough, one hears few calls from the revisionist camp to strike Spenser from the canon, despite the fact that his *View of the Present State of Ireland* entertains the possibility of the wholesale slaughter of the Irish populace as a solution to their rebellion. And, as demonstrated by Essex's murder of every man, woman, and child on Rathlin Island during the Elizabethan campaigns in Ireland, such atrocities were not confined to the printed page.

A cursory glance at the introductions of recent anthologies of Irish writing reveals the extent to which revisionist ideals continue to hold sway over the collection and distribution of Irish texts. Rather than addressing the vexed issue of the place of Irish writers in anthologies of British literature—which is another issue entirely—I have selected the examples that follow exclusively from those texts that explicitly self-identify as anthologies of Irish writing. I will begin with a collection first published in 1979 and revised in 1990, *Poets from the North of Ireland.* Editor Frank Ormsby—himself a highly regarded Irish poet—acknowledges that the authors he has chosen for his anthology

> have been praised for constant resourcefulness in the use of traditional forms, and accused of being technically unadventurous, unwilling to experiment, prisoners of the neat lyric. They have been commended for their restraint in not allowing the brutal realities of their place and time to impair their sense of aesthetic responsibility, and denounced for failure to "confront" their realities directly.[31]

Despite the title's use of terminology more usually associated with Irish nationalism, Ormsby here clearly and unapologetically pledges his allegiance to an aesthetic proceeding directly from Yeats via contemporary revisionists. Simply put, *Poets from the North of Ireland* smacks of literary gerrymandering: only poems suitably free of Longley's "politics" are represented.

Clearly, Republican prison writings need not apply to *Poets from the North of Ireland*, for though certainly not the sole focus of all Republican jail literature, such "confrontation of realities" is a common theme in many texts composed during incarceration and one often sees a deliberate engagement with goings-on contemporary with the moment of composition. To illustrate, in his first "Brownie" column,

"Inside Story," Adams attacks the condescending attitude of both politicians and academics toward Republican writers, in this case, as embodied in the person of Conor Cruise O'Brien. Commenting on his own identity as an author, Adams jokes, "An intellectual Republican—Conor Cruise would never believe it, but then he must know something. He not only refuses to read Republican stuff, he puts our friend Eamonn Mac Thomais in Portlaoise."[32] In this passage Adams's work demonstrates representative features of prison writing, first and foremost in the pervasive use of irony that critics such as Bill Ashcroft correctly identify as a defining characteristic of postcolonial writing in general. As a member of the Labour government, whose duties included education, Dr. O'Brien should foster open debate: instead, as "Inside Story" points out, he uses Section 31 to silence opposing viewpoints, for this law empowered the government of the Twenty-Six Counties to imprison any author espousing Republican views—for no other crime than writing.[33] As Tim Pat Coogan reveals, O'Brien intended to use such powers not only against writers and historians such as Mac Thomais (who was imprisoned twice when editor of *An Phoblacht*), but also against teachers who dared include Republican material in their classes.[34]

Adams's critique in the passage I just quoted centers on events and personages contemporary to the precise moment of "Inside Story's" composition. When it is republished *taoibh amuigh* fifteen years later with the new title "Cage Eleven" in the book of the same name, references to O'Brien and MacThomais are deleted. This, I maintain, is more than mere stylistics. There is a long tradition of Republican prison writing appearing in newspapers; in many ways this is fitting, as jail literature at times shares common ground with journalism. Often, both are more concerned with the immediate, with the here-and-now, than traditional literature generally is, not just in terms of the events occurring outside the prison, but, to an even greater degree, also the events that surround the prison writers themselves. Jail literature frequently is a lifeline cast outward from the depths rather than into them, or a warning beacon to readers outside jail walls.

Despite such compelling reason to attend to them, even anthologists without an antinationalist axe to grind neglect *faoi ghlas* prison writings. It is worth noting that the first three volumes of the *Field Day Anthology of Irish Writing* neglect completely any writings produced *faoi ghlas,* an omission especially glaring given how often and bitterly revisionist critics fault the anthology as nationalist propaganda. In these volumes, editor Seamus Deane reprints excerpts from a few prison memoirs, but the anthology does not include any writings actually composed during incarceration: for instance, noticeable in their absence are any writings by Bobby Sands, arguably the most famous Irish revolutionary of all time. Indeed, among all of the literary anthologies published by major presses only two can be said to contain any texts composed *faoi ghlas*. These are David Pierce's *Irish Writing in the Twentieth Century,* published in 2000 by Cork University Press (which contains only one selection), and the two or three in volumes 4 and 5 of the *Field Day Anthology of Irish Women's Writing,* an improvement tarnished somewhat by the fact that these two volumes are around three thousand pages in length.

Yet, even as I point out these absences, I recognize that academia has made important strides in terms of inclusion in recent decades. However, there is still much to be done. For instance, when critics such as Longley attack Field Day for privileging genres of writing other than traditional literature, their anxiety reveals the extent to which elitist and conservative aesthetic ideologies are still present in arts and letters. I would remind such critics that, as the title itself suggests, *Field Day* volumes I–V collectively make up an anthology of Irish *writing.* In their attempt to reinscribe seemingly apolitical Literature (with a capital L) as the hegemonic center of all forms of writing, revisionists are indeed representative of Magee's "paraliterary wing" of the status quo.[35]

To explore better the counter-aesthetics employed by Provisional Republican prison writing against such attempts to muzzle alternative histories, I center my discussion in this book almost entirely on texts actually composed *faoi ghlas* and not on those about the experience of political incarceration written on the outside. As a result, I must exclude important works such as Áine and Eibhlín Níc Giolla Easpaig's *Girseacha i nGéibheann,* a memoir remarkable not only because of the relative scarcity of Irish language prison writing, but also because it blends the sisters' individual and collective voices. In making this choice, I do not mean to suggest that *faoi ghlas* writings are more accurate representations of the experience of prison than those composed *taoibh amuigh*, for one might easily conceive of the manner in which time and distance might "help" ex-POWs articulate their experience. But this is precisely the point of *Contemporary Irish Republican Prison Writing*: I am not interested in reifying essentialist notions of authenticity, but rather, I hope to analyze the impact of the cell and its often unstable contexts on textual production, pointing out in the process some assumptions about "Literature" that have not been questioned sufficiently.

Similarly, I would be remiss if I failed to point out that this book focuses on the work of authors affiliated (at least at the time that they composed the texts in question)[36] with Provisional Republicanism. Indeed, the admittedly unwieldy title that I proposed for this book was more nuanced, but *Contemporary Provisional Irish Republican Prison Writing* was rejected by the marketing department at Palgrave. The current title might appear to either collapse all forms of Republicanism together or to dismiss other visions as illegitimate, but I intend neither of those implications.[37] In addition, the bulk of the primary sources under scrutiny are by Republican POWs held in the Six Counties. Again, this focus is not intended to discount in any way the experiences of the men and women who served time in the Twenty-Six Counties, England, the United States, or elsewhere in the world—in fact, I hope to turn my attention to their writings in my next book. Rather, I decided on this circumscription because of the markedly different prison conditions endured by those POWs outside of the North of Ireland, a more extreme isolation not least among them.

I have imagined *Contemporary Irish Republican Prison Writing* only as a beginning, one specifically intended for a general audience. Many of the authors whose work I examine here went on to take university degrees during or after their incarceration, and at least four[38] now hold doctorates; however, I do not forget that most of these POWs entered prison and began composing without previous literary experience, and in some cases, without finishing school. I would like this book to be accessible to as many interested readers as possible, and for this reason this book might be criticized as being undertheorized by some academics. Yet, it is one of my abiding frustrations with postcolonial studies in general that those who would benefit most from the discipline's insights are the ones most excluded from it by the sheer density of its theoretical language.

Most of all, I would like to help bring more widespread public attention to writings that either have never been seen before or that appeared only in limited venues decades ago. I share Barbara Harlow's desire to assist in the dissemination of texts that complicate and even contest our understanding of history and literature, and certainly Republican prison writing does this. Readers familiar with Provisional Republicanism only through biased media images likely will find themselves surprised at what these texts offer. Works by incarcerated Republican women in particular have not received the attention that they deserve, and I hope that this book participates in a larger effort to address this neglect. For Ireland to move toward what I pray will be a new era, silence must become a thing of the past.

Chapter Two

"Our Barbed Wire Ivory Tower": The Cages of Long Kesh

A radical shift in hard-line nationalist ideology took place throughout the North of Ireland as a direct result of widespread political imprisonment, a shift not just in terms of Republican paramilitary strategy, but also in terms of the prisoners' self-definition and their relationship with political organizations outside the prison's walls. Like those of the Armagh women, the prison writings originating in the Cages of Long Kesh provide dramatic evidence of how Republican prisoners co-opt and appropriate the space of the prison to at least partially invert the disciplinary structures intended to break them and isolate them from their comrades. In some ways, such Republican resistance to British authority is to be expected. However, what complicates the situation in Long Kesh is the way in which such writings evidence the development of a critical consciousness in the POWs that causes them to disobey and alter the structure of their own political and paramilitary organizations both inside and outside prison. The conflict for incarcerated Republicans has never been that of a simple binary opposition between the British and the Irish, but rather an interlocking system of power relations and tensions—internal and external to their own political groupings and cultural background.

Although the history of Internment and the Republican battle to win and maintain Special Category Status in Northern Irish prisons is familiar to many, this internal struggle of the Provisional Republican movement in the Cages of Long Kesh has received less attention. In 1975, the Irish Republican Army cease-fire was the backdrop for a debate among Provisionals that would redefine the course of Northern Irish political history, as a younger cadre of politicized Provisionals in the Cages contested the tenets of old-guard Republicanism, rejecting an exclusive focus on armed struggle. The ensuing ideological clash threatened to cause a division every bit as devastating as the earlier split from the Officials, for the debate did not remain contained within the barbed wire of the Cages: instead, Provisional POWs on both sides of the debate exported their dialectics to the world outside by means of prison writings published in periodical form. At stake in this textual conflict was nothing less than the future direction of the Provisional movement.

Prison writing in the Cages simultaneously shapes and reflects Republican ideology: in some cases, it is the barometer that augurs the storm, in others, the seed scattered in the clouds that causes the tempest. By contrasting the *Republican News* articles authored by Gerry Adams during his incarceration in the Cages with the prison writings of conservative Republicans published in the short-lived magazine *Faoi Glas* [*sic*][1], I will demonstrate the manner in which the Provisionals radically redefined both their political and military strategy as well as their vision of Ireland. This prison writing dialectic reveals not only the power of discourse, but also the Provisionals' conscious *awareness* of this power: indeed, I argue that Adams's rise to prominence within the Provisional movement came about in part because of his success in the war of words fought in Republican periodicals.

In addition, I insist that study of the texts in *Republican News* and *Faoi Glas* is valuable not only for the insight it gives into the evolution of Provisional Republicanism, but also because prison writing as a genre forces us to interrogate traditional expectations about literature, pulling aside the curtain behind which hides the cultural and political interests served by the traditional canon. Similarly, by analyzing the alterations made to Gerry Adams's prison writings in preparation for their publication in his 1990 anthology *Cage Eleven*, I will argue the necessity of differentiating texts produced during actual incarceration from those produced *taoibh amuigh* (outside). The disparities are stark on the level of both form and intention: as the revisions to Adams's original writings demonstrate, while resistance writing in general often foregrounds the present moment, prison writing produced *faoi ghlas* (locked up) places particular emphasis on the here-and-now rather than the distant "universal" so central to traditional literary aesthetics.

Background: Gerry Adams, POW

In order to gain a clearer insight into the writings produced in the Cages, both the historical moment and the specific conditions of confinement endured by internees such as Gerry Adams need to be understood. Adams was interned twice; once for a period of months in

1972, and once beginning in 1973. One must keep in mind that at this stage in Northern Irish history the Security Forces were empowered to arrest citizens without charge and hold them indefinitely without trial, and this is exactly the treatment accorded to Adams. Although he became a sentenced prisoner during his second detention, the charge was not for "terrorist offenses," but rather for Adams's failed attempts to escape his imprisonment without trial.[2] One positive and remarkable thing did result from his incarceration, however: the short writings smuggled out of the Cages of Long Kesh between 1975 and 1977, in which Adams wrote about his experiences as a political prisoner under the pseudonym "Brownie." These essays and short stories appeared first as a regular column in *Republican News*, the Belfast Republican newspaper that merged with its southern counterpart to become *An Phoblacht/Republican News* on 27 January 1979.[3] Subsequently, a number of these articles were collected and republished in book form in 1990 under the title *Cage Eleven*. The "Brownie" articles mark Adams's earliest entry into print,[4] and, like many Republican prisoners, he continued writing after his release. Adams has become a prolific author who has published a two-volume autobiography, another collection of short stories entitled *The Street*, and a number of book-length political tracts.

Appearing on 16 August 1975, "Inside Story" was the first article published in *Republican News* authored by Gerry Adams under the nom de plume "Brownie" and it gives us a fuller understanding of life in the Cages. The importance of spatial concerns is underscored by the fact that Adams begins with a description of the physical makeup of his home in a prison Nissen hut as well as of the compound that surrounds it. The overcrowding typical in the early days of Internment[5] is very evident when Adams remarks that there are "Thirty [men] to a hut, three huts to a Cage, a washroom, an empty hut and a 'study' hut threw in [*sic*] for the crack. Wired off with a couple of watchtowers planted around, and that's us."[6] Adams's trademark lively pace is clear to see in the passage's clipped, yet humorously descriptive last sentence. His brisk irreverence elevates the seemingly mundane task of setting forth locale, for it does far more than set the stage for the stories to follow; his description becomes a weapon against the compound itself, destroying the secrecy and isolation required by such institutions.

It is no coincidence that such a description is included in Adams's very first smuggled article: the complete success of Long Kesh as a disciplinary machine requires not only the physical separation of its inmates from the outside populace, but also the physical and mental separation of the compound itself from too watchful a civilian eye. As Foucault reminds us in *Discipline and Punish*, prison regimes function very efficiently when they create an environment in which a warder "sees everything without being seen," that is, when the disciplinary apparatus is capable of "dissociating the see/being seen dyad."[7] Prison writing reverses this hierarchy: by smuggling out a description of a prisoner of war camp, Adams is putting the British government's own surveillance under surveillance—an act very dangerous to his captors. The cartography of Adams's writings threatens the compound on every level, from negative fallout in international public relations to potential paramilitary attacks against the camp itself.

Even fifteen years after the initial publication of this first "Brownie" article, the destruction of impermeable spatial boundaries remains a central theme in Adams's 1990 anthology of his prison writing, *Cage Eleven*. "Cage Eleven," the first story in the book, is largely drawn from "Inside Story," and the passage quoted above remains prominent in the anthology's version, though in reworded form.[8] Similarly, it is not by accident that maps precede even *Cage Eleven*'s foreword—which itself gives details of the prison's location between Belfast and Lisburn.[9] This introduction dramatically outlines the development of the Long Kesh compound into unhappy conjoined twins, to recast Ciaran Carson's words, for the H Blocks grew from the Cages both physically and politically, as will be discussed in detail in the next chapter.

However, what makes this cartography particularly interesting is that by 1990 the Cages themselves no longer actually existed as a functioning compound: as a part of the policy of "criminalization," Republican prisoners sentenced for offences committed after 1 March 1976 were incarcerated in the cells of the new prison rather than in the communal huts of the Cages. By 1988, the few remaining POWs in the original prison agreed to be transferred to the H Blocks.[10] In the foreword to his anthology, Adams remarks that Cage Eleven exists now only in the memories of those who once shared its drafty and leaky huts.[11] Thus, in a fashion akin to the narrator of Ciaran Carson's short piece "Question Time," Adams and his fellow POWs become "a map which no longer refers to the present world, but to a history."[12] The cartography of the North is often more fluid on a material level than it is in the minds of its denizens. In the view of many contemporary Belfast writers such as Carson and Gearóid MacLochlainn, people are not just from a place, they *are* the place; they are palimpsests of present and past cartography, the children of the effacements wrought by slow time and the sudden violence of the Troubles. When

Carson's narrator laments "I am this map,"[13] he echoes the dilemma facing Adams in 1990. Because the Cages have been demolished, the ex-POWs must recreate their former prison through testimony alone, they must bear witness to a vanished space of which they still remain a part. Yet, in so doing the writing itself may cause an erasure of *existing* political prisons in physical, if not mental terms. Adams himself argues that the memory of Cage Eleven "is a memory which reminds us, among other things, that the H Blocks, like the British regime which spawned them, will one day be a memory also."[14] The seemingly vanished past can be a weapon in the present, one that at the very least can provide solace to those actually experiencing incarceration.

By keeping Long Kesh visible in past and present form to those outside of its barbed wire fences, acts of witness such as the "Brownie" articles and *Cage Eleven* create not only the possibility of physical interaction with existing sites (for instance, aiding in attacks and/or escape attempts) but also—perhaps more dangerously from the perspective of the British government—the possibility of the connection of hearts and minds to prison compounds. Of course it is in the interests of the Security Forces to keep those incarcerated in these jails hidden from society whether or not the prisons still actually physically exist, especially if inmates are or were treated as cruelly as they were in the Long Kesh compound. To get a better sense of how fearful of Republican testimony the British government has been, one must only remember the degree of state censorship enacted by the Thatcher regime around the time of *Cage Eleven*'s publication. In 1988, Home Secretary Douglas Hurd introduced a broadcasting ban based on clause 14 (4) of the BBC's License and Agreement, and on section 29 (3) of the Broadcasting Act of 1981. As Liz Curtis explains, "Designed for wartime use, and similar to the South of Ireland's Section 31, this legislation empowers the Home Secretary to ban the broadcasting of any matter he/she specifies."[15] Sinn Féin, though defined by the government as a legal political party by this stage, was censored: neither the words of its representatives nor the words spoken by anyone in support of Sinn Féin could be broadcast. Initially the language of the ban was interpreted in as broad a manner as possible and as such Republicans were excluded from appearing on television completely. Later this total media blackout was modified with the strictest literal interpretation of the legislation in mind, with Republican politicians allowed to appear on screen but with their voices replaced either by subtitles or voiceovers. In some cases, actual events such as press conferences were reconstructed in totality, using actors.[16] While at first glance this practice may seem only absurd, the propaganda effect of a Sinn Féin representative's voiceover being done by a sinister-voiced actor cannot be dismissed. In contrast, prison writings such as those collected in *Cage Eleven* allow the victims of such censorship more opportunity to speak in their own unaltered voices.

While undoubtedly many prison authors have an audience in mind while composing a text, in many instances the true impact of words from jail is felt most keenly by the incarcerated writers themselves. The locative effect of description can benefit those imprisoned in what the narrator in "Cage Eleven" terms "some surrealistic limbo."[17] The word choice in that quote is revelatory: just as the souls of the departed are cut off indefinitely from the places and people that they loved, so are the internees with no fixed release date. Yet, in the act of remembering that one is not marooned on a distant desert island but in reality just a short distance from one of the busiest (and to many of the inmates, the most familiar) highways in the North of Ireland, one is able to defeat the sense of isolation with which the prison authorities hope to break resistance. As opposed to the coerced confession of an interrogation, the clandestine words of prison texts are a small but important expression of resistance, a passage out of limbo into actual geography, and as such a qualified freedom.

Special Category Status and Republican Resistance

Throughout Irish history prisons have been sites where identity and political legitimacy have been tested. Most emblematic of this struggle in contemporary Northern Ireland are the repeated battles for Special Category Status, first won for the inmates of the Cages in 1972. Special Category Status granted prisoners in Long Kesh the right to wear civilian clothes rather than the prison uniform, an act that to the Republicans symbolized institutional recognition of the political rather than criminal nature of their confinement. But perhaps the most notable way in which Provisional POWs resisted their incarceration in the Cages of Long Kesh is found in the manner in which they organized themselves. Detainees incarcerated in the Republican Cages followed a military command structure, each Cage led by an officer commanding (OC). Within the confines of the Cages, the prisoners were responsible as individuals only to their officers, not to individual "screws"[18]: relations between prison officials and POWs were negotiated only through the camp or individual Cage OC, the OC speaking for the group.

However, it must be kept in mind that the net of Internment—especially in its first year—was cast widely, and many people without paramilitary (or even Republican) ties found themselves in the Cages. According to Alex Maskey, Sinn Féin councilor and former Lord Mayor of Belfast (who was interned on two occasions during this period), the prison authorities separated internees who were not sentenced of any political offense only along religious lines. While interned, Catholics might share their Cage with prisoners of all shades of the political spectrum, from the completely uninvolved, to members of political parties, to guerillas representing a number of Republican factions. If there was more than one paramilitary group within a particular internees' Cage, each group would have its own separate command structure through which it would deal with prison authorities. Those who did not officially belong to a particular paramilitary or political faction often chose to be adopted by a group as a "civilian":[19] more on this later in the chapter. If formally sentenced, however, the prison authorities segregated prisoners according to specific political grouping, imprisoning Provisionals in their own separate Cages.

This setup proved beneficial to prisoners in many ways. First and foremost, by permitting a group identity the prison administration ceded power and control to the Provisional detainees. As Kieran McEvoy accurately notes,

> the prisoners' de facto control of space within the compounds meant that management could not impose their will without considerable application of resources and the potential for serious disorder. The acceptance of this state of affairs was viewed by some in the [British] army as analogous to the unacceptable challenge to the authorities posed by the no-go areas controlled by the IRA in republican areas . . .[20]

While it lasted in the Cages, Special Category Status allowed a degree of agency for POWs within Long Kesh; in its recognition of Provisional military command structures, Special Category Status conferred an implicit legitimacy upon Republican paramilitary groups as well.

By winning prisoner of war status in all but name, the Republican inmates combat the effects of what Henri Lefebvre terms "dominated space," that which "is invariably the result of a master's project," one that is "usually closed, sterilized, emptied out."[21] In his book *The Production of Space*, Lefebvre further points out "the repressive and assimilative capacity of...dominated space."[22] With barbed wire and watchtowers, the British government seeks to enclose and thus end dissent (or perceived dissent); however, through such actions as refusing to wear a "convict's uniform" and by refusing to deal with prison officials except through their OCs, the Republican prisoners resist assimilation into what the British penal system terms the "Ordinary Decent Criminal" convicted for nonpolitical crimes.[23]

We see more literal appropriation of space in Adams's short story "Sláinte" where Dosser, the Cage "brewmaster," and other Republican POWs use a portion of the plumbing of the shower hut in order to create a still capable of producing some fierce *poitín*—Irish moonshine.[24] In this instance, the POWs literally dismantle part of the system in which they are incarcerated, even using the wet soil of the Cages to their advantage in the construction of dumps where, according to the story's narrator, "some of [the Dosser's] brew survived for six months, simmering gently in the innards of our cage until the potent smell demanded that it be moved on to the next stage of the process."[25] At first, such bootlegging may seem just a small gesture, but in reality it is a symbolic rejection of a system that attempts to transform its inmates into—as Lefebvre correctly recognizes—simple consumers who "passively experienced whatever was imposed upon them inasmuch as it was more or less thoroughly inserted into, or justified by, their representational space."[26] Long Kesh *poitín* results from the POWs' own subversive labor, and in this active appropriation the Republicans reject prison discipline and by extension the repressive system of which it is part, a system that above all (like the worst forms of capitalism) encourages passive consumption. The Provisionals' production of *poitín* is a forceful example of the subversive potential of (and the possibility of recovery of agency through) seemingly commonplace acts of the sort that Michel de Certeau highlights in *The Practice of Everyday Life*. As de Certeau insists, subaltern populations can effectively disrupt disciplinary structures imposed upon them "by using them with respect to ends and references foreign to the system they had no choice but to accept."[27] By its very nature the inescapable fact of imprisonment constrains the POWs; however, in exercising their will whenever possible the incarcerated Republicans reclaim a portion of themselves. Choice itself, however limited, becomes an act of rebellion.

Indeed, in a volte-face of what one would normally expect in such an institution, the prison warders—not the POWs—have passively accepted the position dictated to them by the rules of Special Category Status. In the *Republican News* article "Screws," Adams presents the reader with a picture of how dependent the guards have actually become on the POWs (even in terms of physical motion), through his description of the seemingly simple action of a walk from a cage to the prison hospital. Adams' narrator illustrates:

> When I feel fit enough to go to the doctor's I have my own special screw to keep me company. He is a remarkable piece of machinery.[28] I pause, he pauses_I hobble fast, he hobbles fast_I stop, he stops. I smirk at him, he smiles shyly back_I glare at him, he looks away_I address him as 'my good man,' he grins stupidly_I ignore him, he observes me sleekitly. I go to the doctor's, he goes to the doctor's.[29]

The narrator is keenly aware of the reversal of expected roles: it is not the warder who controls the pace or the destination of the walk, but the POW; perhaps used to dealing with POWs through their OC, this warder is only able to follow the prisoner's lead in one-on-one situations. To Republicans, this attitude is symptomatic of the Security Forces' slipping hold over the POWs in general under Special Category Status[30] for it is the "men behind the wire," the POWs, who are now beginning to find their independence in their state of mind, in their active analysis of the political situation in which they find themselves, and in their active transformation of the world surrounding them.

Hegel tells us that the Master "exists only for himself, that is his essential nature,"[31] a rigid, militaristic self-interest that causes soldiers to brave dangers to preserve their societal position. Nevertheless, this ascendancy is maintained not through creation but negation—negation of Republican freedom through incarceration, and as a consequence, negation of the Masters' own true freedom. After all, *someone* must guard the prisoners. In a passage at the end of "Screws," the narrator shows that the POWs are quite cognizant of the dilemma in which the British have found themselves, recognizing that to maintain its own world order, the British government has, in effect, voluntarily imprisoned itself. This manifests itself on many levels in the Cages, most obviously in the form of the warders who endure much of what their prisoners do, at least in terms of exposure to the elements. "Screws serve their sentences voluntarily," Adams observes, and the deliberate choice to become a part of this disciplinary structure has an effect.[32] Throughout the narratives of inmates such as Adams, the guards appear almost physically inseparable from the wire, gates, and sentry boxes. Such descriptions provide a telling glimpse into the minds of the prisoners, for from the Republicans' perspective the soldiers and warders who guard Long Kesh are themselves assimilated into a machine of the state's devising—a grotesque image redolent of the biomechanics of H.R. Geiger's artwork. In Adams's earlier description of his warder as "a remarkable piece of machinery," the *Republican News* essay further emphasizes the degree to which the warders are seen in this story as an extension of a disciplinary mechanism intended to dehumanize the POWs, a mechanism that in fact has the potential to dehumanize *all* who come in uncritical contact with it, prisoners and warders alike. But this imprisonment occurs at an ideological level as well: by its willingness to detain a civilian population without charge or trial in order to catch a few paramilitaries in the wide net thrown by Internment, the British government has committed itself to a warlike, intransigent stance, one from which it will be difficult to depart. The recurring image in "Screws" of the warders as machines "programmed" to do their soldierly duty, not as beings capable of rational thought, is only ideological petrification made visible.

As the microrebellions of poitín production and "the walk to the doctor's" both demonstrate, no victory is too small to be reckoned in Long Kesh. Such gestures should not be dismissed as merely symbolic; instead, these actions must be considered part of a wider insurrectionary field that the POWs have established within the Cages. Although the POWs remain in the heart of the disciplinary mechanism "behind the wire," they still have won a measured victory by recovering a degree of agency that might go unrecognized by many poststructuralists.[33] However, to acknowledge agency is not to dismiss the important observations that Foucault and his heirs have made with regard to other aspects of incarceration. The POWs' manipulation of the prison environment as a whole cannot be separated from their manipulation of physical space, particularly in terms of the Republicans' success in avoiding the panoptic eye of their warders. As Kieran McEvoy correctly observes in his excellent book *Paramilitary Imprisonment in Northern Ireland*, through Special Category Status

> prisoners physically removed themselves from one of the key components of power and discipline within a prison, the constant surveillance of the authorities. Alternative loci of power were established in the huts...where prison guards could often only patrol with prior discussion and consultation with the prisoners' Officer Commanding.[34]

This appropriation of space in the Cages created the opportunity for rebellions large and small, not the least of which was the development of a critical consciousness through both formal and informal education. The POWs organized lecture and discussion groups and many began to write; this growing "consciousness of consciousness," to borrow Paolo Freire's terminology, had profound results.

Conscientização[35] in the Cages

As Adams himself emphasizes in his autobiography *Before the Dawn*, "When I started to write I began to develop a focused view of things outside...it was only when I began to write that I began to be more openly critical."[36] This critical Republican gaze was not trained solely upon the British: in stories such as "Only Joking," Adams illustrates the extent to which Republican analysis of the wider political situation in the north began with self-critique. This story finds the occupants of the cage reminiscing about all of the pranks played upon fellow inmates, and a debate ensues as to which prisoner was the most skilled practical joker—the "best mixer." Egbert's choice is a man named Dominic, whose trademark faux confessions were set up in the study hut. The "new lads" (that is, freshly incarcerated prisoners) are told that a priest was in to hear their sins and are shown into the hut where a makeshift confessional was constructed. Egbert explains,

> "Dominic would be behind a blanket draped across the hut and he'd have a boxing glove on. You get the picture? He'd begin the confession just as any priest and he'd start to ease all the lad's sins out of him and then, when the lad admitted some particular offense, he'd shout: 'You did what?' and he'd whack out with the boxing glove! It was really something to see. An arm with a boxing glove on the end of it coming round the edge of the blanket. The young lad staring at it in disbelief, then wham!
>
> "And you, ha, ha, you know, nobody ever looked behind the blanket. Even when they got whacked a few times. They just went on with their confession. Ha, ha, ha. One young lad ended up cowering in his seat in dread of the boxing glove as he made a clean breast of things."
>
> "What kinds of sins did they confess?" Your Man asked with interest.
>
> "Oh, nothing much. I mean, no mortal sins; all venial ones. Only telling lies, losing their tempers, masturbating—that was worth two punches..."[37]

Dominic's targets on one level are obvious ones. The new prisoners, usually young and without previous experience of incarceration, are unschooled in the routines of prison life and have not yet been integrated into their cage. Yet, as targets of such practical jokes, they are taken into the fold through common experience of victimization. In effect the "new lads" are running a ceremonial gauntlet before adoption by their new tribe; having successfully negotiated these ritualized obstacles, they will take up a position of equality within the compound, enjoying the protection offered by the Republican command structure.

However, the initiation led by Dominic has other targets also and holds within it lessons that the new prisoners would do well to learn. In true trickster fashion, complete with transgressive discussion of sexuality, Dominic is mocking one of the most sacred rites of the Catholic Church: that of confession and the absolution of sin. In this version, penance is not accomplished through the mind and prayer, but rather through violence against the body. This mild assault is symbolic in two ways. In one respect, it is indicative of how, in a radical departure from earlier, more conservative brands of Republicanism, many POWs of Adams's generation came to equate the Catholic Church with repression and antinationalist sentiment. In "Only Joking," Dominic ritually enacts the hostility of the church toward the Republican POWs, a hostility that church leaders would graphically demonstrate during the hunger strikes of 1980 and 1981.[38]

Secondly, Dominic's "mix" is a forceful reminder to the "new lads" of the need to question their complacency with regard to authority. The dangers of unquestioned obedience and trust in ritual are underscored in the observation that not one prisoner looked behind the "confessional" curtain even after repeated blows, and even after such a striking—pun intended—deviation from the ceremony's usual form. Like the inverted rituals of Native American "contraries,"[39] Dominic's confessional, on the one hand, mocks the sacrament it imitates, yet it also simultaneously reminds one of that sacrament's essential purpose. Rather than settling for the abuse of a hostile church hierarchy and empty, unquestioned ritual, the initiate should instead seek the absolution that is the true purpose of the ceremony. Liberation must be achieved by a combination of spiritual search and political analysis, for in the view of the Republicans the world that the prisoners inhabit is hedged in (and partially constructed) by the violence of state *and* church authority. The initiates learn that they need to develop self-reliance in such an environment, not to cling blindly to old forms and traditions.

Temporality

As Barbara Harlow points out, advocates of a more conservative canon frequently fault resistance literature for its "excessive attention to the immediate exigencies and pressing concern of the contemporary political situation," some of them preferring instead that writers pursue a romanticized vision of "the rewards of posterity and posthumous recognition and acclaim, a 'distant future wrapped in dreams,'" to quote one of the detractors of Palestinian activist/writer Ghassan Kanafani.[40] To many Republicans, such a call to defer a literary dream no doubt has uncomfortable parallels to the rhetoric of some religious officials in the Six Counties: as we saw in the case of Dominic's "mix," it is not uncommon for Provisionals to view clerics within the Catholic Church hierarchy as apologists for a repressive social and political status quo. Republicans such as Adams loudly condemn those cardinals and bishops who, while enjoying a living standard far above that of their parishioners, hypocritically urge their flock to forego material reform in the present in exchange for divine reward after death. Such a critique begins "Christians for Freedom?" an article in which Adams voices the disappointment of Republicans who feel that the church hierarchy has failed to address the "social as well as spiritual needs" of Catholics in Ireland. Adams details his attempt as a representative of his community to meet Bishop Philbin and relates how he

> journied [*sic*] to the Palace (methinks that's the proper jargon) to discuss the affairs of Ballymurphy with [Philbin]. This pilgrimage of mine followed his sudden and unfounded attack on the people of our estate. Unfortunately I wasn't permitted an audience and had to content myself with the sight of Ballymurphy mothers handing in a letter of protest to an apprentice priest who peeked from behind the Bishop's door.[41]

The disparity between the "palace" and the working-class estate from which the delegation originates could not be more stark. In Adams's story, the Bishop lives at a physical and mental remove from his parishioners—a distance made all the more reprehensible to Ballymurphy residents because Philbin *chooses* it. The wealth and willful absence of the church hierarchy witnessed in this passage drives much of the rest of "Christians for Freedom?": Adams similarly reports the manner in which he "nearly met Cardinal Conway" while on a visit to friends living on the Glen Road in West Belfast. Adams portrays Conway not as an active advocate for his flock or one who works shoulder to shoulder with them, but instead as someone whose presence in the working-class ghettos is evident only in "the ecclesiastical limousine, which parked itself across my path. I saw nothing of its owner."[42] To Adams this wealth allows—indeed, encourages—disengagement from the here-and-now of working-class West Belfast.

In contrast to the passivity Adams sees in the church hierarchy, Provisional writings from the Cages frequently are intended to inspire action in a reader. Indeed, in some cases, time is literally of the essence in *faoi ghlas* prison literature, as is the case in Adams's article "Frank Stagg," which appeared in *Republican News* on 10 January 1976. On the day that the article appeared, Stagg had been on hunger strike for nearly a month and was being force-fed every day, a gruesome procedure that from the Republican perspective was done by the prison regime as much to torture POWs as to keep them alive. In his column Adams warns,

> It must be stressed that Frank Stagg will die if pressure is not brought to bear on the Brits immediately. With this horrible eventuality in mind I decided to write a short article on conditions for Republican P.O.W.s in English gaols so that while we go about our daily business, at work or at home, each and every one of us may understand the daily hell which our prisoners in England are fighting against.[43]

Note the use of the first person plural here: on one level, this underscores the solidarity Adams wants to develop among POWs and those outside, as well as between Republicans and the politically unaligned. At another level, imbedded in this use of "we" is a deep understanding of just how greatly prisons can differ from one another with regard to material conditions. Despite the fact that he is incarcerated in a British prison compound, Brownie numbers himself among those *taoibh amuigh* who need further understanding of the plight of Republicans in English jails, for to live *faoi ghlas* in the communal Cages is very different from being *faoi ghlas* alone in Wakefield Prison in England, as Stagg was at the time of the article's composition. To illustrate, unlike Stagg, in the Cages Adams is surrounded by his countrymen and he generally did not have to deal with prison staff except through his OC. As such, Adams is insulated to a certain extent from the brutal discipline imposed upon the isolated Stagg. The disparity between Wakefield and Long Kesh is so great that in the passage quoted above little distinguishes the author in Long Kesh from those going about their daily business outside the Cages, a rhetorical flourish that calls attention to the small comfort the inmates of the "Lazy K" might take in still being in Ireland and thus in being closer to comrades, friends, and family.

In addition, in this first person plural Adams enjoys a curious symbolic escape from Long Kesh: in a fashion reminiscent of Fleur Adcock's ex-queen, Brownie briefly brings the distant close, symbolically moving *taoibh amuigh* with those "at work or at home" even as he brings them into Wakefield Prison through his writings. However, like the ex-queen, Adams looks for something more from his distracted audience. In Brownie's analysis, waiting for a "distant future wrapped in dreams" will do nothing but help consign Stagg, and perhaps other POWs as well, to a horrible death. After all, Adams writes not just on the behalf of Stagg, but on the behalf of *all* Republican POWs in England: as would be evinced in even more dramatic fashion in the H Blocks in 1981, Irish hunger strikers throughout modern history have been synechdochal figures who exist not just as individuals but as expressions of their political and military organizations as well as their nation, irrespective of politicomilitary affiliation.

If Adams does not envision the hunger striker as an entirely autonomous individual, neither does he see the subject position of author as one that always needs to operate autonomously. As Brownie reveals, "Frank Stagg" is a literary collaboration[44] between Adams, Hugh Feeney, and Gerry Kelly. Feeney and Kelly are two former hunger strikers who were force-fed in English prisons in a manner similar to Stagg, and these two POWs wrote out accounts of their experiences. Adams does not hide that in "Frank Stagg" he incorporated Feeney's and Kelly's texts "almost as they were written,"[45] and indeed, the article's account of the procedure itself is an extended quotation from one or both of Adams's coauthors.[46] That Adams does not ascribe individual portions of the quote to their respective authors reveals the communal mindset of the Republican author *faoi ghlas*, a point that corresponds to the article's insistence that Stagg's experience with force-feeding likely will be identical to that of Kelly and Feeney. For instance, after outlining the excruciating ordeal of the insertion of the feeding tube, this quoted section of "Frank Stagg" describes the aftermath of the "successful" force-feeding as the prisoner's stomach is filled:

> Automatically he will vomit [up],[47] the disgorged food being caught in a kidney dish. If the doctor in charge is especially sadistic the vomit will be forced back down his throat again (this happened to Gerry Kelly)... He may be refused a towel or water to wash off his vomit as Hugh Feeney was, and his cell will stink of sour milk and disgorged food.[48]

In this fashion Adams's article blends individual voices to speak for a collective experience of Irish prisoners in British prisons, citing separate experiences only to illustrate what may be happening to Stagg. "Frank Stagg" is at once the individual hunger striker, the ideology for which he stands, the process of composition, and the article that results from this collective effort.

Adams *faoi ghlas*, Adams *taoibh amuigh*

In the introduction to this book, I outline some of the general characteristics differentiating texts produced *faoi ghlas* (during incarceration) from those produced *taoibh amuigh* (outside prison walls, subsequent to release), and the revisions that the "Brownie" articles underwent in their transformation to the texts appearing in *Cage Eleven* provide textbook examples of the manner in which texts composed in prison can differ from those written and revised outside. In stark contrast to the literary canon's traditional fixation on notions of universality, atemporality, and the supposedly autonomous individual, one of the most common hallmarks of the *faoi ghlas* text is its frequently profound grounding in the discrete space and moment of its composition and its deconstruction of the expectations of passive literary consumption. In the editorial choices made to convert the *Republican News* version of "Frank Stagg" to the *Cage Eleven* version, we encounter other examples of the manner in which *faoi ghlas* texts regularly depart from more traditional literary models to an even greater degree than most prison memoirs produced *taoibh amuigh.*

The disparate conclusions of "Frank Stagg" provide dramatic evidence of this contrast between *faoi ghlas* and *taoibh amuigh* prison writing. While both texts include the passage cited earlier foregrounding the need for readers to pressure the British in order to save Stagg, the final paragraphs of the *Republican News* article have been deleted in *Cage Eleven. Cage Eleven*'s "Frank Stagg, 1976" ends with an altered version[49] of the penultimate paragraph of the *Republican News* article, and reads as follows:

> The Dublin government has abandoned its responsibility to its own citizens. It actively undermines their rights. Only the Irish people can guarantee these rights. They can do this by opposing the British presence in Ireland and the injustices and torture meted out to Irish prisoners.[50]

In contrast, the original *faoi ghlas* version concludes with the strident declaration that

> As you finish reading this article, an Irish Prisoner of War is being brutalized.
>
> AT THE TIME OF WRITING FRANK STAGG IS DYING. AS YOU READ THIS, HE MAY BE DEAD!
>
> WILL YOU BE RESPONSIBLE?[51]

On the surface, this alteration is surprising— especially given that the *Cage Eleven* version has not been revised otherwise to reflect contemporary knowledge of Stagg's eventual death after sixty-one days on hunger strike: Adams notes Stagg's passing on 12 February 1976 only in a separate postscript, its italicization making it deliberately identifiable as a contemporary addendum.[52] *Cage Eleven*'s deletion of the original ending certainly reflects the increased attention *taoibh amuigh* texts pay to the formalist aesthetics of traditional literature, not least in its apparent attempts to "improve" the text by eliminating what some critics might consider a "hysterical" tone.

Yet, we would do well to interrogate whatever negative reactions we might have to the original ending: if we prefer the tone of the *Cage Eleven* version, is it because we reckon it evinces more of the subtlety we deem an integral component of literature, or is it because we refuse the notion that we might somehow be culpable in Stagg's death? If the latter, then might our discomfort originate in the *faoi ghlas* text's critique of the autonomous, decontextualized individual and of the still-pervasive model of passive literary consumption? With every drop of its ink, the *Republican News* "Frank Stagg" rejects passivity and quiet contemplation without action: from this perspective there must be recognition of every individual's inescapable connection with and responsibility to the surrounding world. The raw urgency of the *Republican News* "Frank Stagg" derives from the conditions of possibility surrounding its publication: here is a life that might be saved, the article urges, if only one can transcend the inertia often expected in the act of reading.

In contrast, *Cage Eleven*'s "Frank Stagg, 1976" is somewhat more in keeping with the overlapping bourgeois notions of the individual and of literary consumption, most notably in the anthology's shift of responsibility from the reader to "the Dublin government" that "has abandoned its responsibility to its own citizens." Although the *taoibh amuigh* version does raise a call to action, it is a more general one without explicit reference to any contemporary Republican POWs on whose behalf the reader might agitate. Furthermore, *Cage Eleven*'s "Frank Stagg, 1976" firmly casts the reader in the more palatable role of potential solution to the problem rather than the more complex and uncomfortable subject position constructed by the *Republican News* version, one that underscores both individual agency as well as culpability.

Other alterations reveal similar domestication of the original text. For example, unlike the *faoi ghlas* version, the *Cage Eleven* "Frank Stagg, 1976" does not "name names" when describing the actions of the prison doctors responsible for force-feeding the hunger strikers, and similarly the names of the prison warders who brutalized POWs that are mentioned in stories such as "Screws" have been deleted. No doubt the writings in *Cage Eleven* were subject to more traditional editorial scrutiny at the hands of major presses than they received at *Republican News*, not only in terms of canonical literary aesthetics but also with regard to issues of libel.[53] However, while these editorial choices undeniably originate, at least in part, in pragmatic concerns such as staving off lawsuits, they also are entirely consistent with a desire to prod *faoi ghlas* resistance writing away from its usual origins in raw testimony, and, one might cynically argue, from its desire to make oppressors accountable for their actions.[54] *Taoibh amuigh* discourse remains a weapon, though perhaps a somewhat more blunted sword than originally intended by the author.

Indeed, given the fatal outcome of Stagg's hunger strike—a death that was not predetermined at the moment of the article's initial composition—how does one read either version of "Frank Stagg?" Readers sympathetic to Stagg might very easily despair at the apparent inability of discourse to intervene in moments of crisis; after all, Adams's bid to save Stagg's life failed. Is the article included in *Cage Eleven* only as a historical document or as an example of the futility of mixing literature and politics? Quite the opposite: Adams's response to Stagg's death seems clear enough when he concludes that "The Dublin government has abandoned its responsibility to its own citizens. It actively undermines their rights." While the *Cage Eleven* "Frank Stagg, 1976" eschews the overt specificity of much *faoi ghlas* prison writing, the later version nonetheless demonstrates that Adams, like other resistance writers *taoibh amuigh,* remains intent on inspiring action in the present. The *Cage Eleven* version of the story is as much about Anglo-Irish relations in 1990 as it is about a hunger strike in 1976, a point especially evident in its vitriolic denunciation of "the Dublin government." Though in the original article Adams refers to the Republic as the "Free State"[55] and not as the "Dublin government," as he does in *Cage Eleven,* it is the English who receive the harshest critique in the *Republican News* version, a target that is unsurprising considering the similar battles for repatriation that other hunger strikers (including Gerry Kelly, Hugh Feeney, and Marian and Dolours Price) had just fought in the early 1970s. When the article is revised to draw attention to the manner in which Republican POWs felt "the Dublin government has abandoned its responsibility to its own citizens," the *taoibh amuigh* "Frank Stagg, 1976" lends support to the battle for improved conditions in the H Blocks that was in full swing during the year before *Cage Eleven*'s publication.[56] In addition, 1990 marks the midpoint of the years when Adams and Social Democratic and Labour Party (SDLP) leader John Hume began an official dialogue that culminated in the Hume/Adams proposals. In *Before the Dawn* Adams recalls,

> In April 1992 John Hume and I issued the first of several statements of the results of our more than five years of dialogue. We had reached agreement on a process which we believed could create the conditions for a lasting peace; its success depended on the responses of the British and Irish governments and the IRA... The Dublin government pledged its support.[57]

The revisions to "Frank Stagg" should be seen in this wider political context. Because the 1985 Anglo-Irish Agreement formally created an uneasy partnership between England and the Republic with regard to Northern Ireland's fate (thus recognizing British claims to "the Province" in an unprecedented fashion), many Republicans at the time regarded the Dublin government as having betrayed the northern populace: Adams has described the Anglo-Irish Agreement as "an attempt to counter the rise of Sinn Féin."[58] The more pressure that Adams could bring to bear on the Dublin Government to take a proactive role on behalf of the Six Counties (or, some might argue, the more they could be persuaded to support policies amenable to Republicans), the better it would suit Sinn Féin. Considering that *Cage Eleven* received such a wide readership in the Twenty-Six Counties, it is indeed conceivable that the *taoibh amuigh* "Frank Stagg, 1976" played a small role in the success of the Hume/Adams proposals.

As the two versions of "Frank Stagg" demonstrate, both *taoibh amuigh* and *faoi ghlas* prison writing emphasize the present moment, but their emphases differ in important—though subtle—ways with regard to specificity and force. *Faoi ghlas* writing often focuses with laser-like precision and intensity on the concrete here-and-now. I maintain that this tendency to foreground the specifically defined present originates in the desire of political prisoners *faoi ghlas* to remain connected with the outside world from which they are exiled, to remain a part of the political debate outside, and in so doing to discursively deny their imprisonment. After all, as Kieran McEvoy accurately maintains, Internment itself is an act of "reactive containment"[59] intended to disrupt the Republican movement by dividing and isolating its membership. The Security Forces interned Republicans not just in order to prevent possible acts of violence but also to disrupt the development and dissemination of Republican political analysis. A case in point is the particular sort of censorship Adams experiences when as a POW in the Cages he attempts to review Michael Farrell's now well-known book *Northern Ireland: The Orange State* for *Republican News*. As Adams reports in May, 1976 in "A Week in the Life," when his OC inquires about the book's failure to arrive in the Cage, he is informed by the prison administration that "books dealing with events after '69 were not permitted in [the Cages] and that only books about things before that date were allowed."[60] Yet, by self-consciously demonstrating in their writings that they remain informed about current events, Republican POWs such as Adams remind both themselves and their captors that it is possible to defeat the atemporality imposed on them.

Despite this prohibition, Adams points out later in "A Week in the Life" that "they let newspapers in," though these are no doubt censored.[61] Although, on one hand, it is puzzling, this inconsistency in prison policy is entirely typical of Long Kesh; on the other, however, I will go further and argue that the rationale—or lack thereof—for such a distinction between periodicals and books mirrors aesthetics that remain ascendant in academia even today. Just as the prison censors apparently consider newspapers less of a threat than other texts, so the academy historically has not taken seriously "nonliterary" and/or ephemeral writing. Similarly—as is dramatically visible in the relative thicknesses of the last three volumes of the *Norton Anthology of English Literature*—university curricula traditionally deemphasize the importance of the contemporary, encouraging the contemplation of the past rather than the present. As progressive scholars have begun to realize, unchecked such an approach lends itself to a disengagement from the social and political here-and-now, a disengagement in perfect accord with an "apolitical" formalist aesthetic that uncritically reifies the bourgeois status quo.

The ramifications of this removal from the present become clearer when one considers the interrogation techniques used on inmates of the Cages. From the very first moment that the British government reintroduced Internment in 1971, the Security Forces attempted to control the manner in which prisoners experience time, and the experiences of the "Hooded Men" provide grim example of the manner in which time itself can be manipulated into a tool of counterinsurgency. The Hooded Men were nationalists arrested in the first days of Internment who were singled out by the Security Forces for interrogation using techniques subsequently judged to be "inhuman and degrading treatment" by the European Court of Human Rights in 1978, techniques that included both physical and psychological torment.[62]

Sensory deprivation was at the heart of this abuse, and as the name bestowed upon them emphasizes, during their interrogation the heads of these internees were completely covered by hoods. The Security Forces compelled the internees to stand for almost six days in "search position" against a wall, depriving them of food, water, and sleep for that entire period.[63] Similarly, guards denied prisoners all access to toilets: as internee Francis McGuigan testifies, "You just urinated where you stood."[64] POWs were beaten if they could no longer stand in the search position (and sometimes for no reason at all), an experience all the more terrifying because the hoods prevented the prisoners from seeing either their attackers or from which direction they were being attacked. For the greater part of those six days, these internees were subjected to white noise at deafening volume, described by one of the prisoners, Michael Donnelly, as

> a high pitched hissing sound which seems to have been "piped" into the place where we were. After a period this really played on the mind and led eventually to a kind of illusion where I thought I heard someone singing familiar tunes. At times I sang along with them. I remember in particular singing "Henry Joy." Outside of this noise nothing else could be heard except the groans and squeals of other men, I presume, who were undergoing some sort of physical anguish or mortal torture.[65]

These interrogation techniques had a profound effect on the internees, not least in terms of their perception of time. All prisoners subject to this treatment report a loss of temporal perspective soon after they were placed in the room where they were subjected to white noise; Michael Donnelly's statement is representative of other prisoners' experiences when he admits that from that point onward he "cannot at all fix times" when trying to determine the length of his interrogation.[66]

The dislocative effect of this forced atemporality and physical abuse evinces itself in the hallucinations and mental breakdowns suffered by the prisoners. To be cut loose from time is to be vulnerable during interrogation and incarceration—for in Northern Irish disciplinary structures, context is everything.[67] Francis McGuigan reveals,

> on one occasion the interrogator asked me to give my name and address so that he could write it down. He asked me to spell it for him. I spelt Francis but couldn't spell McGuigan. I knew I was spelling it wrong and kept going over it, spelling it from the beginning. They laughed. They kept laughing and saying "You are going mad, you are out of your mind, you are insane." All during this period there were times

> when you thought you were and you prayed. Then they asked me to prove I wasn't mad by counting up to ten. I wouldn't do it for fear I couldn't manage it.[68]

Nor was this erasure confined to mental experience: McGuigan relates how "on one occasion I was being beaten by someone with a stick—thumping me with the stick on back, arms and legs. I thought this was very comical. Here was someone thumping me with a stick and I couldn't feel it."[69]

While he was not hooded during his experiences of interrogation, Adams was nonetheless subject to techniques that obviously were meant to replicate the environment experienced by the Hooded Men. Adams describes the questioning he was subject to after his first arrest as follows:

> In the interrogation center they brought me into a very large room in a barracks-style wooden hut, and this room was divided up into open cubicles: men were seated facing the wall in these cubicles. I was placed in one and left there facing a wall made of board with holes in it which had the effects of inducing images, shapes, and shadows in front of my eyes. Soldiers or branchmen kept coming up behind me, kicking the chair from under me, shouting at me, hitting me on the back of my head.[70]

As they did with the Hooded Men, Adams's interrogators attempt to induce a feeling of helplessness through disorientation and individuation, isolating him from his senses and his comrades. Adams's vision is assaulted not by perpetual darkness, but rather by a surface deliberately designed to confuse the eye. His tormentors remain invisible behind him, announcing themselves only in unexpected blows. And though Adams was not subjected to white noise, his captors attack his ears by dropping steel trays beside him, creating a deafening clatter, again all the more unsettling because it came without warning.[71]

By controlling the POWs' perceptual experience of the world around them (both in terms of the physical senses as well as time), the Security Forces attempt to break individual POWs by decontextualizing them. In McGuigan's case they temporarily succeed, disassociating him from two of the most fundamental aspects of self: his body and his name. Interrogation unmakes McGuigan mentally and physically, for his body is unable to feel and his mind is unable to quantify the world around him alphabetically, temporally, or numerically. In a way, he ceases to *be* as a result of these losses. One must take such experiences of interrogation into account when examining Republican prison writing originating in the Cages of this period, because when POWs foreground the specific moment of composition in their texts, they re-insert themselves into measurable time—thus reclaiming themselves by reclaiming verifiable temporal perspective.

Athghabháil (recovery) of this sort remains important after the actual interrogation ends, for, as Adams reminds us,

> Internment was very unsettling for prisoners, who didn't know whether they were in for twenty days, twenty months or twenty years. If you were sentenced at least you knew how long you had to serve and could settle down to doing your time, but with internment you never knew. This was especially hard to handle for those—and there were many—who had never done anything to warrant being imprisoned in the first place.[72]

The Security Forces utilize forced atemporality as part of Long Kesh's disciplinary mechanism long after the hood is removed and the gross assaults on the body end. The extreme temporal disorientation of the interrogation is a bludgeon to the psyche of the POW, but incarceration without fixed release date is the slow drip of the Chinese water torture, relentless and deriving a large portion of its power from its seeming interminability. To survive, POWs need to reclaim themselves by recovering their ability to perceive the world on their own terms. In a carceral environment such as Long Kesh, to contextualize is to resist.

Adams's prison writings are his *athghabháil*, and through them he recontextualizes himself spatially, temporally, and ideologically. Adams claims that the Brownie articles "tended not to address immediately current events. This was partly because of the practical constraints involved in getting articles written and then getting them out of the camp, but principally because what I wanted to address were more underlying questions regarding the nature and relevance of our political beliefs and practice."[73] Indeed, about one-third of Adams's *Republican News* articles deal only with theoretical aspects of Irish history and nationalism, only slightly fewer than those articles dealing exclusively with prison life in the Cages; however, about half of the Brownie articles specifically refer to events that took place outside Long Kesh less than a week prior to the time of composition. Furthermore, one should not misread Adams's statement about "immediately current events": even those political articles that do not explicitly cite recent happenings on the outside largely remain fixated on the present moment and its possibilities. Even though an essay may nominally focus, for example, on a distant historical occurrence, Brownie generally points the way—explicitly or implicitly—to the manner in which the past might be appropriated for present gain. In the context of Long Kesh, such a move is an *athghabháil* of temporality: time is no longer a weapon of counterinsurgency to be used against the POWs, but rather the POWs reorder it on their terms, and reassert their place in it.

To illustrate, as the title suggests, "Belfast: 1913 or 1976?" suggests that James Connolly's analysis of Orange attacks on nationalists and socialists at a labor rally "are as relevant today as they were [when Connolly wrote his account of them] in August 1913."[74] Similarly, "The Republic: A Reality" points to the prison writings of Liam Mellows to illustrate that "As in 1922, work not done today will be harder to do later and opportunities missed will not reappear so clearly."[75] In this model, 1913 is 1922 is 1976: the precise date has the potential to become tragically irrelevant. Faced with this apparently endless feedback loop of history, one might simply give up and surrender to the impossibility of individual resistance to time's forces in exactly the way the Hooded Men were meant to be broken in a space where time had no meaning. Yet the seeming lack of temporal fixity in the Brownie columns contrasts dramatically with the forced atemporality and individuation of the interrogation or the prison because of the potential agency that Adams finds in the present. In Brownie's view the atemporal cycle can end through properly directed action, for resistance is possible at any time and in innumerable forms, particularly when undertaken as a collective effort.

While many writers censure Republican reverence for the past in general and for martyred leaders such as Mellows and Connolly in particular, I insist that Adams here is not reifying the expected Republican grand narrative. Indeed, in these articles, he calls into question some of the core tenets of earlier Republican ideology—an ideology firmly ascendant in the leadership senior to Adams in the mid-1970s. In "The Republic: A Reality," when Brownie announces to his fellow Republicans that "we are not clearing the way for a more 'Britless Ireland' but for a Socialist Republic and the building of all the alternatives [to the British system] cannot wait until 'after the war.' It must start now," he begins to push Provisional Republicanism away from an exclusive reliance on "armed struggle."[76] The Cage wires are meant to keep Adams and his fellow POWs from active participation in the Republican cause, but if the struggle is redefined as one that also relies on discourse and political engagement rather than physical force alone then he remains a part of the struggle. In his writings, Adams has begun to articulate some of these "alternatives" and as such has discursively escaped the Cages.

Provisional Dialectics: *Faoi Glas* versus *Republican News*

The sea-change in Provisional Republicanism manifest in articles such as "The Republic: A Reality" evinces how even in an era of abstentionism, by means of grassroots periodicals such as *Republican News,* the Provisionals of the mid-1970s were active in political discourse directed at the wider nationalist community. Indeed, dissemination of a particular brand of Republican thought was one of the intentions behind Adams's "Brownie" articles for, as Richard English accurately observes,

> Intracommunal conflict has been a less obvious, but no less vicious, aspect of the northern troubles and of the IRA's story within it. For in some ways the battle for dominance within one's own community was the key one: the likelihood of gaining support from members of the opposing community was negligible, and so expansion of one's role depended upon gaining ground at the expense of one's intracommunal rivals.[77]

Predictably, the moderate nationalist SDLP frequently draws fire from Brownie, but in many cases he reserves particular venom for the Officials, from whom the Provisionals split in 1969–70.

The second Brownie column to appear in *Republican News*, "Out There on the Motorway..." is a harsh critique of the Officials. The article begins with a conversation between the narrator and a comrade:

> "Do you see the Sticks[78] have a Red Star up in their Cage?" I said, pointing over the few acres of barbed wire and corrugated fencing up to Cage 21. "Indeed," said he, as we both squinted to where a large Red Star glared blankly back at us from the gable wall of a hut. "They painted it just after Easter, you know," he volunteered as he slid down off the roof where we had been taking our ease, and more than our share of sunshine.[79]

The physical distance between the Officials' cage and the Provisional cage in which the narrator and his companion are imprisoned suggests a similar ideological one. The passage's reliance on visual metaphor foregrounds the two factions' inability to see eye to eye: the Provisionals squint, straining to comprehend. In contrast, the Red Star's blank glare contains within it a peculiar mix of hostility and vacancy.

Note also that the actual occupants of Cage 21 are not the ones engaged in this ocular joust. Adams's metonymy is more intentional than it may first appear: from a Provisional perspective the Officials privilege empty symbol at the expense of human agency, particularly the agency to be found through guerilla warfare.[80] When the narrator sneeringly remarks in the next paragraph that "Revolutionary theory is a lot easier than the real thing, even in the Lazy K [Long Kesh]," the reader is reminded that the 1969–70 split in the Republican movement was occasioned in part by the Officials' relatively swift move away from armed struggle in the early years of the Troubles.[81] "Out There on the Motorway..." emphasizes action of the most basic sort, cataloging Republican escape attempts past and present, presumably in contrast to the perceived acquiescence of the Officials both to their imprisonment and to British imperialism in general. In addition, the article describes in tragic detail the various ways in which Republicans have, to use the narrator's phrasing, "escaped the hard way" from incarceration, citing the examples of Terence MacSwiney, who died during the Anglo-Irish War after seventy-four days on hunger strike in Brixton Prison, and Adams's own compatriot Hugh Coney who was killed in 1974 during an escape attempt.[82] At the conclusion of the piece Adams's narrator asks,

> Did you ever dig a tunnel? Did you ever drive past [Long Kesh] and not think of Hugh Coney. [*sic*] Out there on the motorway, that he was trying to reach. Out there where the cars and lorries whiz up and down the M1, past [the] whitewashed Church [*sic*], past Long Kesh, past reality.
>
> Maybe it's better to do that than to paint red stars on gable walls. I don't know! Do you??[83]

It is only in these last moments that Adams makes manifest the true import of the article's title. When Coney attempts to reach the motorway, he seeks a hospitable ideological space as much as he does a physical destination. Even if Coney were able to make it to the road, escape would depend upon help from civilians outside—in the best-case scenario,[84] from a sympathetic motorist who would give Coney a lift. And like Coney, Adams also reaches out toward those motorists via his prison writing, in the process interrogating the human capacity to witness suffering without acting to alleviate it. When drivers "whizz up and down the M1" without a second thought about Hugh Coney they ignore—and in so doing, passively support—the unconcealed presence of a concentration camp[85] alongside one of the busiest highways in Ireland.[86] As the photograph appearing below "Out There on the Motorway..." underscores, the "ten thousand lights" of Long Kesh can be seen from the M1; despite witnessing this eerie sight, it seems that most travelers "have somewhere else to go/and sail calmly on" down the highway (to borrow Auden's phrasing). Although Long Kesh may be visible in a raw sense to these motorists, it is not truly present to them. Adams hopes that his prison writing will make the visible present. In the narrator's view, to observe without empathy is merely to look: to truly see Long Kesh is to understand the plight of those within it, to understand the forces that build political prisons, to understand that one may be unintentionally complicit with those forces.

When in the final paragraph of "Out There on the Motorway..." the narrator wonders whether "Maybe it's better to do that than to paint red stars on gable walls," the indeterminacy of to what "that" refers is richly suggestive.[87] In this statement, Adams suggests in bitterly ironic fashion that it is better to utterly forget the active struggle of Republicans such as Coney (as the M1 motorists do) than to be an "armchair revolutionary" of the sort he deems the Officials to be, one's resistance beginning and ending with passive, ineffective symbol. Simultaneously, there is also room to read the last paragraph's "that" as a reference to the commitment and self-sacrifice that "Out There on the Motorway..." finds praiseworthy earlier in the article in the examples of Coney and MacSwiney. While the actions of both men are passive in the sense that they are not actual attacks on the Security Forces, they nonetheless are rooted in both physical and symbolic resistance to the prison authorities. Kieran McEvoy rightly classifies Republican escape attempts under "resistance as ridicule," suggesting that

> Once imprisoned, physically removing oneself from domination is a direct challenge to the power of the prison authorities and the state. Escapes cause disarray amongst the enemy, they lead to official inquiries and calls for resignation (Barker 1998). They are a source of grudging admiration for daring and organization [from the British], they drain resources and offer the potential for propaganda coups. In short, for politically motivated prisoners, they are a rich source of both material and symbolic resistance ridiculing the supposed omnipotence of the state.[88]

When it came to escapes, Brownie did not engage in revolutionary theory alone: Adams takes pride in the assistance he offered in others' jailbreaks.[89] However, in typically self-depreciating fashion in the foreword to *Cage Eleven,* Adams admits to being the internees' "most unsuccessful escapee...I was only caught twice."[90] Yet Adams's recapture is not a defeat in all respects, for on a discursive level his prison writing wins a victory similar to an actual breakout: the very existence of the Brownie columns graphically demonstrates the shortcomings of prison security in Long Kesh, even as the articles themselves ridicule the prison regime in the most literal sense. In many ways these physical and discursive escape attempts are truly emblematic of Adams's ideology at this point in time: guerilla action alone is insufficient, just as is what the Provisionals view as the merely symbolic resistance of the Officials. [91] As we shall see in the next section, as early as 1975 Adams began the move away from traditional Republicanism's exclusive focus on armed struggle and toward an ideology combining physical force, discourse, and electoral intervention—a Republicanism famously termed by Danny Morrison in 1981 as one that held a "ballot paper in this hand and an Armalite in this hand."[92]

While, of course, Republican ideology exhibits many continuities over the years, it is also the case that Republicanism is informed by the individual historical moment, often evincing capacity for dramatic change. Adams's critique of tradition would cause a new generation of Provisional POWs to reevaluate their own command structures. With the benefits of the official recognition offered by Special Category Status, it is no wonder that in the mid-1970s a large number of imprisoned Provisionals defined themselves exclusively in military terms, and foremost among these was Dave Morley, the supreme officer commanding of all of the Republican Cages. Writing in *Faoi Glas* [*sic*], a periodical comprised entirely of texts composed by incarcerated Republicans, Morley declares,

> It has been said that there is a time for war and a time for words and this saying is relevant now, while the British examine the means they wish to implement for disengagement. This period is one for words, but if reluctance is shown in any way by the British, then the time for war will be with us again. Then our simple and straightforward way will come into being once again—DRIVE the British into the sea. No frills and no fancy words. Simply make their existence in Ireland an uncomfortable one and make it an uneconomical proposition for them to remain. The Provisional Army are capable of doing just that and will, if necessary, speak in the only real language the British are capable of understanding, that is force of arms.[93]

Morley's skepticism of the negotiations taking place during the cease-fire are quite evident in the manner in which actual language—embodied in the dismissively feminized "frills and fancy words" of diplomacy—is subordinated to a masculine, metaphoric "language" of uncompromising violence. Moreover, whatever grudging concessions Morley makes to diplomacy are further undercut by the argument he puts forth in the paragraph immediately prior to the passage quoted above. In this paragraph, Morley urges his reader that "It should be obvious to all who have witnessed the struggle for Freedom [*sic*] that the driving force has always been the objective to remove the British from this island, using any means necessary to achieve that aim. It will never be achieved by a war of words."[94]

At first glance this statement seems to support Tim Pat Coogan's characterization of Republicanism in general and the IRA in particular as a tradition "of physical action and separation. It is not an intellectual one."[95] However, I insist that buried in this apparent dismissal of discourse is a real awareness of the power of the word. After all, if Morley truly believed that there was no power to be found in discourse, why would he bother to write at all? In fact, by my reckoning, only one other author appeared more frequently in the pages of *Faoi Glas* [*sic*] during the periodical's short lifespan. This apparent paradox can be resolved with a clearer understanding of prison writing's place in Republican history. Certainly since the time of Michael Davitt, Republicans have produced writing during incarceration. The early years of Internment saw the appearance of a number of internal newsletters within individual Cages, including *Faoi Glas*, which seems to have existed as an internal publication until late 1974 when the burning of the Cages brought publication to a temporary halt.

However, from its reappearance in August 1975, *Faoi Glas* was unique in that it evolved into one of the first periodicals that was written and edited in its entirety by prisoners and was *specifically intended* for widespread consumption outside jail walls. Unlike the individual articles by POWs that made their appearance in earlier Republican periodicals, *Faoi Glas* was an entity of its own. Authors in Republican Cages throughout the compound contributed to the paper, all of their texts smuggled out of the Cages to be printed and distributed by the Cathal Brugha Sinn Féin Cumann in Andersontown.[96] While the bulk of *Faoi Glas*'s content consists of political essays, a number of poems appeared in each issue; a further example of the manner in which *faoi ghlas* prison writing deliberately attempts to undo the partition of "Literature" from other forms of writing.[97]

The lengths to which the Republicans would go in order to produce *Faoi Glas* should be indication enough that, contrary to Morley's insistence in the article quoted previously, the imprisoned authors are in fact *deeply* invested in a "war of words." However, the conflict in which *Faoi Glas* is engaged is primarily a civil war, not one waged against an external enemy. While hawks such as Morley may doubt the power of discourse to sway outsiders, they clearly believe that the nationalist population of the Six Counties may prove more malleable; thus, the writers of *Faoi Glas* seek direct contact with the world outside the Cages. For example, in the article that opens the reborn *Faoi Glas*, Derec Mac Thomais writes,

> In order to help us strengthen the link across the barbed wire, we hope you will not hesitate to contact us with any comments, questions, etc. that you may have regarding Faoi Glas, [*sic*] this will help us make the paper an effective two-way communication. As well as attempting to build a picture of Long Kesh for you we will also write on current happenings as seen from here.[98]

In this passage—essentially the mission statement of *Faoi Glas*—we get a clarification of Morley's message. Far from categorically dismissing the power of discourse in general, the imprisoned writers here are soliciting dialogue with the outside in order to recruit Republicans to their faction of the Provisional Movement. In doing so, writing becomes the instrument through which Moley and Mac Thomais reappropriate the environment surrounding them: *Faoi Glas* co-opts the space outside the Cages, bringing it inside by means of discourse.

The ability of writing to force a collapse of interior and exterior space makes it a powerful weapon of resistance to Republicans: like the command structures themselves in the Cages, the writing in *Faoi Glas* frequently emphasizes the communal voice of Republican POWs, thus combating attempts by the prison administration to individuate, isolate, and control inmates. As Barbara Harlow points out, prison texts in general seek a "re-definition of the self and the individual in terms of a collective enterprise and struggle... [they] are not written for the sake of a 'book of one's own,' but rather they are collective documents, testimonies written by individuals to their common struggle":[99] indeed, from the cover of its first issue onward *Faoi Glas* announces itself to be the "Journal of the Sentenced Republican Prisoners, Long Kesh." This communal voice stands in stark opposition to the aesthetic model that has traditionally governed literature, one that—like the bourgeois society in which this aesthetic was first articulated—values most highly the "solitary genius" who supposedly has managed to break free from contingencies of the historical moment. Just as the worst forms of capitalism encourage passive, isolated consumption of material goods, an exclusively formalistic aesthetics encourages an isolation in readers by bracketing the historical and political context in which literary works are produced and consumed.

At times, however, communality exacts a cost. Many Provisional POWs come to realize that although the militaristic self-governance of the Republican Cages afforded a measure of protection from external pressure, it had the potential to oppress as well. While rigid command structures produce unity, they also often discourage innovation. Indeed, excessive rigidity was one of the complaints that POWs leveled against Davey Morley. Brendan Hughes, who would later be OC of the Provisionals in the H Blocks and leader of the 1980 hunger strike, points out that some important IRA officers in the Cages of the time actually "came from a British Army background and they used to send round these wee manuals. I couldn't stick all that stuff, being trained as non-thinking combatants. You weren't allowed to think."[100] Gerry Kelly, who also became a Provisional leader both in and out of prison, echoes Hughes's evaluation, adding "The Battalion Staff were fairly regimented, a bit copy-cat of the British Army."[101] Ironically, in their fight to rid Ireland of British politicomilitary structures, the older Republican officers replicated these structures in their own chain of command, a contradiction that Adams and others quickly recognized and resisted.

In the story "The Night Andy Warhol Was Banned," Adams unveils the impact of prison-born *conscientização* on the traditional power structures of the Republican movement. As the story's title implies, the conflict in this text centers on the decision of the Camp OC—who is described by the narrator as someone "from the older school of Belfast Republicans"[102]—to forbid all Republican prisoners from viewing a television program about Andy Warhol because of its "'explicit sexual scenes.'"[103] Two of the younger POWs voice their strenuous objection, arguing that "the struggle is about freedom... about freedom of expression, an end to censorship. You can't ban TV programs."[104] Their opposition to this directive indicates how far Adams's generation of POWs has come from the conservative Republicanism of the older Camp Staff, a conservatism that marries extreme Catholic orthodoxy with militarism devoid of extensive political analysis. The two rabble-rousers are dismayed by how, in the narrator's words, "everyone [else] took the news quietly and calmly" and the pair initially mistake their comrades' silence for acquiescence.[105] However, when the program is broadcast, only the Camp

OC's Cage misses it: all the rest—approximately one thousand Republican POWs—tune in. The key component of the other Cages' mutiny is the concerted silence that conceals it. No one mentioned the disobedience to the Camp OC or the members of his Cage, and Adams's narrator slyly remarks that "what he doesn't know will do him no harm."[106]

This insubordination[107] reflects a watershed moment in Provisional Republican history. As Alexandre Kojève observes in his discussion of Hegel's Master/ Slave relationship, "The purely warlike attitude of the Master does not vary throughout the centuries, and therefore it cannot engender a historical change."[108] In contrast to this stagnation, the Republican POWs—like Hegel's Slave—remain dynamic in their active engagement with their world through critical analysis as well as through their continued connection with their own labor. In their act of silent protest, the Republican generation that came of age in Long Kesh set forth on a road that has inaugurated historical change of a sort almost unimaginable in 1975. Indeed, I argue that the shift in mainstream Provisional Republicanism away from a conservative, exclusively physical-force tradition reflects a mode of thinking that flourished—and to a degree, originated—in the prison struggle of contemporary Republican POWs.[109]

Although Special Category Status had its benefits to POWs, I insist that in some respects it actually served British interests in ways that Republicans of the time did not anticipate. For, whether sentenced or interned, within the Cages the Provisionals categorized themselves into three groups, as Laurence McKeown reminds us:

> civilians, "suspended" volunteers and "cleared" volunteers. Being classified in such a manner had very real practical consequences. A cleared volunteer could take a staff position, a suspended volunteer could not. There were certain communications from the...outside which could only be read by cleared volunteers. There were certain meetings and classes which only cleared volunteers were allowed to attend, for example, the military lectures.[110]

In other words, POWs who were members of or sympathetic to Provisional Sinn Féin would be admitted to the Provisional Cages as civilians. These civilian detainees were allowed to vote for the Cage and camp staff; however, as they were not PIRA volunteers in "good standing," they could not themselves be part of that staff. As a result, the Provisional Cages spoke almost exclusively through PIRA volunteers.

Thus, at this point in history,[111] both the Provisionals and the British government confer legitimacy on Republican POWs primarily by foregrounding the subject position of the armed revolutionary rather than civilian political activist. Though Special Category Status forfeits a symbolic victory to the PIRA by implicitly recognizing it as a legitimate army, it simultaneously furthered British propaganda's attempts to blur the distinction between nonviolent civil rights activists and paramilitaries. Such an elision is dangerous on a number of levels, not least that it further emboldens the Security Forces to imprison Republicans whether or not they have paramilitary ties. In an even more sinister fashion, this elision encourages the random violence of Loyalist paramilitaries whose victims tend to be people with no Republican connections, randomly chosen by their killers in Catholic neighborhoods.[112] When Gusty Spence, leader of the UVF in Belfast, declares "If you can't get an IRA man get a *Taig*,[113] he's your last resort,"[114] it is a chilling reminder that, as Martin Dillon aptly phrases it, "within the Protestant paramilitary mind there was a crudely held belief that Catholicism, Nationalism and Republicanism were in some way inseparable."[115] Unfortunately, Republican legitimacy derived exclusively from a paramilitary command structure makes it that much easier for sectarian assassins to imagine that therefore all Catholics are "legitimate" targets. Lest it be thought that I overstate the case here, it must be remembered that such encouragement of countergangs is a central theme of the counterinsurgency techniques advocated by Sir Frank Kitson, who oversaw the British Army in Northern Ireland in the early 1970s.

This Kitsonian sectarian total war both creates and is *created by* the colonization of the private individual, a point raised in Adams's "Brownie" articles. Returning again to "Inside Story," we see Adams's forceful condemnation of the sectarian killings that were particularly frequent in the mid-1970s. Adams laments the artificial division of the Six Counties into

> teagues and orangies, Prods and micks. But it goes deeper than name-calling...and only the Brits reap the benefits. "let you and him fight" sez one wily Sasanach, "while yez are at it I'll be left alone to impose solutions, to build new profits on the backs of old scores. Let you and him fight and me and the privileged few will see things through."[116]

While, of course, Adams's analysis might be criticized as something of an oversimplification, more important to my present purpose is the contrast in tone we sense between the above quotation and the *Faoi*

Glas article by Davey Morley cited previously. Though both articles appear in August 1975, in Adams's article we see a foregrounding of peaceful coexistence between green and orange. Similarly, Adams does not see the problem or the solution only in military terms as Morley did: the "solutions" that the British "impose" are ones that he realizes cannot be ended with the armed struggle alone.

In addition, the previously quoted passage from "Inside Story" contains within it a critique of Morley's faction that might not readily be apparent today. The mid-1970s were a dark time indeed, and it is during this era that the PIRA committed many of the actions for which it was most harshly criticized, including no-warning bomb attacks against Unionist civilians. Thus, when Adams censures sectarian attacks, he censures some PIRA operations of the time: a perilous thing to do in Morley's Cages. To illustrate the risk that Adams takes in writing such an article one need only refer to the experiences of Brendan Hughes, who recalls

> being accused of dissenting and threatened to be thrown out of the Cages and of being dismissed with ignominy because of my opposition to the leadership. "Did I not understand I was arguing against the leadership of the Republican Movement?" Someone had heard me talking about what was happening on the outside. I was arguing against sectarian bombings and so forth.[117]

Prisoners cast out of the Republican Cages would face much more peril to life and limb: at the very least they would be at the mercy of their warders, many of whom were militant Loyalists. Though such exile was imposed infrequently—perhaps because POWs cannily realized the difficulties of isolation—it must have happened enough to warrant the reservation of Cage Eight for those POWs who voluntarily broke ties or who were expelled from the paramilitary group with which they were associated. According to Alex Maskey, the inmates of Cage Eight enjoyed the same facilities and privileges afforded to other prisoners under Special Category Status but unlike the Provisional Cages, where the POWs were sheltered by and reclaimed agency through their command structures, the prison authorities "more or less controlled the Cage" of the exiled.[118]

Yet despite the threat of Cage Eight, as time goes on Adams's opposition to Morley's regime grows less subtle. To illustrate, in "The National Alternative," which appeared in *Republican News* on 3 April 1976, Adams critiques OCs who act in a "purely 'military'" fashion, arguing that "as the tearing down process intensifies so can the rebuilding.

They're not two separate phases."[119] By contending that Republicans must develop "an alternative [to the British system] in keeping with the peoples' needs, with the war effort and with national policy," Adams advocates a fusion of military and political action that directly challenges the simplistic "Brits Out" approach of an exclusively military Republicanism.[120] It is also important to note that Adams emphasizes the need for popular input into the process of politicization when he maintains that such development of Republican policy "can't be left to Sinn Féin, the leadership or anyone else": grassroots-level Republicans must participate in the dialogue.[121] When Adams articulates these points, he begins a sea-change in Republican ideology, one that eventually results in the abandonment of electoral abstentionism, the Provisional IRA cease-fire, the Good Friday Agreement, and the total decommissioning of PIRA weapons that took place in September 2005.

As the next chapter will demonstrate, certainly the 1981 election of IRA hunger striker Bobby Sands to the British parliament influenced such a reevaluation of tactics;[122] however, other precedents were set even earlier in Long Kesh. Speaking about his own experiences in the H Blocks, Dr. Laurence McKeown reveals that in analyzing the pyrrhic victories of such actions as "burning the camp,[123] the riot in the Crumlin Road Prison, the blanket protest and the hunger strikes," by the late 1980s, the POWs "knew that head-on confrontational, physical battles were not the way to wage prison struggle"; instead, future prison protests were won "by intellectually undermining the prison rules by pointing to the inconsistencies and incoherence that underpinned many of them."[124] Beyond the fact that these new tactics decentered physical force as a resistance technique, this shift in approach by the Republicans is important to note because it demonstrates their growing confidence in their own agency as writers and thinkers. The critical consciousness to which McKeown refers was both developed in and exported out of the Cages and the H Block cells via prison writing. As the Brownie articles demonstrate, prison walls historically have never been able to isolate incarcerated Republicans completely: at most, such walls prove to be a semipermeable membrane that contains the body, but not the thoughts of POWs. Far from remaining in a "barbed wire ivory tower,"[125] as Adams terms it in the foreword of *Cage Eleven*, through the written word, the Republican POWs exercised agency as people who "were not just prisoners but political activists and theorists whose intellectual influence could expand beyond the confines of the prison camp."[126]

Such attempts by the new generation of POWs to become active shapers of Republican policy are unmistakably evident in Adams's article "An Ard Fheis," which appeared in *Republican News* on 18 September 1976. Outside, the Ard Fheis is the annual meeting where party policy is debated: in this essay, "Brownie" describes how Republican prisoners in his Cage organized their own ard fheis. The open dialogue of equals *taobh amuigh* (outside) and *faoi ghlas* (locked up) is noticeably less present in 1976 than it would be in later years, when Adams rather tentatively reports in "An Ard Fheis,"

> Last night in an exclusive interview the Cage O.C. and Adjutant told me that they considered the Ard Fheis to have been a great success. They hoped Sinn Fein [*sic*] Cumann [*sic*] outside would give a favourable reception to proposals sent out to them. The interest that POWs maintained in events outside was amply illustrated by the high level of debate and by the informed arguments put forward...They would wait with interest a report from the Ard Fheis outside and promised, somewhat *pessimistically* that the Cage would probably have another one next year.[127] (emphasis in the original)

The pessimism Adams describes above is not just an acknowledgment of the likelihood of continued political imprisonment in Northern Ireland: it also proceeds from the possibility that the prisoners' proposals might be ignored by the conservative leadership outside. Such a dismissal would effectively imprison the POWs a second time, for they would be simultaneously isolated from the outside world and formally rejected by the political party they turned to most for support. Yet, in prison writings such as "An Ard Fheis," the POWs hedge their bets, for they are putting their proposals directly in front of Republican community as embodied in the general readership of *Republican News* rather than indirectly, filtered through the elite delegates attending the Sinn Féin Ard Fheis. Like the POWs who ignore the Camp OC's command in "The Night Andy Warhol Was Banned," Adams alters the locus and directionality of power: it ceases to operate only in a vertical, hierarchical structure, shifting instead to a more horizontal one. Crucially, Adams and the other internees effect this change (and indeed, in the process appropriate a degree of this power) through the written word composed *faoi ghlas*.

Adams's challenge to conservative Republicanism via his prison writing is especially striking when one takes into account the events contemporary to the composition of the "Brownie" articles. Given that Loyalist strikes in 1974 shattered hopes for a constitutional settlement of the Troubles through the power-sharing executive envisioned by the Sunningdale Agreement, any Republican move away from an exclusively physical-force tradition in the mid-1970s is remarkable. The Sunningdale Agreement was the product of talks among delegates from the British and Irish governments, along with representatives from the Unionist Party, the Alliance Party, and the nationalist Social Democratic and Labour Party. It suggested an executive with five seats allocated to Catholics and six to Protestants[128] Historian and journalist Tim Pat Coogan maintains that Sunningdale was "the most important constitutional experiment to take place in Northern Ireland since the setting up of the state," and its failure caused some Catholics to question whether reform by constitutional means was possible in the Six Counties.[129] Yet, it is precisely this disaffected population—those that might be tempted to join the exclusively "physical force" brand of Republicanism—that the "Brownie" articles attempt to recruit.

In addition to the collapse of Sunningdale, other events contemporaneous with the "Brownie" articles created an atmosphere that easily could have ensured the continuance of conservative Republicanism. The years during which Adams's writings appeared in *Republican News* coincided exactly with the reign of terror of the Shankill Butchers, whose sectarian murders Coogan ranks as "the worst single set of atrocities of the entire troubled era."[130] Between 1975 and 1977, the Butchers—whose members were affiliated with the Ulster Volunteer Force (UVF), a Loyalist paramilitary group—targeted people they assumed to be Catholic, abducting them and torturing them for hours before murdering them, often with knives and axes. Martin Dillon describes the brutal excess that earned the Shankill Butchers their collective name, noting that one victim was

> suspended by a rope from a wooden beam and stripped of his clothing. A knife was used on his body much in the manner a sculptor would chip away at a piece of wood or stone. Long cuts were made down his back and thighs and in all there were 147 stab wounds on his body.[131]

Eleven of the Butchers were eventually convicted of a total of 112 crimes, including nineteen murders; for their offences, forty-two life sentences were handed down.[132] However, while the Shankill Butchers' murders are perhaps the most gruesome committed during the period, they represent only a fraction of the deaths caused by Loyalist paramilitaries: between 1974 and 1976, the UVF alone killed 250 people.[133]

Historically, a sizable portion of the Catholic population of the North has turned to the Irish Republican Army for defense against such physical attacks—though, as David Lowry notes, "often with some misgivings."[134] Indeed, in the nationalist interface areas that suffered the most in the early years of the Troubles, some residents faulted the IRA for not coming to their defense. As Caroline Kennedy-Pipe reminds us, "During the outbreak of the conflict in the North the IRA leadership was incapable of mounting an effective response to the Unionist [*sic*] onslaught on the Catholic communities," and in the Catholic Bogside area of Derry in 1969 and 1970, graffiti implied that "IRA had become synonymous with 'Irish ran away.'"[135] With potential for similar backlash from nationalist communities terrorized by sectarian killers such as the Shankill Butchers, Adams's public call to revision the Republican Movement as something beyond a military force is all the more noteworthy: after all, hardliners could—and did—criticize Adams's position as one that privileged politics at the expense of community safety. Yet, such a conservative Republican critique misses the complexity of Adams's analysis. Although the Brownie articles never dispute the traditional Republican belief in the right of violent revolution (nor do they suggest a de-escalation of the IRA's campaign), even at their most militant, not only do they always reject a sectarian response to sectarianism, they also insist that the armed struggle can only be a part of an overall rebellion that takes its direction according to the needs of the communities on the ground rather than from arbitrary dictates from a distant leadership.

Adams's call for the implementation of such dialectic within the Republican Movement appears to have been heeded, certainly by later Republican prisoners. The change from the atmosphere prevalent at the time of "An Ard Fheis" is perhaps best demonstrated by the appearance of such formal publications as *Iris Bheag* in the later years of the H Blocks. As chapter five of this book discusses in detail, *Iris Bheag* was a booklet produced monthly by Sinn Féin's Education Department between 1987 and 1990, and it established a direct dialogue between *taobh amuigh* and *faoi ghlas* that centered on critical reflection. Such debate is one of the most important legacies of Republican prison writing. If Long Kesh must be situated within the wider scope of the "Troubles," then by the same token Republican thought must be examined in the context of the evolution of the Republican prison struggle. To be sure, Sinn Féin's participation in the Peace Process is surprising only if the precedents evident in Republican prison writing are ignored. Hard-line nationalist support of the Good Friday Agreement is in many ways the inheritance of the internal debates sometimes initiated by, sometimes continued in writings such as the "Brownie" articles, *Cage Eleven*, *Iris Bheag*, and *An Glór Gafa*. Republican prison literature at times mirrors Republican philosophy, but it also constructs that philosophy. In the most powerful appropriation of power possible, not only are POWs able to co-opt the space of the prison, they also are able to change Republican minds and policy through their writings, and in so doing they provide an example of human agency that poststructuralists would do well to remember.

Chapter Three

"Comrades in the Dark": Writing in the H Blocks, 1976–1981

> The Men of Art have lost their heart
> They dream within their dreams.
> Their magic sold for price of gold
> Amidst a people's screams
> They sketch the moon and capture bloom
> With genius, so they say.
> But ne'er they sketch the quaking wretch
> Who lies in Castlereagh.[1]

This stanza from the first section of Bobby Sands's long poem "Trilogy" encapsulates some of the most crucial preoccupations of the Republican POWs who were composing their texts in the H Blocks between 1976 and 1981. Like many texts written during incarceration, the space of the prison intrudes, the fearful interior of Castlereagh interrogation center standing in stark opposition to the beauty of the natural world exterior to jail walls. Indeed, this violent juxtaposition propels Sands's poem: as the POW is dragged inside the cell, so is the audience metaphorically incarcerated alongside him. While the "quaking wretch" found in the cell at first may appear to be a solitary figure, the stanza insists that all of this takes place "Amidst a people's screams." The political prison is but one locus of a larger, shared trauma—a trauma willfully ignored, Sands asserts, by the artists and writers whose duty it is to communicate such injustice to the rest of the world.

In the composition of "Trilogy," whether or not Sands had in mind the poem "The Tower" and the dream with which it concludes, his critique might certainly be directed at Yeats's desire to sequester himself from the external world, all the while praising those "Bound neither to Cause nor to State, / Neither to slaves that were spat on, / Nor to the tyrants that spat."[2] To Republicans, the aloof middle ground that "The Tower" valorizes here is precisely what guarantees the continued existence of tyrants and slaves. Far from the miraculously autonomous individuals that the poem imagines as exempt somehow from the web of power relations that trap everyone else, these people ultimately assist the system in replicating itself. Even more troubling, no doubt, is the particular phrasing that Yeats utilizes to describe the Protestant Irish nationalists Edmund Burke and Henry Grattan, who, he claims "gave, though free to refuse—/ Pride"[3] to Irish Catholics. While these lines perhaps were intended to point out the admirable manner in which Burke and Grattan went against their own class interests by campaigning for Catholic emancipation, "The Tower" nonetheless frames pride and basic civil rights as privileges to be bestowed or refused as a political elite saw fit. Surely Sands would find such a characterization repugnant, for as will be described below, the post-1976 prison struggle itself centered on the Five Demands being recognized as rights, not as privileges to be withheld on a whim. In addition, Yeats's self-absorption certainly runs counter to the vision of the responsibility of the artist endorsed by the men in the H Blocks whose collective gaze turned relentlessly outward from the solitary self. In this chapter, I will explore in detail the specific ways in which through this collectivity Republican authors in the H Blocks not only contest romanticized notions of writers as individual geniuses cut off somehow from the brute world surrounding them, but also how in so doing the POWs resist their incarceration, critique structures internal and external to their cells, and attempt to recover agency through their writing.

Furthermore, the chapter will analyze the textual history of these prison writings, for these histories provide similarly valuable insight into another coercive and assimilative disciplinary regime: that of the contemporary literary canon. By studying the varying forms in which Republican prison texts appeared, we can not only gain an understanding of the editorial interventions to which Sands's texts were subject but also discover the manner in which prison writing frequently flouts bourgeois literary conventions. The activist shape of pamphlets, like the two versions of *The Writings of Bobby Sands*, stand in radical opposition to collections of Sands's work published by larger presses, including *Skylark Sing Your Lonely Song*, *Bobby Sands: Irish Rebel*, and *Writings from Prison*. While the editorial decisions made in all of these compilations lay bare the uncomfortable alterity of Republican prison writing, in their formal departures from the standard literary text, locally published collections of Sands's work subvert most completely the conventions of bourgeois literary production, aesthetics, and consumption that creep into later editions of Sands's work. In diametric opposition to the activist approach to textual composition and consumption advocated and practiced by Sands, larger publishing houses discipline his writing in a manner uncomfortably reminiscent of the ways in which the H Block prison regime attempted to discipline the Blanketmen themselves.

To better understand some of the connections between academic and carceral discipline, a bit of background regarding the prison struggle in the North of Ireland between 1976 and 1981 is in order. Indeed, among all of the watershed moments in Irish history, the British government's decision to end Special Category Status for paramilitary prisoners must rank as one of the most tragic and crucial in shaping the decades that followed. As outlined in the previous chapter, between 1922 and 1976, the Special Powers Act empowered the Security Forces to intern subjects indefinitely without charge or trial. In part as the result of a hunger strike by Republican POWs, between 1972 and 1976, prisoners incarcerated for "scheduled" (paramilitary) offences had been granted Special Category Status in prison compounds across the North of Ireland. Those with Special Category Status could wear their own clothes rather than prison uniform, were permitted to have free association with one another, were granted access to educational facilities, and were not compelled to do ordinary prison work. In addition, the prison authorities implicitly recognized paramilitary command structures, conducting all communication with the POWs through the prisoners' officer commanding (OC). In the Cages of Long Kesh, prisoners endured communal incarceration in a compound reminiscent of the prisoner-of-war camps of World War II, each Cage housing about ninety POWs in Nissen huts: the POWs were locked into the huts only at night. In short, detainees with Special Category Status were treated as political prisoners in all but name.

Internment had always been a public relations nightmare for the British government, not least because by definition it required the suspension of juridical procedures normally taken for granted in supposedly democratic regimes. Only 727 prisoners were in Northern Irish jails in 1968, the year prior to the ignition of the "Troubles": by 1974, there were 2,650.[4] How could Westminster explain to the world the sudden imprisonment without trial of such a large percentage of what it claimed as its own populace? The answer was found in a strategy that came to be known as "criminalization." Following the Gardiner Report's recommendations in 1975, the British government began phasing out both Internment and Special Category Status: in Northern Ireland, this shift in policy prompted the replacement of the Special Powers Act with the Emergency Provisions Act (EPA).[5] However, critics of the EPA correctly point out the manner in which this new legislation provides only the veneer of due process, denying nearly all of the protections that the U.S. Bill of Rights nominally affords its citizens, for example.[6] The EPA did away with indefinite internment, but suspects can still be held *incommunicado* and without charge for up to seven days. Additionally, the EPA denies its victims protection from self-incrimination: in diametric opposition to the rights guaranteed by the Fifth Amendment of the American Constitution, silence legally imputes guilt under this system. Similarly, the courts that try suspects arrested under this emergency legislation are juryless: one judge decides the case in these so-called Diplock courts. This is all the more flawed given that in Northern Ireland these judges frequently are members of the Orange Order, an organization known for its anti-Catholic prejudice. Furthermore, the EPA dramatically lowers the standards of evidence in Diplock courts, as is particularly manifest in the practice known colloquially as "verballing." The sworn statement of a member of the Security Forces that s/he heard a suspect "verbally confess" to a crime is frequently all that is necessary for a conviction. In fact, as Queen's University professor of law David Lowry notes, 80 percent of Diplock court convictions between 1976 and 1980 relied solely on the practice of "verbaling": no other evidence of any sort was produced by the prosecution. To appreciate more fully how problematic this system is, consider also the fact that 93 percent of Diplock court cases during this same time period ended in conviction, a suspiciously high rate.[7]

Successful counterinsurgency requires the defeat of insurgents not only in military but also in public relations terms; in short, victory is incomplete—and is perhaps impossible—without the control of discourse. By phasing out Special Category Status and by creating the appearance of due process, the British state hoped to redefine paramilitaries not as guerillas but as gangsters, to borrow Pat Magee's phrasing.[8] As historian Tim Pat Coogan rightly insists, this policy of "criminalization" was not just a revision of military and carceral policy, but also a propaganda move on the part of the British government

> aimed at taking away whatever dignity the Special Category Status conferred and making the IRA not an organization with a political ambition and its roots in history, but a mafia-like conspiracy differing only in its methods from what the North of Ireland Secretary of the time...termed "ODCs"— Ordinary Decent Criminals.[9]

Subsequent to 1 March 1976, paramilitaries sentenced by the Diplock courts would be sent to a cell in the newly constructed H Blocks. Here, the POWs became mere prisoners: rather than being housed in large groups in shared Nissen huts and allowed communal association, inmates of the H Blocks were separated, isolated one or two to a cell; rather than negotiating through OCs, prisoners had to negotiate individually with prison officers; in addition, the prisoners were required to wear the regulation prison uniform. In short, in the words of Allen Feldman,

> the first IRA men to enter the H-Blocks encountered a regime that refused to recognize any social unit larger than the individual inmate. The depoliticization of the paramilitary's former political status conversely meant his extreme individualization and a refusal on the part of the prison administration to recognize his organizational affiliation.[10]

Under this regime the prisoner is no longer recognized as a part of a larger politicomilitary body, rather, s/he *is* a body—and nothing more. To counteract this depoliticization the Republican POWs refused the most obvious signifier of criminality: the regulation prison uniform. Thus began what came to be known as the Blanket Protest, as the Republicans covered themselves only with prison-issued blankets and towels.[11]

As months went by, protesting prisoners—especially the "YPs," the young prisoners—were subject to ever-increasing brutality, suffering frequent beatings as well as the denial of access to toilet facilities. In response to this abuse, the Republicans' protest intensified: the OC of the H Blocks "decided that if YPs were not allowed to wash then no one would wash. If screws were trying to control the pace of their lives, [the POWs] had to take back control by acting together."[12] This was the commencement of the No-Wash Protest: beginning on 20 March 1978, the prisoners stopped using the washroom facilities and cleaning their cells. The warders' reactions were extreme, and as one former prisoner's welfare officer admits, "The instructions to break the prisoners came from the highest levels of government."[13] Because the Republicans refused prison regulations their warders stripped their cells bare: even the prisoners' thin, frameless foam mattresses were removed during the day. All that the POWs were permitted were a copy of the Bible and the blankets covering their naked bodies. It was in these unforgiving circumstances, in a freezing, empty concrete cell, all writing material forbidden, that Sands composed his most famous works.[14]

Conditions of Literary Possibility: H Block Manuscripts

Scholars such as Allen Feldman have done important work analyzing the H Block protests in terms of the physical body as site of dominance and resistance. Feldman insists, for instance, that "The H Blocks teach us that within the ecologies of violence, knowledge, representation, and cultural genesis begin and end in the body."[15] Yet, to focus exclusively on the corporeal (and only on orality as the privileged extension of that corporeality) is to ignore the full of spectrum textual resistance that has been a crucial component of Irish prison struggles since at least the nineteenth century. Just as Republicans physically challenged carceral discipline in their refusal to wear the prison uniform, so they also engaged in textual transgressions that are arguably even more important manifestations of rebellion and co-option of agency. Every stage of literary production in the H Blocks was a microinsurrection.

The ingenuity that Sands and his comrades demonstrated in circumventing the authorities' prohibitions on writing is nothing short of astounding. Unlike the Cages of Long Kesh where luxuries such as typewriters were apparently permitted,[16] for literary production to occur at all in the H Blocks, the Republicans were obliged to import writing implements: passed to POWs by visitors, cling-wrapped pen refills and pencil stubs made their way into cells inside the prisoners' bodies, hidden in mouths and recta. While the Blanketmen had some access to paper in their cells in the form of toilet tissue and leaves torn from the Bible, frequently their warders deprived them of both of these items. As such, smuggled cigarette papers became a treasured raw material in the cells, not only because their miniature size made them ideal for concealment but especially because one could write on both sides of the paper, unlike toilet tissue. When complete, the text exited the H Blocks the same way the raw materials had entered: wrapped in cling film and secreted inside the body of a prisoner going to a visit.

The body of both the Blanketman and his outside contact thus become vessels for text. Feldman's point that rebellion begins with the body holds true here; however, in this case the bodies are merely the *conveyance* of the more dangerous rebellion. Indeed, it is tempting to liken the *bearta* (smuggled parcels) to the spirit within the flesh—connected to and dependent on the body in some complex ways, yet separate in others. Interestingly, the transmission of text in the H Blocks cuts loose the POWs and their comrades *taoibh amugh* from expected corporeal certainties, blurring sex roles. For instance, as Fairweather, McDonough, and McFadyean have demonstrated, it was usually women who passed the raw material of literary production to the Blanketmen, "small bits and pieces . . . which we will try to smuggle into the prison in our vaginas."[17] In a moment such as this, it is the women who provide the seed that is deposited into the male body, the male who then completes the creation of literary life within his cell, carrying the raw materials of composition as well as the manuscripts inside him until the text is ready to be passed out of the H Blocks again. As O'Hearn recounts, in the case of Sands's epic prose work *One Day in My Life,* "Bobby kept the manuscript, written on dozens of sheets of toilet paper, stuffed up his anus, carefully folded like an accordion to keep it as small as possible";[18] to gain some sense of the difficulty of this gestation, one must note that the "bulky package" of *One Day in My Life* was but one of the manuscripts that made up "the considerable library [Sands] carried around in his back passage."[19]

In the works of Samuel Beckett, we certainly find precedent for the concept of "writing in the shit," as David Lloyd has phrased it. Yet, unlike works such as *First Love* where, as Lloyd observes, "the turds of the subject of history represent the condition of alienation,"[20] this anal birth is necessary in the H Blocks to *combat* separation from self and others. Furthermore, it points toward the POWs' acceptance of the grim necessity of overcoming the shame of the body and its functions stereotypically associated with Irish Christianity. In this fashion the transmission of text actually results in a certain *transcendence* of the body and the repression—sexual and otherwise—heaped upon it by religious institutions in particular.

Blank space is a precious commodity to an author incarcerated in these conditions; indeed, the absence of usable writing space mirrors the claustrophobic space of the cell in which the POWs are kept. However, no Republican POW was more adept at utilizing every available millimeter of paper than Bobby Sands. His prose manuscripts are astounding in their economy: Sands could easily fit three hundred words on a single cigarette paper. An interesting new aesthetic arose in H Block manuscripts, one that harkens back to early monastic texts: occasionally in their desire to conserve space, Sands and his comrades wrote their prose without utilizing paragraph breaks. It is not that the POWs were ignorant of grammatical conventions, as demonstrated by other manuscripts with emphatic paragraph breaks; instead, this alternative form points toward a number of issues that literary criticism would do well to ponder. First, it forces us to consider to what extent rigid formalism—even on as basic a level as paragraph format—is a product and indication of luxury. Although the POWs had developed a very efficient system to smuggle in the raw materials required to engage in literary production, paper was never a commodity that could be wasted in the H Blocks of this era. Beyond this, however, the economical utilization of blank space is not merely evidence of a utilitarian ethos but also in part an indication of an alternative aesthetic common in prison literature. In short, the actual content of their prose writings is more important to the POWs than precision in form. While arguably there are corresponding traditions in more traditional literature, it is striking the degree to which formalistic concerns are secondary in Republican prison prose of this period.

Interestingly, the *poetic* manuscripts of Republican POWs from the same period and place evince a diametrically opposed aesthetic. In sharp contrast to the dense hedge of letters one frequently encounters in Sands's prose compositions, his verse manuscripts are remarkable for their comparatively vast expanses of white. For instance, as we see in the photoreproduction of the original manuscript reproduced in *Skylark Sing Your Lonely Song*, Sands leaves almost entire lines unfilled in the original draft of his poem "The Fair People."[21] Similarly, precision in line breaks and stanza form is clearly more important to Sands than "wasted space" in the manuscripts of his epic poem "Trilogy." In the manuscript of "Diplock Court," the second part of "Trilogy," the first six stanzas appear—by H Block standards—in almost leisurely sequence along the left side of the paper. Yet, the limitations of prison intrude even into this poetry: in an attempt to maximize available space, Sands includes stanzas seven through nine in the right margin of the paper. To permit the full line length, these three stanzas are written sideways in the margin, perpendicular to the first six stanzas. They are clustered together in a triangle, stanza seven appearing alongside stanza eight, stanza nine neatly centered immediately below them and to the right of the first six stanzas.[22] Because of this less-than-ideal layout, Sands takes pains to ensure that the stanzas appear in the order he imagined them, devoting more than a full line of available space to stanza numbers, emphatically underlining each Roman numeral twice. The rest of "Trilogy's" manuscript further illustrates the extent to which the H Blocks fragmented literary texts produced within them. Sands writes stanzas 40–46 of "The Torture Mill—H Block," the final section of "Trilogy," on the title page of the only book permitted to the POWs: these stanzas are neatly bisected by the words "THE HOLY BIBLE," the book having been turned at a ninety degree angle from how one would normally hold it. Likewise, the words "THE OLD TESTAMENT" create an odd, block letter caesura in the midst of stanzas 83–88 of "The Torture Mill—H Block."[23]

As the 226 stanza sprawl of "Trilogy" proves, it was not impossible to compose lengthy texts in the H Blocks; however, the physical constraints involved in writing and eventually transmitting the literary text outside of Long Kesh produced measurable consequences both in manuscript as well as in final form. Lengthy documents were necessarily divided into several minute parcels or, in Republican parlance, *bearta.* Even relatively short texts generally necessitated multiple miniature pages, and, of course, every page that was written increased the difficulty of exporting the complete work. The more pages, the more times the gauntlet had to be run, and consequently the greater the possibility that part of the text would be discovered by the warders—with grim consequences for the POW. In short, the conditions in the H Blocks were such that a certain amount of fragmentation was unavoidable in texts produced during the period 1976–1981. Sands's "Trilogy" is representative: written on many different types of paper, the complete poem made its way to the outside in a series of *bearta.* The segmentation at every stage of the process of what I will term the *téacs pluide* (blanket text) necessitated Sands's precise directives to the outside.

Physical and spatial concerns shaped the *téacs pluide* with regard to content as well as form. In fact, in the aggregate, I insist that the carceral space intrudes into these texts in a far more dramatic manner that those prison memoirs composed or completed *taoibh amuigh.* The contrast is vividly evident in the disparity between the atmosphere—and the polish—of Gerry Adams's "Cage Eleven" and Bobby Sands's *One Day in My Life.* Like Adams's "Cage Eleven," Sands's text begins with a description of the place of incarceration. However, whereas the physical environment is a backdrop in "Cage Eleven," it is an active participant in *One Day in My Life.* To demonstrate this, it is worth quoting the entire first paragraph of Sands's narrative:

> It was still dark and snowing when I woke. I don't think I got more than an hour's sleep during the long, restless, torturous night. The cold was intense, biting at my naked body. For at least the thousandth time I rolled over on to my side, hugging the blankets close to my body. The sleep that the bitter cold had denied me hung above me, leaving me

> tired and drowsy. I was somewhat exhausted, and every bone in my body seemed to be protesting at the ordeal of spending yet another night on a damp foam mattress on the floor. No sleep again worth mentioning! I was frustrated, cross and curled up in a little ball to get warm. If I had something to boot, I would have booted it, that's just how I felt. I had tried lying in every sort of position to get warm, but the cold still penetrated. My three flimsy blankets were no match for the bitter, biting cold that came creeping through the bars of my window, situated above my head.[24]

Contrast that passage with the one that begins Adams's story "Cage Eleven," where, although huddled under a blanket, the narrator has the benefit of an actual bed. He is "covered in breadcrumbs," has a nice cup of tea, and chuckles at his companion's "pink pajamas," making light of the depression settling in on the hut resulting from a lack of visits.[25] While the narrators of each of these stories are first encountered in a fetal position, that pose beneath identical British Army blankets is one of the few similarities between the conditions endured by the two POWs. Adams's story takes on the quality of a surreal sleepover, with his companion's comical appearance figuring strongly in the scene. The narrator in "Cage Eleven" is found in the attitude of a quiet Sunday in an odd university dormitory, remnants of comfort food close at hand, the humorous tone downplaying what was undoubtedly a real sense of loss at the removal of visits. In stark contrast to this, Sands's narrator is huddled under his blankets not out of depression, but out of real need. Images of the cold fill almost every sentence of the passage quoted above, becoming an almost sentient enemy in the pathetic fallacy of the final sentence quoted above, creeping toward him through the open windows like a predator.

In both "Cage Eleven" and *One Day in My Life*, sleep is sought as a balm, an escape from the immediate. Yet the crucial difference between the two situations is that the stresses on the POWs have entirely different origins: for the inmates of the Cages, it is largely external to their space, as visits have been denied to them. In the H Blocks, however, the immediate stress comes from the physical experience of the space that they occupy, a stress too invasive to flee even in sleep. The carceral space thus invades Sands's mind as well as his body, making even mental escape from the cell nearly impossible. The cell is so frigid that Sands seems to run out of words to describe it, the staccato repetition of the word "cold" reminiscent of chattering teeth.

In Sands's writings, the reader can again and again see the way in which the physical environment of the cell intrudes upon the world of the mind. By way of example, the short prose piece "I Once Had a Life" spends almost the entirety of its length leading the reader along a pleasant trail through the outdoors: the birds are singing, the sun is shining, the scenery is beautiful. However, at the sound of a gun this world shatters, and the speaker is revealed to be imprisoned in the H Blocks. The shift is a melancholy one, perhaps even more so to the readers outside prison walls who encountered the article on its initial appearance in *AP/RN* on the usually joyful Saint Patrick's Day, 1979: "I arose, not from my panoramic platform, but out of the inky blackness in the corner of my filthy, cold cell, where, wrapping a dirty, flimsy blanket around me to cover my naked body, I stepped towards the barred window and leaned my head against it."[26] One is unsure whether the gunshot is part of the fantasy or if it arises from the real world of concrete and razor wire that surrounds the speaker; either way, that the liminal moment is one of violence is telling. In the H Blocks, the violence enacted against the mind is just as dangerous as that directed against the body, if only because it brings the POW back to his body and the physical discomfort of the frigid, dirty cell. The dissociation between mind and body is that of sleep and wakefulness, as can be seen in the peculiar, almost third-person perspective in which the prisoner observes and describes himself emerging from the blackness of sleep into the blackness of the cell.

Again and again, brief respites from the immediate surroundings are short lived. "Christmas Eve," which begins as a prose piece and ends as a poem is yet another example. The poem itself finishes with the brave lines "But I tell the Screws and Mason[27] too/ To break a blanket man you cannot do!" but this is not where the writing ends. In emphatic capital letters Sands writes "—I HATE THIS PLACE": unlike the other lines in the poem, this one is not paired into a neatly rhyming couplet; rather, it ends the poem on an odd-numbered, jagged note, the lack of any punctuation underscoring the line's movement toward frenzy.[28] In this conclusion the text is heartbreakingly honest and stark, revealing that, although the POWs will fight bravely to the death for political status, the suffering they endure permeates their existence—Sands's word choice illustrating that it emanates from a spatial, physical source.

This pattern exhibits itself again in the concluding passage of *One Day in My Life*. Sands's autobiography has come full circle at this stage; in its last pages, the POWs are settling in to try to sleep. Yet, the pattern that emerges is not just a cyclical one of prison routine or of nature's rising and setting sun. It is a cycle of resistance against the four walls that confine the POWs, a space that is as physically punishing as any beating. As the night falls, Sands writes,

> It was cold, so very, very cold. I rolled onto my side and placed my little treasured piece of tobacco under the mattress and felt the dampness clinging to my feet.
>
> That's another day nearer to victory, I thought, feeling very hungry.
>
> I was a skeleton compared to what I used to be but it didn't matter. Nothing really mattered except remaining unbroken. I rolled over once again, the cold biting at me. They have nothing in their entire arsenal to break the spirit of one single Republican prisoner-of-war who refuses to be broken, I thought, and that was very true. They can not or never will break our spirit. I rolled over again freezing and the snow came in the window on top of my blankets.
>
> "Tiocfaidh ár lá,"[29] I said to myself. "Tiocfaidh ár lá."[30]

This concluding passage is remarkable in the pendulum regularity with which the narrative switches between mental resistance and recognition of physical discomfort. It is only with near superhuman willpower that the POWs are able to match their cells, to endure and keep the equilibrium. The physical environment in the cell is the same as it was in the morning—even the POW's postures are the same—but he and his comrades remain unbroken. It must be remembered too that at this stage those windows are at once friend and enemy to the prisoners: though the bitter snow and air passes through them, they at least provide some form of optical escape from the cell. In a short while, however, all of the windows in the H Blocks will be sealed up, preventing even that modicum of escape from the cell walls. This particular type of confinement is the origin of the hatred seething in the POWs of the H Blocks, a hatred not seen in the Cages, "a hatred so intensive that it frightens me," as Sands confesses in the essay "The Harvest Britain Has Sown."[31]

This passage again demonstrates a quality earlier touched upon in the discussion of the opening paragraph of *One Day in My Life*: that of repetition. The reader will note that the first paragraph and the last passages of *One Day in My Life* both exhibit an almost uncontrollable repetition of the word "cold." Yet this reduplication cannot be simply written off as a stylistic error, for it also speaks to other issues—those of literary production and the aesthetic expectations of the academy. To a sophisticated literary audience, perhaps Sands's technique seems lacking in finesse and polish, and hence unworthy of study. I would argue that these jagged edges and sometimes visible seams reveal as much, if not more, about the politicized nature of the academy than about the prison writer producing the works, a nature that the academy often deliberately conceals in a mantle of false neutrality. Because it is so much more difficult to engage in the sort of revision championed by composition departments across the discipline, prison literature remains discourse at its rawest, least edited, and at times, most powerful. I concur with Elaine Scarry who argues in *The Body in Pain* that

> Physical pain does not simply resist language but actively destroys it, bringing about an immediate reversion to a state anterior to language.... to be present when a person moves up out of that pre-language and projects the facts of sentience into speech is to have been permitted to be present at the birth of language.[32]

The cold that Sands writes about is not a distant memory that is written down in tranquil recollection: he must suffer that same cold again tonight, he must endure it even as he writes. In addition, the act of writing and revising texts in the H Blocks is, of course, fraught with difficulty. While revision is indeed valuable, sometimes allowing writers to express their points or describe a scene with improved clarity, in visceral documents such as those smuggled from the H Blocks we see the struggle with the physical environment actually inscribed in the words. The repetition of the word "cold" indicates its cyclical, physical assault on the POW: we must realize that where the text "suffers" can be a marker of where the human creator suffers.

Unsurprisingly, this suffering produces the sort of hatred described above in "The Harvest Britain Has Sown." Even more tragically, Sands imagines it as having the potential to become a generational one that transcends the temporal and spatial boundaries of the H Blocks, predicting that the Blanketmen will pass it on to their daughters and sons.[33] Without doubt, a number of Sands's texts exhibit a strong reliance on physical force tradition that Adams reevaluates and redefines in his own prison writing. For instance, in the final two lines of the poem "Teach Your Children," Sands's speaker concludes that it is best to "Teach your children the only law and word that fat men fear/ The power of an AK47."[34] As a folk music enthusiast, Sands surely must have chosen his title in deliberately ironic reference to the Crosby, Stills, Nash and Young hit of the same name. Yet, to observe such militaristic tendencies in Sands's writings is not to dismiss his contributions to the development of Republican dialectics. By all accounts, Sands was at the forefront of creating a system of education in the

Republican wings of the H Blocks that centred on "a culture of discussion" (to utilize the words of Dr. Laurence McKeown, who was himself on the 1981 hunger strike).[35] Furthermore, as OC of the H Blocks, Sands directly went against the wishes of the leadership outside when he and the other Republican POWs embarked on the 1981 hunger strike; certainly other actions of Republican POWs during the worst years of the H Block struggle between 1976 and 1981 also demonstrate a continued questioning of internal Republican hierarchies on the part of Sands and others.

Nor should such violent imagery be seen as evidence that Sands was an inherently violent person. Instead, I maintain that such images reveal more about the specific environment in which they are composed than about the author who composed them. The *téacs pluide* is prison literature in its rawest form, a visceral response to the world immediately surrounding the incarcerated writer. Because the POWs in the H Blocks were subject to greater isolation, more frequent beatings, and generally worse physical and mental deprivation than the Republicans in the Cages, it should not be surprising that Sands's images are at times so violent. Though he did write during his time in the Cages,[36] it was after his second arrest and subsequent incarceration in the H Blocks in 1977 that Sands composed his most familiar works, and it is exclusively these "H Blocks texts" that have been anthologized in books such as *Skylark Sing Your Lonely Song*. In short, Sands's words at times are more brutal than those of Adams because his surroundings were correspondingly so.

The Early Publication History of Bobby Sands

While the material conditions of confinement in the H Blocks did impact the compositional strategies of the Blanketmen, other factors too came into play. The relative brevity of the typical *téacs pluide* frequently proceeds from the venue in which the text typically was first published. There is a long history in Ireland of Republican prison writing appearing in nationalist newspapers[37]; as Sands was the public relations officer (PRO) of the Provisional Republican POWs in the H Blocks, perhaps predictably his writings were published first in *Republican News* (the Belfast paper that describes itself as the "[o]fficial organ of the Republican Movement" in an early collection of Sands's writings).[38] In the pages of *Republican News*, Sands's writings—like the H Block prison writers themselves—are immersed in a larger political matrix. One expects individual newspaper articles to be surrounded by other images and texts, yet the frequency with which *Republican News* published creative writings by POWs (often literally alongside expository writing) remains noteworthy. The ramifications of the paper's layout are clear: there are no artificial boundaries between the literal and the literary, the poetic and the political. Creative, critical, and journalistic writing coexist remarkably in Republican periodicals: no Peace Walls need divide them.

Significantly, from the first appearance of his work on 5 November 1977, an emphasis on collective voice is evident even in the pen names under which Sands's texts are published in *Republican News*: all of them point away from the construct of author as "autonomous individual." In addition, and perhaps even more importantly, all of these pen names metaphorically destroy the impermeable inside/outside binary that disciplinary regimes such as the H Blocks seek to impose on inmates as well as on supporters *taoibh amuigh*. Bylines such as those of his articles "How Much More?" and "I fought a monster today" [*sic*] identify Sands only as "a Republican prisoner in H Block 5,"[39] thus certainly highlighting the subject position of prisoner; however, this identity is not the passive, isolated one that the prison authorities seek to impose through the policy of "criminalization." After all, the whole purpose of the authorities' removal of Special Category Status was to deny the legitimacy (and hence the *existence*) of politically motivated prisoners, to sever them from their group identities. As Bill Ashcroft correctly argues in another context, the "key to resistance" in an environment such as the H Blocks is "the capacity to produce one's own identity through representation":[40] from the byline onward, Sands's *Republican News* articles contest the government's attempt to equate POWs and ODCs by calling attention to the Republicanism of the prisoner.

An even more complex rhetorical move is made in the byline of Sands's 1 April 1978 *Republican News* article, credited to "OUR YOUNG COMRADE FROM WEST BELFAST PRESENTLY ON THE 'BLANKET PROTEST' IN THE H BLOCK [*sic*]."[41] This establishes dense layers of communal identity. By foregrounding the author's participation in the Blanket Protest, the byline emphasizes Sands's place within an active, communal resistance both inside and outside Long Kesh, a point further underscored by the use of the term "comrade." However, perhaps the most crucial—yet deceptively simple—rhetorical move is the specification that the author hails from West Belfast. This reminds reader and author alike that Sands is *in* the H Blocks, not *of* them: he has other identities separate from the carceral one that he must come to terms with in Long Kesh. As we witnessed in the last chapter with regard to Adams and his fellow authors in the Cages, through the evocation of space *taoibh amuigh* the prisoners symbolically reach out from the "surrealistic limbo" of their prison and back into the familiar, empowering space of home.[42] This is an *aide memoire* to themselves and to those *taoibh amuigh* that the POWs inhabited spaces other than their cells prior to their incarceration, and that they hope to do so again in the future. In a sense, the Blanketmen continue to live outside the prison in their minds, for, as discussed elsewhere in the chapter, the mental escape outward is a cornerstone of survival in the H Blocks.

The cartographic specificity of this byline no doubt contained particular resonances of home and safety to Sands, especially given the fact that he and his family settled in the relative safety of the West Belfast district of Twinbrook after they were intimidated out of the predominantly Loyalist North Belfast neighborhood of Rathcoole in the early 1970s.[43] Yet this foregrounding of location not only allows passage out of the prison but also compels simultaneous passage *into* the H Blocks. Readers are introduced to the author not as an individual, but—for those living in West Belfast—as a neighbor, possibly translating into greater connection to and potential support for the Blanketmen. The article, the byline implies, could have been written by *any* prisoner, by anyone from West Belfast, and thus the horrors of the H Blocks become a communal experience. The importance of this locative move evidences itself in the fact that so many of Sands's early articles are credited to variants[44] of "A YOUNG WEST BELFAST REPUBLICAN": it is a key component in the destruction of the outside/inside binary that the prison authorities seek to impose. In yet another way, the prisoners are no longer contained and defined by their cells, nor are those *taoibh amuigh* forcibly prevented from contact with the POWs *faoi ghlas*.

Sands also emphasizes the communal voice in those *Republican News* articles that he writes in his capacity as PRO of the Republican prisoners but often does so in unexpected ways. In fact, these articles provide the most forceful demonstration of the degree to which "I" and "we" are essentially interchangeable in most of Sands's writings: "The harvest Britain has sown" [*sic*] is representative. One might expect the exclusive use of the first person plural in a statement from the Republican PRO; after all, the primary function of this staff position is to speak on behalf of the Blanketmen. Yet, with the exception of the final paragraph, the entire essay is written in the first-person *singular*. In so doing, Sands deliberately transgresses both literary and carceral discipline, simultaneously destroying the division between inside and outside prison, between the conventions of the Anglo-American autobiography and the communal tendencies of resistance writing in general and of the Latin American *testimonio* in particular.[45]

If one were to ignore the byline announcing the essay to be a communiqué from the PRO of the Republican prisoners in the H Blocks, the first paragraph of "The harvest Britain has sown" appears to be standard autobiographical fare as the "personal I" dominates every sentence: "A stretch of tarmac surrounded by barbed wire and steel is the only view from my cell window. I'm told it is an exercise yard. I wouldn't know. In my fourteen months in H-Block 5 I haven't been allowed to walk in the fresh air."[46] As with all of Sands's writings, these apparently simplistic lines contain within them strata that readers would do well to excavate. Note the clever manner in which Sands underscores the extent of the isolation imposed on the Blanketmen. Given this introduction, the reader might expect Sands's account to merely lament the grim landscape to which the POWs' eyes and bodies are limited, but in a tragic twist the narrator is deprived even of the unwelcoming space of the H Blocks exercise yard. The conditions are surely deplorable when one longs for such a sterile barbed-wire enclosure. However, as unwelcoming as this cage is, it offers the possibility of a movement outside the opacity of concrete, a fleeting experience of fresh air, and, if one was lucky, the potential of less-fettered interaction with other POWs. The denial of the communal association of the exercise yard is simply another manifestation of the British government's shift to a more panoptically minded prison regime of the sort imagined by Jeremy Bentham. To frame it in Foucaldian terms, by refusing communal association "[t]he crowd, a compact mass, a locus of mutual exchanges, individualities merging together, a collective effect, is abolished and replaced by a collection of separated individualities."[47] The prison regime hopes that this cellular isolation will encourage despair and malleability in the POWs, reducing them to the "docile bodies" of which Foucault writes.

Yet, as a Republican POW and as a member of the H Block command structure, Sands knows that his individual experiences are shared by his comrades who suffer unseen next to him in their own cells. He writes, "There have been many attempts to break my will but each one has made me more determined. I know my place is here with my comrades."[48] Personal trauma only pushes Sands to greater solidarity with the other Republican POWs. These two sentences are a model of the essay's larger structure and point. While the "personal I" is deceptively insistent throughout "The Harvest Britain Has Sown," in the final paragraph Sands completes his move into the collective voice: "Every aspect of H Block life, from cold empty cells and denial of every comfort, to refusal of medical treatment is designed to grind down our resistance but it will not succeed. They may hold our bodies in the most inhuman conditions but while our minds remain free, our victory is assured!"[49] In this abrupt move, the "I" of the preceding paragraphs is revealed to be synecdoche, each POW not an isolate mote, but instead part of a group that extends to his wing, his block, and the H Blocks in their entirety. Nor do the connections end there, for the POWs remember that they are a vital part of the Republican Movement as a whole.

"Marcella," the pen-name most frequently associated in the popular mind with Bobby Sands, offers yet more evidence of Sands's conception of author as communal subject position. On 25 November 1978, Sands's article "The window of my mind" [*sic*] appeared in *Republican News* under the nom de plume "Marcella, H5 Block."[50] The few academics who have taken note of Sands's prison writings generally misinterpret the intent of this new byline, focusing on what they misread as its assertion of individualism. Even a scholar as astute as Denis O'Hearn claims in his otherwise excellent biography of Sands that the appearance of this particular article with its byline

> marked a significant new phase of Bobby's writing, reflecting both a transition in his own consciousness and the beginning of public awareness of his stature as writer, poet, and propagandist.... He is transformed, from caterpillar to cocoon and now to butterfly. No longer is he a faceless "young West Belfast Republican." He is now Marcella, on his way to becoming the enigma the world knew as Bobby Sands.[51]

It does seem reasonable to assume that recurring appearance of the byline "Marcella" created a degree of "brand name recognition," aiding in the development of a following among the readership of *Republican News*. Like Gerry Adams's "Brownie" articles and those of Adams's immediate successor "Solon," the "Marcella" columns were intended to draw even casual readers into critical awareness of the prison struggle and, by extension, into a larger dialogue about Republicanism in general.

However, O'Hearn's metaphor of the chrysalis overlooks several important issues and as a result overstates the importance of individualism in many of the writings emanating from the H Blocks in 1978. A linear progression is assumed here, a "march of progress" from the lesser, undifferentiated voice to that of the superior, individualized

"Marcella." O'Hearn mistakenly claims that "Between July 1 and late November [1978], *Republican News* did not publish any of his articles. According to Ginty Lennon he was still writing constantly. But he concentrated on press releases and coordinating information that was coming in from different blocks and wings."[52] This period O'Hearn likens to the ugly pupal stage of the butterfly, a stage that ends upon the emergence of "Marcella" from the cellular chrysalis. Unfortunately for the metaphor, a number of Sands's writings appeared in *Republican News* during the period between 1 July and 25 November. On 16 September 1978, "The harvest Britain has sown" and "The Gloves Have Been Removed" are published as the work of "PRO H Blocks 3, 4, 5."[53] "I fought a monster today" and "How Much More" are published in the paper as the work of "a Republican prisoner in H Block 5" on 7 October 1978.[54] Nor does the emergence of the pen-name "Marcella" end the anonymous publication of Sands's prison writings: on 16 December 1978, his article "The Birth of a Republican" appears in *Republican News* credited only to "a Blanket Man."[55]

Even setting aside the continued use of "faceless" alter egos, Sands's choice of his best-known *ainm cleite* (pen-name) "Marcella" merits more careful scrutiny. For example, the gender inversion of Sands's alias would not have been lost on his *Republican News* readership: as they would have been painfully aware, the H Blocks housed only male prisoners. Why then use a manifestly feminine name? Sands's own Republican ideology provides the answer. Rather than an assertion of extreme individuality, Sands's decision to use his sister's name points forcefully—if perhaps at the time, privately—toward the comforts of home, to a reimmersion in the absent family, to the world outside the H Blocks. Marcella Sands was—and is—one of her brother's most fervent advocates: O'Hearn recounts that "[Bobby] felt tremendous support from his parents and Marcella" at all stages of his incarceration and especially during his hunger strike, noting that few people visited Sands more frequently than Marcella.[56] It must be remembered that while visits were important for the POWs' morale, in addition they were nodes in the network through which all forms of contraband and communications were transmitted, a task at which the Sands women were apparently very adept.[57] Sands's choice of *ainm cleite* honors his female relatives' active engagement in the prison struggle, simultaneously highlighting the communal ideal of the cutting-edge vision of Provisional Republicanism[58] so actively articulated in the writings of prisoners in Long Kesh and Armagh. As Sands would later insist in his hunger strike diary, everyone—male and female, outside and inside prison, "Republican or otherwise"—has a role to play. The byline

"Marcella" unites male POW and female activist *taoibh amuigh*, simultaneously highlighting their successful resistance to the state's attempts to render both of these subject positions passive and docile. Without the material support provided by comrades *taoibh amuigh,* Sands's writings would be impossible: this *ainm cleite* publicly recognizes these men and women, in effect crediting them as coauthors.[59]

In fact, to see how unimportant his own public "stature" was to Sands, one only need consider how few of his texts were published under his own name. As best as I am able to determine, only a handful of Sands's published texts appeared under his own name before he began his hunger strike, all of them poems, and all of them using the Irish version of his name: "Roibeard." Although the most individualized of aliases, even this name directs one to larger cultural and political issues when one considers that Sands is deliberately rejecting his Anglisized self. Certainly this rhetorical move actively subverts the imposition of an institutionalized identity.

Such an ideology is common in *téacsanna pluide* (Blanket texts): the manuscript of a letter[60] to the *Irish Press* written on a strip of toilet paper in H6 by Laurence McKeown in 1980 is representative [see page xiii]. I will postpone my examination of the content of the three discrete sections that make up this single text in order to concentrate on the manner in which McKeown signed each part, for these signatures embody the same communal ideal, the same layers of identity evident in Sands's bylines [see page xiv]. I will begin with the final section of McKeown's text, a brief note in English addressed to McKeown's mother instructing her how to send the letter to the *Irish Press*. This is signed "LAURENCE," not in cursive script but in the neat block letters so prevalent in *téacsanna pluide*. The second segment of the text, a private note to the editor of the *Irish Press* written *as Gaeilge* (in Irish Gaelic), bears the signature "LORCÁN MAC EOGHAIN BLOC 6 CEIS FADA." Even readers without competency in Gaeilge might recognize the first three words as the Irish equivalent of Laurence's name: the final portion of the signature specifies the author's place of incarceration in H Block 6, Long Kesh. The first segment might be termed the primary one, for it contains the portion of the text intended for actual publication in the *Irish Press*; the text is a letter *as Gaeilge* briefly outlining the history of the H Block protest. In total congruence with Sands's insistence on communal anonymity, this portion of the manuscript is signed "FEAR PLÚIDE SAN BLOCANNA H": as I would translate it, a faceless "blanketman in the H Blocks," one who refuses to specify even the individual block in which he is held. Interestingly, in the manuscript, McKeown encases this block letter signature in quotation marks, drawing further attention to the deliberate anonymity of his *ainm cleite*. In its signatory layers this document underscores the intentionality of the Republican prison writer's decentering of the individual. Of course, this rhetorical strategy is wholly in keeping with Republican resistance in the H Blocks and must be read as a further attempt to undermine the forced individuation of cellular incarceration and the refusal of prison authorities to recognize the POWs' political or paramilitary organizational affiliation. Group identity is of utmost concern to the *téacs pluide*, an identity that transcends prison walls.

In highlighting this communal drive, I do not mean to deny that security concerns in some part motivated the anonymity of published versions of H Block writings of this era, for POWs faced very real dangers at every stage of textual production. Indeed, one of Sands's first appearances in *Republican News* is accompanied by the editorial commentary that Sands's work was "smuggled out written on minute scraps of paper. Each [*sic*] article being signed in Gaelic by the author. We are not printing his name for fear of 'disciplinary action' being taken against him by the prison regime."[61] However, as the preceding quote emphasizes, and McKeown's manuscript demonstrates, the typical *téacs pluide* was signed sometimes with an *ainm cleite* and sometimes with the author's own name. McKeown's name appears on his manuscript twice. Had his letter been intercepted by the H Block warders, McKeown would have been easily identifiable and could certainly have been targeted for reprisals.

Consider also the case of Sands's poems that appeared in *Republican News* with the byline "Roibeard H5." One would think that this *ainm cleite* would be transparent enough to prison authorities, especially given that Sands actually identifies the Block in which he is incarcerated. In the case of "Poetic Justice," which appeared in *Republican News* in December 1978, if the Irish version of his name was too difficult to decipher, in the middle of the poem itself God even addresses the speaker as "Bob!"[62] Similarly, the work of other H Block poets was being published without *any* attempt at concealing authorial identity. On 9 September 1978, for example, *Republican News* devoted an entire page to a feature entitled "Poems from the H Blocks": five of the six poets are identified by first and last name, and in Noel Ferguson's case the editors specify the H Block in which he is incarcerated.[63] What might explain this apparent reversal in policy on the part of the editors of *Republican News*? Certainly the prison authorities had not relaxed carceral discipline during this period. In fact, the brutality would continue to worsen. The last week in April 1979—just over four months after the "Roibeard" texts appeared—is still remembered as the *seachtain dona* (bad week) by Republican POWs, especially those in H4. Leo Green, the Block OC, describes the conditions during that period as "the worst I ever knew" with regard to beatings and other maltreatment.[64] It seems plain that the deliberate anonymity of the majority of Sands's published *téacsanna pluide* cannot be attributed solely to a desire to shield Bobby from harm. Instead, in addition to a self-conscious urge toward the communal, the commentary cited above illustrates the manner in which Republican editors rightly viewed the stakes as being higher when widespread dissemination of these texts was accomplished, for the consequences of actual publication are in some ways of even greater import than the rebellion of composition and smuggling. In the years before the Hunger Strikes, Republicans believe POWs' texts would be disseminated most widely and would be truly *heard* by the greatest number of people through the utilization of a voice that consciously elides the individual *faoi ghlas* with the communal *taoibh amuigh.*

The Editing of Bobby Sands

In the case of prison writing, Republican editors largely prefer to absent themselves as much as possible from the shaping of a creative work—an approach differing dramatically from that of most academic editors in the twentieth century, at least those editors dealing with the works of living authors. Contrast the largely collaborative relationship of F. Scott Fitzgerald and his editor Maxwell Perkins with Danny Morrison's approach to editing Sands's work. Morrison edited Sands's writings for their initial publication in *Republican News* and acted in the same capacity for *Prison Poems*, the first collection of Sands's poetry that appeared in pamphlet form in October 1981 three months after Sands's death on hunger strike. In that pamphlet Republican editorial *modus operandi* is clearly manifest when Morrison opines that

> It has been said that were Bobby alive to see these poems today he would have rewritten or changed some of the simpler rhyming words. But that is to miss the point. These poems were written by a young man under the most depressing of conditions. More importantly his poetry is the raw literature of the H-Block prison protest which hundreds of naked men stood up against their cell doors (in the late of night when the Screws left the wings) to listen to and to applaud.

> It was their only entertainment, it was a beautifully rendered articulation of their own plight. Out of cruelty and suffering Sands harnessed *real poetry*, the poetry of a feeling people struggling to be free...[65] (emphasis and ellipsis in original)

Despite his admission that—by the standards of the academy anyway—Sands's poetry might have been improved on a technical level by editorial intervention, strikingly Morrison emphasizes authorial rather than editorial agency here: he frames it as *Sands's* prerogative—not an editor's—to alter the text in any substantive way. In this statement, Morrison is representative of the vast majority of Republican editors who view such writings as inviolable, any substantive alteration obscuring their readers' glimpse into the world of the prisoner of war. Morrison and others keep these texts situated in the prison environment that produced them, even if it requires the sacrifice a certain amount of aesthetic polish.[66]

Such was the attempted practice with regard to Sands's writings both before and after he became world-famous on hunger strike: illustrative of this avoidance of editorial intervention is the short story "An Scéal." "An Scéal" appeared in *Republican News* on 10 December 1981, seven months after Sands's death, and has not been reprinted in any form since that time. The story as well as the editorial comments are written entirely *as Gaeilge*, with no translation offered. At the end of the brief introduction to the text the editor writes, "Scríobh Roibeard an scéal seo ar bhluirí phápéir leithris. Ní raibh leabhair nó foclóir ag Roibeard. Is í gaeilge [*sic*] na mBlocanna atá le léamh thíos":[67] as I would translate it, "Bobby wrote this story on bits of toilet paper. Bobby had no books or dictionaries. It is the Irish Gaelic of the Blocks you read below." Like Morrison's comments cited earlier, this implies a particular editorial stance. Because many of the POWs learned Gaeilge from their comrades in prison, the patois written and spoken in Long Kesh was frequently nonstandard Irish: by pointing out that Sands spoke "the Irish of the Blocks," the editor here explains both grammatical irregularities that Irish speakers might notice as well as the reason for which those irregularities were not corrected before publication. One cannot help but admire the honesty of this editorial *modus operandi*, given that everyone involved must have anticipated the hostile scrutiny to which Sands's work would be subject. After all, as I discussed in greater detail in this book's introduction, though they often simultaneously attempt to claim their own aesthetics to be apolitical, according to revisionist foes of Republicanism such as Edna Longley, poetic skill is somehow indicative of the validity of the author's ideology.[68] Given this hostility, a temptation on the part of his editors to "improve" Sands's work would be understandable, particularly given the propaganda value that might have been lent to the prison struggle by the construction of an "imprisoned Heaney."

In their decision to be minimally invasive, Republican editors rightly underscore the contrast between the conditions of possibility within Long Kesh and the conditions in academia outside. For instance, by commenting on the unavailability of books and dictionaries in the H Blocks, the uncredited editor of "An Scéal" praises Sands's level of fluency, simultaneously questioning the actual necessity of those reference texts and by extension the factions within academia that privilege grammatical precision over political engagement. Like Morrison's prefatory remarks to *Prison Poems*, the introduction to "An Scéal" puts a premium on the "real poetry" slouching its way out of the H Blocks to be born in local Republican presses, much to the chagrin of revisionist critics.

However, despite the unquestionably heartfelt desire on the part of editors to remain true to the original text, complications soon arise in achieving this goal. One of the first issues facing any editor is to determine what base text will be used for the edition, a decision with far-reaching implications. Sands's song "Nuair a thigeann ar [*sic*] lá" encapsulates such an editorial dilemma. O'Hearn has pointed out a disparity between the last line of the song as Sands apparently sang it in the days before his hunger strike and the version that Sands wrote in his hunger strike diary. The latter version is the best known: "Nuair a thigeann ar [*sic*] lá aithíocfaidh mé iad go mór (When our day comes I shall repay them dearly)."[69] However, according to O'Hearn, POWs such as Phillip Rooney[70] remember Sands singing "Nuair a thigeann ar [*sic*] lá, is feidir ní bheidh mé ann," a line he translates as "When our day comes I'll probably not be there."[71] O'Hearn does not explicitly comment on the ramifications of this alteration, though the orally transmitted version appears as the epigraph of *Nothing but an Unfinished Song*'s twenty-second chapter, a chapter entitled "The End," wherein he traces Sands's last sixty-six days of life on hunger strike. The oral tradition's vision of death sadly proved true, for Sands did perish; however, by foregrounding this version in an epigraph, *Nothing but an Unfinished Song* partially obscures the defiant move that Sands makes in his diary. After all, in the diary's version, not only does the speaker of the poem survive his ordeal in prison but he also triumphs in apparently vengeful fashion.[72] The revelation that this imagined outcome was altered in dramatic fashion from an earlier, hopeless version should only stress the degree to which Sands was steeled to the fight even thirteen days into a hunger strike.

Complicating the matter further is another text I discovered among the holdings of the Linen Hall Library in Belfast, a pamphlet titled *Faoi Ghlas ag Gaill*, published in 1981. With the exception of one essay by the anti–H Block and Armagh activist Father Raymond Murray, this pamphlet is entirely comprised of prisoners' writings *as Gaeilge*. Notable among these is a version of "Nuair a thigeann ar lá" that departs radically from either of the two discussed above. Credited to "Roibeard Ó Seachnasaigh," the song is titled "An Mhaidin" and reads as follows:[73]

> Mhúscail mé ar maidin mar tháinig an coiméadóir,
> Ag réabadh mo dhorais go trom is gan labhairt.
> Dhearc mé ar na ballaí is shíl mé nach raibh mé beo.
> Títear domh nach n-imeoidh an t-ifreann seo go deo.
>
> D'oscail an doras is níor druideadh é go ciúin,
> Ach ba chuma ar bith mar nach rabhamar inár suan.
>
> Chuala mé éan ach ní fhaca mé geal an lae.
> Is mian mór liom go raibh mé go domhain faoi chré.
>
> Cá bhfuil mo chuimhne ar laethe a chuaigh romhainn?
> Is cá bhfuil an saol a smaoinigh mé a bhí sa domhan?
> Ní chluintear mo bhéic is ní fheictear mar a rith mo dheoir.
> Nuair a thigeann an lá, monuar,
> Athíocfaidh mé iad go mór!

Even to a reader unable to speak Irish, some of the departures from other published versions should be readily apparent, most obviously in this text's uncharacteristic division into stanzas. Despite the irregularity of the middle two verses—one wonders whether stanzas two and three were meant to be joined in order to parallel the structure of the first and last stanzas—arguably this stanza format makes "An Mhaidin" appear more clearly as a song by Western formal conventions, less as a poem than the usual unbroken block of twelve lines that one encounters in more widely available versions. Whatever the editorial intent, the formal variants of "An Mhaidin" and "Nuair a thigeann ar lá" ask their readers to consider the divisions between popular and "literary" verse, particularly given the place in Irish traditional music of *Siún Ní Dhuibhir*, the song to whose melody Sands sang his song.[74]

The first word of "An Mhaidin" diverges from that of "Nuair a thigeann ar lá" in a manner that will make many learners of Irish grin in remembrance of early attempts at precision. In Gaeilge, the verb "múscail" means "to awaken," not necessarily to physically arise in the manner that "éirigh" connotes. On the surface, this might suggest that the speaker's behavior in "Nuair a thigeann ar lá" is more active, particularly when one considers that the initial verb has strong associations with rebellion. The phrase "éirí amach" means "to rise in insurrection"; "Éirí na Cáisca" is an often-heard term for the Easter Rebellion of 1916. The physical force tradition of Republicanism thus suffuses the background of the hunger strike diary version of this text from the first line, adding an additional menace to the final line's assertion that the speaker will settle scores in the future. A more active tone might seem to be struck in line 9 of "Nuair a thigeann ar lá" where the speaker references his "smaointí" (thoughts) rather than his "chuimhne" (memory) of days gone by that is specified in the same line in "An Mhaidin." However, the use of "Mhúscail" in "An Mhaidin" permits just as important a rebellion: one of the mind. As in English, the word can be used to suggest an awakening on many levels, particularly the intellectual and political—a rise to consciousness in the broadest and most radical sense. Although unarguably tragic and painful, the leaving behind of the past as embedded in forgotten memory might present an opportunity for forward motion—at least if that memory encouraged only passive suffering or "doing heavy whack," as wallowing in depression was termed in Long Kesh patios.

Also notable in "An Mhaidin" is the final phrase of the eighth line: "go domhain faoi chré."[75] In addition to the alteration of the spelling to "doimhin," every other published version of this poem fails to include the word "chré" (clay, earth). This omission is surprising on a number of levels, not least in that the absence of "chré" interferes with the insistent end rhyme pattern of the poem: the word "faoi" that concludes other versions at best creates an off-rhyme with the "lae" of the preceding line and is certainly not the spot-on match of "An Mhaidin's" version. Similarly problematic is the issue that without "chré" the reader must rely on inference to determine precisely what the speaker desires to be under ("faoi"). The English translation of this line that appears in other published versions accurately reflects the apparent intention of "An Mhaidin": "Would that I were deep in the earth."[76] However, without that crucial noun this translation is strictly speaking, conjecture.

Whatever editorial decisions that might have been posed by the existence of these three variants of Sands's verse,[77] their divergences collectively reflect the new brand of Republican ideology being forged in Long Kesh and Armagh. It is entirely appropriate, for example, that "An Mhaidin" emphasizes a mental awakening while "Nuair a thigeann ar lá" dwells on the physical, for in their separate ways these embody the uniting of political engagement and armed struggle that Adams wrote about in "The National Alternative" and that Danny Morrison famously termed the strategy of ballot box and Armalite. Contemporary editorial and textual theory proves useful here in soothing anxieties about determining which of these is the "right" version. By reimagining these variants as "texts" that jointly compose a "work," we can draw greater insight into the carceral space that formed them. An individual text is then only part of the story, certainly interesting and important in and of itself but not necessarily the hermetically sealed object imagined by Matthew Arnold and exponents of New Criticism.

Until recent decades, three divergent texts of the sort analyzed above might have caused undue anxiety even in textual scholars who, historically, attempted to work their way backward in a work's history to a hypothetical, uncorrupted ur-text. Instead, as I will argue later with regard to the radical forms of locally produced Republican prison writing collections, it would be better to conceive of "An Mhaidin" and the two versions of "Nuair a thigeann ar lá" with, as Jerome McGann terms it in a slightly different context, a more "socialized concept of authorship and textual authority."[78] We would do well, as McGann urges, to be aware of the manner in which the desire for a single, unproblematic, authoritative text evinces and reifies a rather petrified notion of textual production. Indeed, as McGann correctly muses, it is possible for there to be "more than one 'final' version" of any given text, particularly when it originates in an oral tradition such as the one that flourished in the H Blocks.[79] As researchers and his own companions have affirmed, Sands, like all skilled storytellers and musicians, had a knack of both responding to and creating a mood. For instance, according to his comrades, Sands performed his ballad "Sad

Song for Susan" only during rare moments of peace in the H Blocks: he did not regularly sing it.[80]

Indeed, one cannot overestimate the extent to which many of Sands's poems spring from and return to a more overtly oral tradition than most contemporary literature. Many of the works that we have come to know as poems are actually songs and thus in a certain sense cannot be fully experienced—and, arguably, commented on—sans melody. A different critical apparatus might be in order when dealing with lyrics severed from their active, consciously musical performance. Writers such as McKeown, Campbell, Feldman, and O'Hearn have documented the intensely aural and oral atmosphere in the H Blocks of 1976–81, driven by the grim necessity of isolation and lack of access to standard literary texts. Given that memory frequently was all that the POWs could count on, we should not be surprised then that most of Sands's poems follow an insistent, sometimes admittedly simplistic, rhyme scheme. Without, I hope, absurdly overstating the case—and while noting that the H Block poets themselves consistently have downplayed the importance and skill of their literary endeavors—I cannot help but characterize this era in the H Blocks as one reminiscent of earlier times when oral and scribal technologies more equally participated in the transmission of text; I am not averse to comparing poetry readings in the H Blocks to performances of medieval ballads and, dare I say it, Homeric recitations. At least one of Sands's works was of epic length at any rate: in the eyes of his comrades, his master work of fiction was one that came to be known as *Jet*, a story of such length that it took "many nights to tell" out of the door of his cell.[81] Yet, because Sands never wrote it down, this work exists now only in the minds of the comrades who heard it. Likewise, O'Hearn recounts the demise of the original melody of Sands's song "McIllhattan." The tone-deafness of the ex-POW who attempted to communicate it to the well-known Irish musician Christy Moore (who eventually recorded it) was such that Moore and Donal Lunny needed to compose an entirely new melody as they could not recognize an actual tune in the ex-POW's well-meaning warblings.[82] The fragility of the *téacs pluide* manifests itself in a multiplicity of ways, yet it is strengthened if viewed as part of a larger work.

Published versions of Sands's prose evince a more active editorial hand than does his poetry. In most instances, this intervention is confined primarily to the formal level, what the editorial theorist G. Thomas Tanselle terms "horizontal revisions" that "do not reflect an altered intention and do not produce a new 'work,'" as opposed to "vertical revisions" that "do represent a changed intention and thus do result in an essentially different 'work.'"[83] Such editing is understandable given that the manuscripts not infrequently lacked paragraph breaks. As I have argued earlier in this chapter, prose form seems less critical than verse form in Sands's mind and it is reasonable to assume that he trusted his editors to sort out his paragraphs for him. Certainly there is precedent for such trust: Gibson insists that no less skillful a writer than Mark Twain "expected a publisher to impose a consistent texture on his accidentals."[84] Later in this chapter, I will discuss the variants of paragraph breaks imposed by editors in succeeding collections of Sands's writings, as there are enough to merit a separate subsection. In this more general section, I will focus on a peculiar formal disparity that evinces itself not between the manuscript and the print version, but rather between the English and Gaeilge texts in the version of Sands's hunger strike diary that appeared in *Skylark Sing Your Lonely Song*—a disparity that has been reproduced in every subsequent print version by major publishers.

Fair portions of the diary are written entirely in untranslated Gaeilge, particularly the latter part. For example, I cannot help but find significance in the fact that in manuscript the last entry contains not a word of English. Bobby knew that his death approached swiftly and chose Gaeilge to write what he knew might be his last public words. It is fitting, then, that whoever was to read those lines had to know Irish, had to know something about the culture for which Sands was giving his life. Translation would occur later, but to experience that lonely moment near its occurrence one needed to be a part of his world. In fact this is *still* the case for those who know the diary only through editions published by major presses because in all of those editions subsequent to the diary's inclusion in Mercier's *Skylark Sing Your Lonely Song,* the English translation omits several key sections of Sands' Gaeilge text. In the third paragraph from the end of the final diary entry in Irish, the English version fails to translate the second and third sentences, and the fourth sentence could be interpreted in a radically different fashion. This passage and my translation of it are as follows:

> Is é an mheabhair an rud is tábhachtaí. Mura bhfuil meabhair láidir agat chun cur in aghaidh le achan rud, ní mhairfidh. Ní bheadh aon sprid troda agat. Is ansin cén áit a dtigeann an mheabhair cheart seo.[85]
>
> [The mind is the most important thing. Unless you have a strong mind to oppose everything, you will not live. You would not have any fighting spirit. It is there where this proper mentality comes from.]

While I acknowledge that the act of translation is often at best a negotiated loss, the amount of text left unaddressed here begs examination. One must wonder why omissions of this relative magnitude occur in the translation, particularly given that all of those involved must have known that the overwhelming majority of readers would enter the text through English. Was it merely carelessness on the part of the translator and editor? Was this a deliberate attempt to make the passage seem more polished or self-assured and less repetitious? If one returns to the first published version of the hunger strike diary, the issue becomes more vexed. As a "special supplement" to the 13 June 1981 edition of *An Phoblacht/Republican News*, readers were given the hunger strike diary in its entirety. Sure enough, this version's English translation includes an additional two-sentence paragraph (the fourth from last) that addresses a portion of the absence above. It reads, "If you don't have a strong mind to resist all, you won't last. You wouldn't have any fighting spirit."[86] However, even this translation refuses to address the final sentence of the original Irish text. Subsequent pamphlet editions of the diary published locally by Sinn Féin retain this more accurate translation, including both the first version published outside of the pages of *AP/RN* and the version published on the ninth anniversary of his death.[87]

Other editorial intrusions evince themselves in structural disparities between the Irish and English texts in the versions disseminated by major presses. Certainly the English paragraphs are divided differently than the ones in Gaeilge. In the Irish, the third-to-last paragraph ends with the sentence translated as "perhaps from one's desire for freedom" and the penultimate paragraph begins with "It isn't certain that that's where it comes from."[88] These final paragraphs of the diary are quoted below in their entirety to illustrate, and I have included English glosses as markers at critical moments:

> Is é an mheabhair an rud is tábhachtaí. Mura bhfuil meabhair láidir agat chun cur in aghaidh le achan rud, ní mhairfidh. Ní bheadh aon sprid troda agat. Is ansin cén áit as a dtigeann an mheabhair cheart seo. B'fhéidir as an fhonn saoirse. ["Perhaps from the desire for freedom."]
>
> Ni [*sic*] hé cinnte gurb é an áit as a dtigeann sé ["It isn't certain this is the place where it comes from."] Mura bhfuil siad in inmhe an fonn saoirse a scriosadh, ní bheadh siad in inmhe tú féin a bhriseadh. Ní brisfidh siad mé mar tá an fonn saoirse, agus saoirse mhuintir ns hÉireann I mo chroí.

> Tiocfaidh lá eigin nuair a bheidh an fonn saoirse seo le taispeáint ag daoine go léir na hÉireann ansin tchífidh muid éirí na gealaí.[89]

The differing structure of the final four paragraphs of the English translation given in *Skylark Sing Your Lonely Song* is as follows:

> The body fights back sure enough, but at the end of the day everything returns to the primary consideration, that is, the mind. The mind is the most important.
>
> But then where does this proper mentality stem from? Perhaps from one's desire for freedom. It isn't certain that that's where it comes from.
>
> If they aren't able to destroy the desire for freedom, they won't break you. They won't break me because the desire for freedom and the freedom of the Irish people, is in my heart. The day will dawn when all the people of Ireland will have the desire for freedom to show.
>
> It is then we'll see the rising of the moon.[90]

The English translation ends with one dramatic, succinct phrase, yet it should be obvious even to someone without any knowledge of Gaeilge that the final sentence in the Irish original contains a great deal more. Indeed it does. The last sentence in the English translation is actually just the last six words of the final paragraph in Gaeilge: "ansin tchífidh muid éirí na gealaí."[91]

Certainly the editorial choices manifest in *Skylark Sing Your Lonely Song* provide the translation with more technical prowess; Sands thus seems to be a more precise writer than he appears to be in the original. Although strictly speaking this English translation abides by the usual Republican editorial *modus operandi*, to avoid substantive alteration of the author's words, the formal intervention we see here produces a rhetorical impact more pronounced than the average modification of a paragraph break. Yet, because published editions of the diary generally foreground the Gaeilge text for those with the desire to experience it in the original, perhaps this might be rationalized as a less serious departure from a policy of nonintervention than it first might appear. Ultimately, given Sands's emphatic choice to compose this entry *as Gaeilge*, any translation must be viewed as distinct from—though at this point in history, an entity inextricably linked to—the original.[92]

While no explanation of the editorial apparatus accompanies *Skylark Sing Your Lonely Song*, the "Publisher's note" immediately preceding the text in the Mercier edition of *One Day in My Life* demonstrates the manner in which larger presses approach volatile political texts such as

Republican prison writing, for it admits that "Certain sections of the original manuscript have been omitted from this book on legal advice. Otherwise only minor textual changes for consistency and clarity have been made."[93] This desire for "clarity" may have prompted the alterations to Sands's diary mentioned above: certainly the "Publisher's note" authorizes a more invasive hand than either Morrison or the other editors at *An Phoblacht/Republican News* seem ready to employ. This is especially evident with regard to the legal issues raised in the first sentence of the quote above. In the *An Phoblacht/Republican News* version of Sands's diary, for example, Sands is allowed to "name names," angrily and unambiguously identifying the "collaborating middle-class nationalist" priest who visits him on the seventh day of his hunger strike, though he pulls himself back from his own invective, chiding himself to get "off the man's back O Seachnasaigh, for now anyway!"[94] Both the priest's name and Sands's partial retreat are deleted in the Mercier edition of this text (and as a result, in all subsequent versions except Sinn Féin's miniature pamphlet reprints), an excision that deemphasizes Sands's capacity both for balance and self-parody, even in the extremity of hunger strike. In subsequent editions, similar deletions also are made with regard to the prison governor, one of the doctors, politicians north and south, and the Officials. In the last entry of the Mercier version of Sands's diary, for instance, both the original Irish and English terms are replaced in order to make Sands's tormentor into a generic "oifigeach / official."[95] Similarly, the *An Phoblacht/Republican News* version of the 13 March diary entry specifies the particular H Block in which Sands reports brutality during a wing shift, a specificity removed in larger press editions.[96] Given the ferocity of libel laws, these deletions are understandable on an intellectual level at least; however, we also see the fashion in which these laws (and the editorial decisions that they provoke) potentially might lend themselves to counterinsurgency as well, whatever their intent and their legitimate value in defamation cases. To the editors' credit, at least the Mercier version intentionally notes with ellipsis marks the deletions seemingly motivated by "potentially libelous" statements, thus calling attention to an absence and consequently inviting readers to question what might have necessitated the alterations in Sands's texts.

The Anthologization of Bobby Sands

Given that Sands's work initially got widespread public exposure in the pages of *An Phoblacht/Republican News*, it is fitting enough that the newspaper offered its readers the first collection of Sands's texts on 21 March 1981 in the form of a two-page spread titled "The Writings of Bobby Sands." This marked the first time the prose pieces "I am Sir, you are 1066!" [*sic*], "The Battle for Survival," and "The Lark and the Freedom Fighter" appeared in print specifically credited to Sands, the first text having previously been the work of "a young West Belfast Republican," the other two that of "Marcella." The ending of anonymity coincides with the end of Sands's third week on hunger strike and indicates a subtle shift in Republican publishing tactics, one that complimented the larger Republican anti–H Block/Armagh strategy. Rather than using an anonymous image to represent the collective as was the rhetorical move of the byline "a West Belfast Republican," specific individuals now would stand for the collective. Because Sands was "the most prolific writer amongst the H Block blanket men," as the editor writes in the introduction to these three texts, he became an obvious figure around whom Republicans could rally support.[97] The editor continues,

> There is a premonition of personal tragedy running through Bobby Sands' [*sic*] articles: that his H Block cell will, literally, become a tomb, when the monster of British imperialism and the prison regime it has created, kill him, following their failed attempts to destroy his spirit.
>
> Bobby Sands' [*sic*] tragic premonition can now only be averted if the widespread passive support for the prisoners which exists nationwide, is transformed into active support, building up sufficient political pressure to urgently force the British government to grant the five humanitarian demands which constitute political status.[98]

The "five demands" to which the editor refers in the passage above are the distillation of the Republican POWs' wider struggle to regain the political status that the British government revoked with the institution of the policy of "criminalization" and the consequent end of Special Category Status in British prisons. As Bik McFarlane, who became the OC of the H Blocks during Sands's hunger strike, summarizes, the five demands were formalized in January 1980 and were

> 1) the right to our own clothes; 2) no prison work; 3) free association with other POWs; 4) a visit, parcel and letters per week; 5) the return of remission lost due to protest action on the Blanket. Supporters could campaign around a specific programme. The five demands, we felt, also gave the Brits plenty of room to manoevre since no emotive terminology was attached.[99]

Frustrated by the failure of the Blanket and No-Wash Protests, to achieve these goals, seven male Republican prisoners went on hunger strike on 27 October 1980. Three women in Armagh Gaol joined them on 1 December and thirty more men in the H Blocks began their fasts on 15 December. These men and women ended their hunger strike when the British government convinced them that "a resolution was imminent. The episode finished in despair and confusion, however, when the prisoners realised [*sic*] that a settlement was still not in sight."[100] However, several months of inertia convinced the POWs that the British government was not going to deliver on any of the concessions they had suggested were forthcoming, and in protest the POWs in the H Blocks began their second hunger strike on 1 March 1981, a strike lead by Bobby Sands.

Sands's writings proved to be an integral part of the Republican campaign surrounding the second hunger strike. As noted above, *An Phoblacht/Republican News* reprinted three of Sands's articles on his twenty-first day on the strike and ran his essay "The Birth of a Republican" again on 4 April. The choice of the latter essay in particular is interesting, and the editorial commentary revelatory. On its initial anonymous publication on 16 December 1978, in smaller font beneath the title, *An Phoblacht/Republican News* described the article as an account in which "A Blanket Man recalls how the spirit of Republican defiance grew within him."[101] The 1981 reprint backs away somewhat from this statement, describing the article instead as a "semi-autobiographical" work.[102] In the post–*A Million Little Pieces* literary landscape, some readers might rush to judgment about this recharacterization. Instead, I will remind the doctrinaire of the manner in which Sands had long considered his own story to be representative of others—why should he not feel justified in taking inspiration from his comrades' stories? Similarly, as recent scholars of autobiography remind us, all attempts to describe the personal necessarily rely on a certain fiction, the establishment of certain constructs that might not be "objectively" true. Description is necessarily subjective.

At very least, Sands's ultimate intention remained the same in 1981: to focus attention not just on one solitary individual, but on *all* POWs as represented by the hunger strikers. In addition, the fact that *An Phoblacht/Republican News* continued to publish Sands's writings in the months after his death indicates that his texts were viewed as representative of the struggle as a whole. In the period between 5 May and 3 October, the newspaper printed what would become Sands's most famous poem, "The rhythm of time" [*sic*],[103] as well as two prose pieces, "The Captain and the Cowards" and "All God's Children."[104] The hunger strike, of course, did not end when Sands expired on 5 May 1981: nine other men fasted to the death after

Sands, and men continued to fast until 3 October 1981 when the POWs announced the strike's termination.

There is no denying, however, that the anthologization of Sands's writings outside *An Phoblacht/Republican News* overlaps in significant ways with the campaign to elect Sands to British parliament, a candidacy that Sinn Féin announced on 26 March 1981.[105] The earliest collection of this sort that I have been able to unearth is a plain affair, a booklet whose white, heavy paper cover bears the title "The Writings of BOBBY SANDS" [*sic*] beneath a black and white image of the famous photograph of Sands's grinning face. The pages are plain white paper, and while the individual story and poem titles are in slightly more elaborate font, that of the texts themselves suggests the Courier style of a standard typewriter. No publisher is noted, though above the foreword, the Linen Hall Library has penciled in "Sinn Fein [*sic*] Belfast c. 1980s." Internal evidence suggests a much more precise date: the introduction by Gerry Adams recounts that "Bobby Sands commenced [his] hungerstrike [*sic*] on March 1st 1981. He was followed a fortnight later by Frankie Hughes who was joined this weekend by Raymond McCreesh and Patsy O'Hara."[106] The fact that Adams's introduction fails to reference Sands's bid for British parliament also aids in determining a potential publication date: this absence strongly suggests that the pamphlet appeared between 22 and 26 March 1981, a matter of days before Sands's electoral bid is announced. That the collection certainly is not a posthumous one evinces itself in Adams's admonition "that the hungerstrikers and blanketmen and protesting women are political prisoners is without question . . . Whether [Sands] has to die to prove it remains to be seen. It also depends absolutely on you."[107] As I argued in the previous chapter regarding the revisions evident in the anthologization of Adams's own prison writing, it would be uncharacteristic for Republican editors to allow a call to such specific action to remain unaltered after such action is no longer relevant to the political moment.

This version of *The Writings of Bobby Sands* contains seven of Sands's prose pieces and two of his poems.[108] Interestingly, in the introduction, Adams remarks that he "was drawn particularly to four [of Sands's stories]. 'I once had a life,' 'I fought a monster today,' 'I am Sir, You are 1066' and the interesting use of a small rodent as a medium in "A Mouse-Eye View' [*sic*]."[109] The last text in Adams's list is a short story that does not actually appear in the collection, one that does not even seem to be authored by Sands. This puzzle might be solved by looking back to the original publication of "I once had a life" in *An Phoblacht/Republican News*: Sands's story, credited to

"Marcella," occupies the top half of the page, while the lower half is devoted to "A Mouse-Eye View, A tale by an H-block prisoner."[110] Two possibilities suggest themselves here: either Adams had this newspaper page in front of him when writing the introductory remarks, or the manuscript of *The Writings of Bobby Sands* to which he refers originally contained "A Mouse-Eye View" as a result of a similar misattribution and, realizing their mistake, the editors subsequently excised it. I raise this issue not to criticize Adams or the editors of *The Writings of Bobby Sands* but rather to emphasize the manner in which this error actually highlights Republican notions of collective identity. In content and style, "A Mouse-Eye View" was evidently similar enough to Sands's texts to confuse the editors initially: in this we can certainly see evidence that one voice from the H Blocks can speak for all, or rather, that all of the POWs spoke with the same voice.

Nevertheless, *The Writings of Bobby Sands*'s decision to focus on a single voice potentially runs the risk of foregrounding one experience over others and in so doing seemingly contradicts the ideal of collectivity. Such an anxiety at first appears to be justified by the collection's cover, for, as mentioned earlier, the now-iconic photograph taken during Sands's previous imprisonment in the Cages dominates the available space. The formatting of the title similarly pulls the eye to Sands himself, not his writings. Beneath the photo, the first three words of the title appear in slender cursive but a reader's attention is swiftly drawn to the strikingly larger boldfaced type announcing the author's name in heavy block letters. The layout of the title thus places primary emphasis on the man, not his texts—a layout uncharacteristic of anthologies except among those of the most famous or canonical authors.[111] It certainly goes against the previous practice of *An Phoblacht/Republican News* as demonstrable in their usual habit of printing prison texts by multiple authors on the same page. Although certainly the work of some incarcerated individuals was occasionally highlighted, apart from regular columns such as that of "Brownie," this appears to be the exception rather than the rule before 1981, particularly with regard to poetry. In fact, it is worth mentioning another example of a divided page of the sort encountered above. On 10 June 1978, the top half of page three of *Republican News* is dominated by "One of those Days that Never Ends," a prose piece by Sands as "a young West Belfast Republican." Occupying the lower half is "Thoughts from H Block by a blanket man's brother," another prose text that centers on excerpts from—and the author's reactions to—two letters smuggled out of Long Kesh. Though the author wrote comfortably outside jail walls, in so doing he hopes that "it will give you, the reader, a much clearer picture of not only what the men in the H Blocks must endure, but also how they endure it."[112] In such a moment *taoibh amuigh* and *faoi ghlas* become one voice, each a part of the same struggle, a point emphasized by page layout.

Despite concerns raised by the initial image, however, *The Writings of Bobby Sands* avoids becoming a truly monovocal collection not only through the deliberately collective focus of the texts contained within it, but also via the layout inside the covers. Like Sands's *Republican News* articles, this pamphlet reemphasizes in its physical layout the extent to which Republicans conceive of prison writing as inseparable from a wider political—and politicized—context. I insist that in its activist shape *The Writings of Bobby Sands* and its immediate successor of the same title stand in radical opposition to subsequent collections of Sands's work, including *Skylark Sing Your Lonely Song*, *Bobby Sands: Irish Rebel*, and *Writings from Prison*. In their own ways, each of these compilations underscores the otherness of Republican prison writing. Of them, however, *The Writings of Bobby Sands* subverts most completely the conventions of bourgeois literary production, aesthetics, and consumption—a textual insurgency that only grows more sophisticated and radical in its second edition of April 1981.

Like the texts contained within it, this anthology consciously works to destroy the binary of inside and outside, those apparently free and those behind jail walls. One manifestation of this emerges in the manner in which the collection's layout decenters and deconstructs the bourgeois subject position of author. *The Writings of Bobby Sands* does not concern itself with bolstering the idea of the individual genius, a writer somehow set apart from all others. Even a casual glance at the illustrations reveals the surprising extent to which the collection draws attention away from Sands himself, refocusing it on the H Blocks in general and Sands's comrades who suffered alongside him. Sands's face appears only on the cover: the other three images of men in the pamphlet are those of unidentified Blanketmen, and in two of the three cases the images depict POWs in pairs. In fact, a photograph of two Blanketmen—neither of them Sands—precedes the first text in the collection, an unambiguous foregrounding of the group.

The other three images are drawings that all point toward the cooperative in their own way, and two of them have become iconic in the prison struggle. The first is a small drawing of a clenched fist apparently in shackles, surrounded by barbed wire. The implications are clear: despite—indeed, partially because of—their brutal incarceration, the POWs remain defiant. The synecdoche should not be lost on the viewer: the Republicans' bodies, their identities, have been distilled into a single fist.[113] Like this image, the second drawing that appears in *The Writings of Bobby Sands* has become synonymous with the larger prison struggle—so much so that it is possible that some might have forgotten its origins in Sands's prison writings. Next to the title of the last story in the collection, "The Lark and the Freedom Fighter," the reader encounters the image of a skylark perched on a field of barbed wire, its wings spread wide and its beak parted in the midst of defiant song.[114] The connection between this illustration and the story is clear: the central image of "The Lark and the Freedom Fighter" is a skylark, imprisoned by a cruel man who desires to bend the bird to his will. The man employs increasingly extreme tactics against the bird, covering its "cage with a black cloth, depriving the bird of sunlight. He starved it and left it to rot in a dirty cage, but the bird still refused to yield. The man murdered it."[115] To the story's speaker, the parallels to POWs in British prisons are clear: "I am now in H-Block, where I refuse to change to suit the people who oppress, torture and imprison me, and who wish to dehumanize me. Like the lark, I need no changing."[116] Par for the course in nearly all of his writings, Sands does not let the first person singular remain the sole focus, asserting near the end of the story, "while I remain alive, I remain what I am, a political prisoner of war, and no one can change that. Haven't we plenty of larks to prove that?"[117]

In a related manner, it is important to recognize that *The Writings of Bobby Sands* forces the reader into contact with all of the phases of resistance in the H Blocks. The two drawings of POWs capture the agonies of the early stages of protest, both images depicting half-naked, bearded men clad only in their blankets. As is all too obvious from the excrement visible on the walls, the photograph mentioned above captures the horrors of the No-Wash Protest. Yet, strictly speaking the horrifying spectacle of human waste on H Block walls was already an anachronism at the time of the collection's publication: the POWs ended the No-Wash Protest at the start of the 1981 hunger strike (1 March 1981) in order to focus attention on Sands and the other Republican POWs who began the fast in swift succession. There is more to this amalgam of illustrations than a relative paucity of visuals available from the H Blocks, for by presenting older images along with more contemporary ones *The Writings of Bobby Sands* visually emphasizes the continuity of the prison struggle in Long Kesh, the determination of the POWs not to be broken.

The POWs' appearance adds to this sense of collectivity for the No-Wash Protest broke down visual distinctions among the Blanketmen, long hair and beards obscuring distinctive facial features. Feldman is correct in his assertion that the Blanketmen "had generated a counter-textualization of their bodies, a self-inscription that could not be effaced by defiling contact with the prison uniform"; however, his analysis does not go far enough in highlighting the importance of collectivity.[118] While refusing prison garb and the criminality it implied to them, the Republicans' own bodies created uniforms in the root sense of the word: their protest made the POWs look alike, made solidarity visible. Each of these images literally could be anyone on the protest, and in being anyone each becomes everyone. In visually highlighting this kinship, *The Writings of Bobby Sands* merely continues the tradition established from the first moment that Sands's writings from the H Blocks appeared in *Republican News,* where Sands's texts were frequently accompanied by illustrations of this sort.[119]

Events on the ground appear very quickly to have necessitated a revised edition of *The Writings of Bobby Sands* published, as the title page informs us, by Sinn Féin's POW Department in Dublin in April 1981. While perhaps not befitting the status of the member of parliament that Sands had become in the interim, this version of the text is, as pamphlets go, a more luxurious outing. The bright orange cover, though still just heavy paper, more dramatically frames the same black and white photograph of the smiling Sands that graces the cover of the first edition. The glossy pages and a switch to a more clearly professional font and typesetting evince a similar upgrade between the covers, further manifest in the table of contents and page numbers not present in its predecessor. Again Gerry Adams provides the introduction and, as before, his words help us date this version—which I will henceforth term the Dublin edition—more precisely. With obvious pride, Adams recounts Sands's election to the British parliament as MP for Fermanagh and South Tyrone on 10 April 1981:

> The election, held against a background of harassment and intimidation of his election workers by British crown forces, was unique, not least because of the pressure put upon the nationalist electorate by the SDLP leadership, the Catholic church, and British politicians. Despite these pressures, Bobby Sands received 30, 492 votes, a clear sign—for those who doubted it—that the nationalist people recognize republican prisoners as political prisoners and support their prison struggle.[120]

Further reference to an April 12 *Sunday Times* editorial pushes the moment of publication to at least mid-April. Because no mention at all is made of Sands's death on 5 May 1981, the pamphlet likely was published before that tragic moment.[121]

In addition to being a more polished collection in terms of physical construction, the revised Dublin version of *The Writings of Bobby Sands* is also an expanded edition: to the seven prose pieces in the first edition, this collection adds "The harvest Britain has sown" [*sic*], "A break in the monotony," and "The battle for survival." The two poems remain the same, although "And the woman cried" has been retitled "The woman cried." The number of illustrations has also increased to seventeen, eleven of them photographs. This expansion and the more professional layout swell the pamphlet's length to thirty-six pages, sixteen more than the original. While precise sales figures are impossible to determine, the Dublin edition of *The Writings of Bobby Sands* appears to have been the most widely available of the two versions and is likely the one that first exposed a readership outside *An Phoblacht/Republican News* to Sands's descriptions of the carceral excesses of the H Blocks.[122]

As mentioned earlier, the physical layout of the Dublin edition's cover is identical to its predecessor. However, an important alteration is made in the inside cover of the later version, and the rhetorical move that it makes is striking, one that is more complex than it may initially appear. Here, we encounter a full-page photograph of a young woman captured in mid-shout, in the midst of a political rally. With both hands she holds a large poster mounted on cardboard, one dominated by the same image of Sands used for the cover of *The Writings of Bobby Sands,* the words "Bobby Sands" in bold white letters amid the black border of the poster's bottom edge. In the crowd in the background above her right shoulder one can glimpse a young man wearing a t-shirt reading "SUPPORT THE HUNGER STRIKERS" its image of Francis Hughes partially obscured by another marcher. The *sequence* of images is important here: because in the act of reading, the reader likely has experienced the cover first, it is almost as if the woman is holding a copy of *The Writings of Bobby Sands* and not a placard. In this moment the cover of *The Writings of Bobby Sands* has been revealed as part of a much larger politicized matrix, one that invites the reader to abandon the passivity and isolation historically associated with bourgeois literary consumption. As with the earlier edition of *The Writings of Bobby Sands,* in isolation, the outside cover initially seems to reify a unidirectionality of text, perhaps causing us momentarily to imagine that we might just sit back and hear the words of the solitary author whose image we encounter first.

However, the inside cover presents the consumer of these texts with the possibility—even the necessity—of literally speaking out subsequent to our textual encounter with Bobby Sands. If the text speaks to us, this photo suggests, we in turn must speak to others: the act of reading does not end with the completion of the text. Testimony begets further testimony and the joining of individuals into a community.

The Writings of Bobby Sands visually articulates the necessity of active engagement again in one of the last photos in the collection. This one captures a march in support of the POWs, one that may very well be a rally in support of Sands's bid for the British parliament.[123] Owen Carron—Sands's election agent and the man who would later replace him as MP for Fermanagh/South Tyrone—stands in the middle of a line of five well-dressed marchers, two women on his left, two elderly men on his right. Carron's four companions each carry large posters, three of them bearing the ubiquitous image of Sands, one bearing that of Raymond McCreesh. The placard carried by the woman on Carron's immediate left—who may be Marcella Sands—merits specific commentary. Unlike the other two posters of Sands, which simply comprise his photo and name in black and white, this poster identifies Sands as an "IRISH HUNGER STRIKER" in words appearing above Sands's image. In addition, we see one of the central rallying cries of the hunger strike and the 1981 election campaign in which Sands was elected MP: "DON'T LET HIM DIE!" printed in dramatic block letters beneath the photo. The placard is aimed as much—and likely, *more*—at passive nationalists as it is at the British government. Inaction is tantamount to participation in the deaths of the men in the H Blocks, a view that *The Writings of Bobby Sands* similarly stresses by reproducing this photograph. By rallying behind Sands, the photo implies, one rallies behind *all* POWs, a point underscored by a large banner visible in the background of this photo that reads "IRELAND UNCONQUERED BACKS THE PRISONERS!"

There are overt echoes of Sands's *ainm cleite* "Marcella" in the photograph accompanying "A Thought in the Night" in the Dublin edition. Here the reader comes face to face with some of Sands's family, his mother and his younger sister Marcella, apparently at an outdoor hunger strike rally as both women are seen wearing coats.[124] On one level, of course, this can be read simply as an emotional ploy to garner support by further humanizing Sands, forcefully reminding the reader not only of the sufferings of the hunger strikers but also of the sufferings of their loved ones. "A Thought in the Night" echoes this point as its speaker temporarily escapes his H Blocks cell through a dream vision of his family. Before his eyes appear

> the faces of my family, my sisters and brother, growing up in my absence. And I knew just how much I loved them, and how I longed to share this short life with them and my poor mother. Lord, my poor tortured mother, grey and marked with a lifetime of worry and hardship that only she knows the entirety and toll of. And I said: "I'm sorry that you have suffered through my sufferings, mother." As ever, she replied: "Don't be humble. You're my son, and I'll always stand by you."[125]

Suffering passes through the cell walls in both directions in this passage, yet this suffering is ameliorated for the prisoner by the unconditional support of family. Similarly, the courageous endurance of the POW inspires further devotion and encouragement on the part of those on the outside. The photo accompanying "A Thought in the Night" precisely mirrors this implicit call for active engagement and support. The microphones in the foreground are not an inconsequential detail: Sands's mother is captured in the act of testimony—she adds her voice to that of her son, *literally* in the case of the event at which the photograph was taken, as well as *symbolically* within the collection itself in the presence of this image. Before her son's incarceration, Roseleen Sands was certainly not an active Republican: in fact, when Bobby was born in 1954, she reportedly stated, "if the Troubles ever flare up here, and the IRA gets going, we'll go to the South."[126] Yet, her actions and this photo suggest that all of us, Republican or otherwise, might have a voice and a duty to use that voice against injustice. The gathering captured in the photo may be the one Sands refers to in the second entry in his hunger strike diary, where he writes, "I heard that my mother spoke at a parade in Belfast yesterday and that Marcella cried. It gave me heart. I'm not worried about the numbers of the crowds."[127] Sands's statements here parallel the concerns that his story, the photo, and *The Writings of Bobby Sands* attempt to address. Observe the emotional lift that Sands experiences as a result of the support of his family; similarly, though he downplays it, the quote above also implicitly recognizes the never-ending need to reach others.

There is something of Freire's critique of the "banking concept of education" in this sequence of images, for like Freire *The Writings of Bobby Sands*'s paratext here argues against passive accumulation of knowledge for its own sake. Instead, it urges critical engagement and activism of the sort that we see in Sands's texts themselves. For example, in "The Battle for Survival," one of the new additions to the Dublin edition, after cataloging the abuses to which the POWs were subject in the H Blocks, Sands admonishes his readers to "think about it, but just don't leave it at that."[128] In the intersection of those concluding lines and the title he chose for his essay, Sands implies that his readership outside Long Kesh plays a role in the "battle for survival" of POWs within the H Blocks, not just when the essay was initially published in 1979 but also especially in the crisis surrounding the moment of republication. This conception of literature assigns a terrible agency and a terrible *responsibility* to its reader, for it posits the ability of spectators to intervene in the prison struggle, a responsibility all the more awesome as Sands's hunger strike progressed. As noted in the previous chapter, in his own prison writing, Gerry Adams made similar demands of the public *taoibh amuigh* during Frank Stagg's hunger strike, and the ultimate failure to intercede successfully on Stagg's behalf no doubt magnified Republican anxieties during the moment of the Dublin edition's initial appearance. Sands, after all, was only weeks—possibly days—from death.

Like the first edition of the collection, the Dublin version of *The Writings of Bobby Sands* attempts in other ways to obliterate the binary of *taoibh amuigh* and *faoi ghlas* and to contest the idea of the autonomous individual. This collection also refuses a complete fixation on Sands alone and likewise does so through visual imagery. There are almost as many illustrations of Sands's fellow Blanketmen as there are of Sands himself: in fact, images of unidentified Blanketmen actually outnumber images of Sands on his own. Sands appears alone in only four of the seventeen illustrations, including the cover, in *The Writings of Bobby Sands*, and two of those four instances utilize the same photograph of Sands. In a related manner, the Dublin edition continues the tradition of including illustrations depicting all stages of the H Block protest, from the Blanket, to the No-Wash, to the Hunger Strikes: it reproduces the same photograph of the two Blanketmen standing in their excrement-covered cell that the first edition did, for example. Further continuity of H Block resistance is also argued with the inclusion of a photo of Brendan Hughes in the early stages of the 1980 hunger strike.[129]

Yet, the Dublin edition goes further back in time in the prison struggle and devotes a full page to a photo of Sands, Tomboy Louden, Brendan Hughes, and Gerry Adams taken outside one of the huts of the Cages of Long Kesh in the mid-1970s.[130] If readers were at all in doubt of Sands's Republican credentials, this image certainly establishes him as someone with long-standing ties to the Provisional elite.

As hard as it might be to imagine today, one must remember that Sands would have been an unknown quantity to the vast majority of nationalists in the North of Ireland, partly as a result of the anonymity of his writing in *An Phoblacht/Republican News*. By contextualizing him alongside a well-known Blanketman, the former OC of the H Blocks, and the vice president of Sinn Féin in a moment when all of them are being held as political prisoners in the infamous Cages, the collection visually lends Sands credibility through obviously longstanding group identity.[131]

Undoubtedly—and interestingly—all versions of *The Writings of Bobby Sands* privilege prose over poetry, as did the reprints of Sands's work in *AP/RN* during his hunger strike. Readers would have to wait until 29 June 1981 for the appearance of "The rhythm of time" in the newspaper's pages to encounter any verse specifically attributed to Bobby Sands. As the introductory remarks note, this poem was written "in H3-Block of Long Kesh about two years ago . . . and is previously unpublished."[132] The first compilation of Sands's verse did not surface until October 1981, when Sinn Féin's Publicity Department released *Prison Poems*, a collection of seventeen poems with an introduction by Danny Morrison.[133]

Prison Poems eschews the relatively lavish visuals of the Dublin version of *The Writings of Bobby Sands*: only one black and white image appears inside it, the publicity photo of Sands used for the covers of the two earlier collections. That *Prison Poems* does not continue the tradition of the previous pamphlets with regard to illustrations—particularly cover illustration—merits attention on several levels, not least in that its cover insistently foregrounds the space of Long Kesh rather than Sands. On the green, glossy cover, the impressionistic black silhouettes of two of the guard towers on the perimeter of the H Blocks loom and, unlike its predecessors, the large white block letters of the title actually draw attention away from the much smaller, lowercase letters that announce the author's name. The pamphlet does its best to deliver on its title, for at eighty-two pages it is more than double the length of the longest version of *The Writings of Bobby Sands*. Its stripped-down layout and tiny font permit seventeen of Sands's poems to reach the public, no mean feat considering that the epic "Trilogy" on its own spans forty-two pages.

Prison Poems concludes with "The Rhythm of Time," the poem that just over three months earlier became the first to have been published in *An Phoblacht/Republican News* credited to "Bobby Sands"; however, in doing so the collection completes the circle back to Sands's most famous *ainm cleite*. Beneath the final line of this poem appears the italicized, signature-like inscription "—Marcella, H-Block, Long Kesh Prison Camp. [*sic*]," the full stop bringing both poem and collection to a dramatic close. In this manner *Prison Poems* interrogates the subject position of author, for the attribution of the poetry to "Bobby Sands" does not suffice, it seems. "Marcella" is part of Bobby Sands, but Bobby Sands is only part of "Marcella," only one of the many people whose lives Sands sought to commemorate in verse. It is a particularly fascinating move given that so few of Sands's poems were initially published using this *ainm cleite*: "and the woman cried"[134] was one of the few poems given the byline "Marcella." "Poetic Justice,"[135] for example, was credited to "Roibeard, H5 Block."

Nevertheless, the inclusive movement of the pen-name "Marcella" is entirely appropriate to this poem, for "The Rhythm of Time" meditates on archetypical moments of resistance from cultures around the globe. It does so in a fashion that seems almost deliberately designed to refute some of the traditional critiques of Irish resistance writing. Deriving their views more from the overtly Christological imagery of Irish writers from early in the twentieth century than from the work of more recent Republican authors, hostile critics frequently—and inaccurately—attempt to dismiss contemporary Provisional Republicanism as a militant Catholicism. At first glance, the evocation of the crucified Jesus in the poem's fourth stanza seems to lend itself to this claim, for such a rhetorical move is common in nationalist texts such as those by Pearse. To focus overmuch on this stanza would result in a grave misreading of Sands's ideology, however. Three stanzas later, Sands references the "holy innocence" of non-Christian Native Americans who faced the greedy swords of European missionaries and colonizers in Columbus's time, an imagery echoed in the eighth stanza's allusion to the massacre of Lakota men, women, and children by the United States's Seventh Cavalry on the Pine Ridge Reservation in South Dakota in 1890. Revisionists should observe also that Sands highlights *English* heroism in the sixth stanza, when he praises the courage of "Wat the Tyler's poor."[136] In fact, "The Rhythm of Time" references Ireland only twice: once in the context of the Anglo-Irish War, and once in the indirect evocation of the H Blocks in the final stanza. Far from imagining it as a unique trait, the speaker affirms that the battle against injustice "knows no bounds nor space," for it originates in a desire for freedom that "is there in every race."[137]

From his first prison text onward, Gerry Adams urged readers to develop precisely this expansive, nonsectarian stance, so it must have been with satisfaction that he witnessed its continued growth in the H Blocks. The tactic of "divide and conquer," after all, did not just apply to the segmentation of Republicans in individual cells, but also could be seen on a societal level in the counterinsurgency efforts of military strategists such as Sir Frank Kitson, who were known for their use of "gangs and counter-gangs" to divide rebel groups. Strength, Republican theorists such as Adams and Sands knew, can proceed from connection with others, from the establishment of common ground. Literature is a powerful teacher in this regard, one that can reveal overlooked connections between ourselves and others. In his review of *Prison Poems* Adams asks,

> How many Bobby Sands [*sic*], ignored or unknown to us, have we in our midst? By reading Bobby's poetry, a profound experience, perhaps we will appreciate not only what he is saying but what others, less articulate than he, are forced to bottle up within themselves under the insidious but no less vicious and smothering burden of what passes for the quality of life in our materialistic, modern day, partitioned, unfree consumer society.[138]

The experience of reading, Adams insists, must point away from the autonomous author, away from the passive enjoyment conventionally associated with literary consumption. Instead, literature is the starting point for social critique and the building of community, of hearing the "ignored" subaltern. In short, literature is an insurrection against an enforced powerlessness, an escape from an imprisonment within the solitary individual, a freeing of the collective voice, a creation of solidarity that might be extended outward to a global level. Such a conception of literature has unmistakable resonances of some of the more democratic aspects of Romantic poetic theory. When Adams contends that "real poetry is not written solely for academics. Real poetry is written for people,"[139] he echoes Wordsworth's admonition almost two centuries earlier in the Preface to *Lyrical Ballads* that poets "must descend from this supposed height" of obtuse, academic language and speak in ways that all might understand, for "poets do not write for poets alone, but for men"[140] and presumably for women as well. Unlike the Romantics, however, the material conditions of composition faced by Republican prisoners often ground their work in the present to an extent that Shelley and Wordsworth at times resist, for, as Shelley put it, a poet "would do ill to embody his own conceptions of right and wrong, which are usually those of his place and time, in his poetical creations, which participate in neither."[141]

In the review above, although Adams deemphasizes a scholarly aesthetic, *Prison Poems* actually makes a move toward academia in its layout. In its increased length and lack of internal illustration, this collection begins a divergence from the overtly political pamphlet: in short, by traditional academic standards, Sands's work looks "more serious" in such a setting and is less easily dismissed on a purely formalistic basis. *Prison Poems*, I argue, begins the textual embodiment of Bobby Sands in a more self-consciously traditional way and marks the beginning of an increasingly insistent co-option of his texts by an academic formalism that in some crucial ways actually decontextualizes his work.

The first collection of Sands's work to be published by a larger, independent press was *Skylark Sing Your Lonely Song: an anthology of the writings of BOBBY SANDS* [*sic*], which appeared in 1982 under the imprint of Mercier. Unlike *The Writings of Bobby Sands*, the vast majority of texts contained between its covers are verse: there are twenty-five prose pieces and forty-one poems. Despite the twenty-page length of the hunger strike diary, this volume, like *Prison Poems,* is dominated by "Trilogy," which stretches to forty-three pages. Although undoubtedly many concerns informed the selection of the particular texts that were anthologized, one can hardly avoid the obvious shift in the verse/prose ratio toward a genre so strongly valorized as the "most literary" of forms. It is worth noting as well that the back cover pointedly remarks that Sands's work will be enjoyed by a general audience, "whether they are interested in politics or not."[142] In direct contrast to the activist drive of *The Writings of Bobby Sands* (and somewhat surprisingly, given Mercier's long history of publishing unapologetically nationalist texts), the back cover points the reader not toward engagement with the political moment but instead to rather safe apolitical abstractions such as "courage." Although inarguably Sands and his comrades demonstrated an extraordinary amount of that quality, the term itself as used here seems plucked from a prompt for a tepid university essay. That is to say, not only might Sands's courage be passively admired, one is encouraged to admire him as an extraordinary individual—not as a member of an extraordinary collective, or as a part of an extraordinary political moment.

However, the photoreproductions of nine of the original *teachtaireachtaí* that carried Sands's texts out of Long Kesh ameliorates the depoliticization enacted by the back cover. In the inclusion of these photos of Sands's manuscripts, *Skylark* consciously foregrounds the disparity between the uniformity—the sterility—of mechanically reproduced text and the painstakingly crafted lettering visible on the scraps of cigarette paper and toilet tissue. In so doing, the collection goes a long way toward a demystification of the authority of the modern press. This inclusion of a relatively large number of photographs suggests that the *teachtaireachtaí* actually help valorize the regularized text rather than vice versa, an inversion of the usual publication process wherein the manuscript and any "mistakes" it may contain are concealed from the public. Such an exposure of the "man behind the curtain" remains relatively uncommon, particularly in classroom or "practical" editions: intentionally or not, the act of publication frequently obscures the nature and extent of editorial interventions or at best relegates them to footnotes. Such an opacity downplays the extent to which editing is an appropriation of power, one that has striking similarities to the disciplinary technologies described in detail by Foucault. As Foucault reminds us in *Discipline and Punish*, prison regimes function very efficiently when they create an environment in which a warder remains unseen during surveillance.[143] Just as invisibility helps prison warders to create their desired product, docile bodies, so the concealment of the editor assists the manufacture of an apparently inviolate, authoritative text, one whose form and content are passively accepted by its readers. Both situations require the participation of the "object," of course, an internalization of and acquiescence *to* vertical hierarchies of power. In its presentation of Sands's manuscripts, *Skylark Sing Your Lonely Song* realigns power along a more horizontal axis, nudging the reader to question the role of editor. If manuscripts are normally the prisoners in the panopticon of publication, the inclusion of Sands's *teachtaireachtaí* turn a critical eye back on their warders, making their editorial interventions visible. Sands's texts now police their editors and the literary world to which those editors are the gatekeepers.

As *Skylark*'s photos make evident, Sands's prose works frequently were subject to a quite invasive editorial hand on the level of form throughout their textual history. As has been outlined earlier in this chapter, due to the relative scarcity of paper and the size restrictions required to smuggle texts out of the H Blocks, many Republican POWs used every available millimeter of paper when writing prose. Like others among his comrades, Sands often seems unconcerned with paragraph breaks. The photos of *teachtaireachtaí* make it clear in retrospect the degree to which the journalistic conventions of the time determined the form of Sands's texts printed in *AP/RN* and in both editions of *The Writings of Bobby Sands*: these conventions necessitate what in *literary* circles might be considered an excess of paragraph breaks, an atomization intensified by internal paragraph headings. It is perhaps for this reason that *Skylark Sing Your Lonely Song* does away with these subheadings: Mercier's editors may have been preempting a dismissal of Sands's writing on formalistic grounds. By smoothing the rougher paragraph breaks, *Skylark Sing Your Lonely Song* pushes the reader to experience Sands's prose as Literature with a capital "L" rather than mere "writing," that genre so abhorred in revisionist circles.

Other manifestations of the technologies of control and representation are made visible by these *teachtaireachtaí*. These nine photos make concrete exactly how laborious the act of composition in the H Blocks was, and in this fashion *Skylark* visually underscores the alterity of the *téacs pluide*, demonstrating its intense connection to the space of composition. Yet, while the disciplinary regime forces their particular form, the survival of the scrap of paper bears witness to the carceral regime's inability to completely implement its controls. Furthermore, these fragmentary manuscripts force the reader to confront the aesthetics that remain puzzlingly ascendant among the revisionist critics of contemporary Irish literature. For example, Edna Longley insists that "Poetry and politics, like church and state, should be separated": yet, after witnessing the fragile manuscripts photographically reproduced in *Skylark*, how could readers reasonably expect writers incarcerated in the H Blocks of this era to conform to such a directive?[144] It is easy to see why Republicans view Longley's revisionist aesthetic as just another disciplinary regime like the one in which the POWs are imprisoned, one that similarly maintains the status quo by isolating and delegitimizing dissent.

Yet, in some ways *Skylark*'s exclusive reliance on these photos simultaneously *reifies* traditional literary expectations. In the absence of other kinds of illustrations, Sands visually *becomes* his texts in *Skylark*. Such a move contributes to the fetishization of the insular text evident in varying forms throughout literary history, certainly in the excesses of New Criticism as well as most recently in the branches of discourse studies that insist that no agency, no resistance—and if one proceeds to the bitter end of such a theory, no real *existence*—can be found outside text. In related fashion, because this anthology contains no images of Sands and his fellow POWs, Sands might seem a more isolated figure than he was, thus reinforcing the all too familiar image of the autonomous author. The individual—the basic unit of exchange in bourgeois literature and society—implicitly ascends again, a move reinforced by the back cover's likening of Sands's work to a "self portrait."[145]

In contrast to the Mercier anthology's foregrounding of original manuscript and its drive toward a more self-consciously literary form, the next compilation of Sands's work evinces a rather less consistent approach to Sands's texts. *Bobby Sands: Irish Rebel, A Self-Portrait in Poetry and Polemics Issued on the 10th Anniversary of His Death* was published by Mellen Research University Press in 1991. In a reversal of *Skylark*'s editorial decisions with regard to Sands's prose, this collection reproduces the journalistic internal headings of the Dublin edition of *The Writings of Bobby Sands.* I would hazard a guess that in his return to the earliest anthologized form, the editor of *Bobby Sands: Irish Rebel* was attempting to preserve rather than alter Sands's work. In addition, the title of the collection suggests yet another explanation: to the editor, Sands's prose is not "Literature" or even "literature," but "polemic"—a genre apparently better represented by journalistic conventions.

However, the most striking feature of *Bobby Sands: Irish Rebel* is its failure to include any texts *as Gaeilge.* For instance, though Sands wrote the final entry of his hunger strike diary entirely in Irish, this collection presents the reader only with the English version of the text. One might forgive the absence of a dual-language text if there was some acknowledgment of the act of translation: one waits for such an acknowledgment in vain. If readers were unaware of Sands's fluency in Irish before encountering *Bobby Sands: Irish Rebel,* they remain unaware afterward as well. Editorial interventions of this nature are puzzling, particularly given that the stated intention of this collection, like that of the back cover of *Skylark Sing Your Lonely Song*, is to present readers with a "self-portrait" of Sands. Translation is at best a vexed proposition and this collection leaves its readers with a very mediated text indeed, rather than a "self-portrait"—especially given the translation issues I outlined earlier. But the absence of Gaeilge is more deeply problematic than this, for it undermines some of the issues central to Sands's work, not least of which is his call for the Irish language to be put on equal footing with English. In privileging an English translation, in the literal erasure of the Irish original, *Bobby Sands: Irish Rebel* unintentionally recolonizes Sands's work, implicitly suggesting that in the end the Irish language is irrelevant.

While it is heartening that Mellen Research University Press saw enough value in Sands's prison writing to publish *Bobby Sands: Irish Rebel*, the book's subtitle reveals much about the expectations of the academy when it frames Sands's work as a "self-portrait." Again, this reifies the image of the solitary—even self-obsessed—author, an image in direct conflict with majority of Sands's texts. As I have asserted at length, Sands views his experiences as representative of all Republican prisoners throughout history, not just those of his comrades in Long Kesh and Armagh. Even in Sands's hunger strike diary—a genre one might reasonably expect to focus primarily on individual experience—Sands's text always points away from himself. In the diary's first entry, for example, Sands insists that he is "but another of those wretched Irishmen born of a risen generation with a deeply rooted and unquenchable desire for freedom."[146] Authorial ego has been shifted from the background—as embodied in *Skylark's* back cover—to one of the most visible components of the book, the title itself.

Some of these issues were addressed in the next (and the most recent) collection of Sands's work, *Writings from Prison,* which was published by Roberts Rinehart in 1997. This anthology is superior in many respects to its immediate predecessor, not least in that it literally foregrounds the Irish language texts. For example, when reproducing Sands's hunger strike diary, the Roberts Rinehart version presents the original, *as Gaeilge* diary entry *before* the English translation. This may seem a small detail, but such symbolism is important in Ireland in general, especially in the context of the prison struggle. The Blanketmen, after all, had gone naked for five years and Sands and nine Republicans after Sands met their deaths on hunger strike for the right to wear their own clothes rather than what in their view was a criminal's uniform.

At first glance, however, *Writings from Prison* appears potentially problematic in its approach to Sands's texts, for the cover of this collection engages in a rather dangerous semiotic move. An out-of-focus photoreproduction of one of Sands's manuscripts has been used to create an impressionistic background. Although certainly a striking visual, the cover aestheticizes these texts out of existence: if *Skylark Sing Your Lonely Song* turned Sands *into* his texts in its emphasis on the manuscripts, the cover of *Writings from Prison* turns Sands's texts into elevator Muzak. This layout likely can be traced to Roberts Rinehart's marketing and design departments, entities likely less concerned with the semiotic ramifications of their cover design than the unnamed editor; however, the peril remains that the cover anesthetizes the reader somewhat, authorizing a purely aesthetic response to these writings, a reaction that is, of course, the reverse of what Sands and the first collections desired.

However, the cliché about a book and its cover is applicable in this case. *Writings from Prison* creates a rather more complex matrix than it externally suggests, for it strikes something of a balance between the images presented in the first two collections and those reproduced in *Skylark Sing Your Lonely Song.* The same image of Sands appears in this book three different times: once on the cover, once on the title page, and once at the beginning of the long prose piece entitled *One*

Day in My Life. It is the usual photograph taken in the Cages of Long Kesh and later cropped and used for posters and for the cover of the first collection of Sands's writings.[147] *Writings from Prison* also includes a single image of one of Sands's manuscripts: several stanzas of the long poem "Trilogy," written on a page torn out of the Bible.[148] The inclusion of these items complicates the presentation of Sands's writings on the cover, for this binary creates an oscillation between Sands the person and Sands as textually embodied. Although neither of these photos contest the image of Sands as solitary individual, at least the Roberts Rinehart edition prevents an absolute fetishization of text.

One final collection of Bobby Sands's prison writings deserves mention: miniaturized photocopies of the Dublin edition of *The Writings of Bobby Sands* made their way back into the H Blocks. Literature was not just an export of the H Blocks, but was an import as well. Assuredly the activist format of that tiny pamphlet must have provided comfort to the POWs, the photographs of women, men, and children marching on their behalf a reassuring reminder that they were not alone. The defiant textual circuit complete, the POWs could physically witness the active solidarity *taoibh amuigh*. They could see that cell walls failed to isolate them from the world outside, and that these walls similarly failed to isolate the outside world from *them*. Those *faoi ghlas* and those *taoibh amuigh* shared the same textual space in the images of this collection; through the text itself, outside and inside *saw* one another even through the darkness of Long Kesh.

Chapter Four

"Silence or Cell?": Women Writing in Armagh, Maghaberry, and Durham

If literary critics have been slow to address the writings of male prisoners, they are doubly so with regard to the writings of women imprisoned for political reasons. In the case of Ireland, this critical silence in part originates in the paucity of readily available texts by Republican POWs in general and by Republican women in particular. Of the few books written by female ex-prisoners, only two achieved anything approaching wide circulation: *Sisters in Cells* by Áine and Eibhlín Níc Giolla Deacair, and *Tell Them Everything* by Margaretta D'Arcy. Unfortunately, these works fall outside the purview of this study for a number of reasons, first and foremost that both are memoirs written *taoibh amuigh* after release. To reiterate the argument I put forth in the introduction, in this exclusion I do not mean to suggest that writings produced *faoi ghlas* are somehow more "authentic" than memoirs produced after the fact. Rather, I am concerned more with ascertaining the manner and extent to which the space of incarceration shapes the literary production that takes place within it. Distance, time, and greater freedom to write and revise often obscure the traces of incarceration present in both subject and form, particularly in works such as the *téacs pluide* (Blanket text) discussed in detail in the preceding chapter.

D'Arcy's book in particular must be excluded for another reason as well: although sympathetic to the POWs with whom she shared a cell in Armagh, D'Arcy does not define herself primarily as a Republican. While attending a 1978 poetry reading in support of political prisoners in the North of Ireland, she was arrested along with eleven other women from the Twenty-Six Counties for vandalizing the walls of the museum in which the event was held. In D'Arcy's words, disgusted with what was only "an impression of radical protest against censorship and the brutality of repression on the Falls Road,"[1] which in her view was personified by the well-known writer Paul Muldoon dedicating a poem to a banned seventeenth-century Spanish painter, she "leant against the wall, took out a red marker and wrote H Block."[2] In her brief examination of D'Arcy in *Barred*, Barbara Harlow reveals that in fact "the British courts, in the face of adverse publicity, proved reluctant to prosecute the southern women, much less send them to jail."[3] D'Arcy and one other woman chose not to pay a fine and voluntarily went to prison in Armagh for three months.

What resulted from this incarceration, I would argue, is prison literature that cannot be categorized with that of POWs such as Sands, if only for the reason that at times D'Arcy seems to envision her project more in terms of an anthropologist studying a target group than as an actual member of the group.[4] Though D'Arcy does join the Republican POWs on their No-Wash Protest, she admits "I was not only an observer, I was also a participant and I had to retain my own individuality as a civilian."[5] In a sense, D'Arcy's desire for a separate perceptual framework is predictable. Though D'Arcy is a sympathetic outsider, she is an outsider nonetheless and as a result cannot expect to be allowed into the secretive inner sanctum of paramilitary prisoners. Nor does she seem to desire such a total entrée: at various points, D'Arcy's narrative suggests a certain tension—even incompatibility—between her conception of feminism and the radical nationalism espoused by the POWs, a difference in ideology shared by some in D'Arcy's group Women Against Imperialism. However, D'Arcy's statement above also treads into the vexed territory of similar claims to "journalistic objectivity" evoked by some literary critics. The drive to retain one's individuality contrasts sharply with the collectivity of the Republicans on the level of both gender and politics. Despite evincing undisputed and admirable bravery in submitting to voluntary incarceration, in her desire for individuation, D'Arcy participates to a certain extent in the sort of enforced fragmentation that prison regimes seek to bring about through their disciplinary structures. Ultimately, as *Tell Them Everything* reveals, we must not confuse the project of the outsider—and my own, of course, also included—with texts actually written by Republicans in carceral space.

Unfortunately, as of the time of this writing, Gerry Adams, Bobby Sands, and Danny Morrison are the sole representatives of Provisional Republicanism among prison writers whose works are distributed by international presses. While arguably the Internet has ameliorated some of the difficulties of obtaining texts published by smaller presses outside the mainstream, few titles of this subject were ever released in the first place, and the ones that were released were generally in such limited runs that they are nearly impossible to unearth, even if one is specifically searching a text out. For example, *An Phoblacht/Republican News* and Sinn Féin's Women's Department both have demonstrated commitment to prison literature, but their publications generally are ephemeral in nature: newspaper features and card-cover pamphlets. The sad fact remains that apart from the excerpt from *Sisters in Cells* by Aine and Eibhlín Nic Giolla Easpaig included in the *Field Day Anthology of Irish Women's Writing*, critics generally must engage in archival research to uncover examples of Republican women's prison writing. There is some hope for improvement, as former POW Eileen Hickey is currently in the process of collecting Republican women's prison writing for eventual anthologization. However, the question remains to what degree their words will be heard. This is not just a question of the brute numbers of texts disseminated locally, regionally, or internationally, but also of how readers of these texts approach them.

After all, the admitted lack of readily available texts can only be part of the explanation for the critical silence surrounding incarcerated Republican women. As this chapter hopefully will demonstrate, with a bit of diligence (and a lot of time in the Northern Ireland Political Collection of Belfast's Linen Hall Library) some remarkable writings might be discovered by interested literary critics. One must conclude then, that this past and present silence points to much larger issues of power and representation. As Barbara Harlow rightly observes, conservative discomfort with the intersection of the feminine and the political "is continuous with, if not derivative of, a historically dominant project of patriarchy—and academic humanism—to maintain the self-interested conveniences of an unequal division of labor."[6] Indeed, even taking into account that there were far fewer female POWs than male, the disproportionate lack of extant texts is probably best conceived of, not as an excuse for a failure to engage with such issues of power and representation, but rather as dangerously symptomatic of a larger structure that continues to deny women their voices, even in nominally liberal extensions of this structure such as academia. Mary Corcoran insists that female POWs faced a "double bind in that the circumstances of their confinement were practically effaced by normative conceptions of offending women and official denial of the politicality of their lawbreaking."[7] Female activists—and especially female paramilitaries—doubly challenge the norms that both the state and its carceral system attempt to enforce: in the North of Ireland dissent is threatening, *female* dissent even more so because of its transgressive repudiation of an expected passive domesticity.

In important ways the academic rejection of the prison writing of Republican women implicit in critical silence mirrors the reaction of the carceral regime described above. Like the "uppity woman"—Yeats's characterization of Maude Gonne in "Easter 1916" only one example—the politicized text has frequently been dismissed as shrill and unseemly in its polemic. This ideology apparently believes that literature, like women, is best when at a genteel remove from the uncouth world of politics. In fact, at least since Shakespeare's time, this ideology's proponents suggest that politics unnaturally "unsexes" women such as Lady Macbeth, driving them to imbalance, madness, and murder. As is argued at length throughout this book, such conservative expectations with regard to the production, form, and subject of literature remain ascendant in many unacknowledged ways; furthermore, these expectations generally do not take into account the conditions of possibility inside a political prison. As Harlow correctly insists, given the alterity of the space of its composition and given the activist nature of so many of the texts produced in such a volatile matrix, "Reading prison writing must in turn demand a correspondingly activist counterapproach to that of passivity, aesthetic gratification, and the pleasures of consumption that are traditionally sanctioned by the academic disciplining of literature."[8] Critical rejection of prison writing often proceeds from the text's failure to live up to an uninterrogated set of assumptions that proceed from a privileged space of composition and reception historically rooted in a bourgeois status quo. I concur with Benita Parry's critique of Gayatri Spivak and Homi Bhaba, whose work—while undeniably motivated by a desire to effect positive change—nevertheless is sullied at times by a marked

> incuriosity about the enabling socioeconomic and political institutions and other forms of social praxis...their [Spivak and Bhaba] theses admit of no point outside of discourse from which opposition can be engendered; their project is concerned to place incendiary devices within the dominant structures of representation and do not confront these with another knowledge.[9]

Parry here accuses Spivak and Bhaba of a failing often cited by critics of Foucault and other poststructuralists: the failure to imagine any alternative locale from which insurgency—textual or otherwise—might be mounted. If resistance is kept confined within traditional discourse or traditional canon, it is even more easily controlled. In contrast, I submit that prison writers present us with the opportunity to move toward "another knowledge," one distinct from the technologies of "colonial production"[10] that Spivak seeks to either enter or destroy.

Complicating matters further, female POWs sometimes must face rejection by fellow feminists who see their Republicanism as potentially regressive or even wholly incompatible with "true liberation." Critics such as Kirsten Holst Petersen are rightly suspicious of male postcolonial authors' use of nationalist mythos that conscript traditional—usually repressive—notions of gender roles "in the service of dignifying the past" in their attempts to contest colonial discourse that images the indigenous as disorderly and chaotic.[11] Although Petersen herself describes as an "ideal" starting point Ngũgĩ Wa Thiong'o's ideology that cultural, national, and women's liberation need to be undertaken simultaneously, she does not sufficiently interrogate views such as those she ascribes to Buchi Emecheta who, Peterson says, "lays claim to no ideology, not even a feminist one. She simply ignores the African dilemma, whereas Ngũgĩ shoulders it and tries to come to terms with it."[12] If, as Petersen suggests, Chinua Achebe must be decried for not employing adequate invective against the violence enacted against women in *Things Fall Apart*, surely we must more aggressively question the possibility of "*not* having an ideology" before setting such a position up as a school of thought from which a careful critique might be launched. The simple fact that Emecheta ignores the "African dilemma" certainly suggests a theoretical framework, even if it is not one to which she explicitly lays claim. While Petersen seems more interested in pairing Ngũgĩ and Buchi Emecheta as the starting point for a "vigorous debate" rather than to posit a more specific thesis regarding the topic, I cannot help but find problematic the implicit revalidation of academia's traditional false claim to apolitical neutrality imbedded in such a binary. This same assertion of a naturalized, "ideology-free" perspective historically proved to be a powerful discursive tool against women and colonized peoples and remains a tool capable of misdirection even when a doubly subaltern author employs it. Such an approach is entirely compatible with—and perhaps unintentionally encourages a return to—the critical framework that Chandra Talpade Mohanty finds ascendant in Western universities, one used to "discursively colonize the material and historical heterogeneities of the lives of women in the third world."[13]

As Mohanty urges, we must resist too easy a connection between the experiences of women in the ghettos of Northern Ireland and those of women in developing nations elsewhere in the world. However, we must also address the reasons why many working-class women in the Six Counties have felt abandoned by the larger women's movement, particularly in the early years of the present conflict. For example, despite her activism in Women Against Imperialism—which, as we will see later, brought her in conflict with sexist male Republicans—Anne Marie Loughran insists "I don't want to be called a feminist—not yet—it's remote, somehow, not earthy enough for what I'm struggling with. I want liberation from all oppression. I want the people to be free. I'm against imperialism. Feminists won't deal with that, from what I can see."[14] Loughran made this provocative claim in 1980, and although undoubtedly many Irish Republican women today would find much less of a tension between their feminism and their anticolonialist ideals, one wonders the extent to which conventional academics will be permitted to find common ground—at least publicly—with them in the reactionary climate in post–September 11 United States and post–July 7 Britain. The writings of Republican women POWs at least afford the opportunity to begin an exploration of these vexed issues in a place close to home for those in the West, perhaps one that will assist in a more constructive dialogue regarding similar issues elsewhere in the world arguably more radically "Other" (and "Othered") than Republican Ireland.

Despite their active participation in politics and warfare alike throughout history, the story of women in Ireland is one that only now is beginning to be told. In the modern era, women literally have fought alongside the men at every stage of the nationalist struggle, yet historians and critics alike tend to ignore the contributions of Republican women, and at times so has the nation for which they made so many sacrifices. The example of the Ladies' Land League in the 1880s is representative. When the male leaders of the Land League were imprisoned, Anna and Fanny Parnell—the sisters of Charles Stewart Parnell—formed their own organization to fight for the same causes of fixity of tenure, fair rents, and the right to free sale for Irish farmers. However, as the filmmakers responsible for *Mother Ireland* relate, the men upon their release disbanded the women's organization, thinking it "too radical."[15]

This sexism remained almost completely unaddressed in many ways until recent years, even among organizations that claimed to battle for equality: although women worked in vital roles in organizations such as the Civil Rights Association and although Máire Drumm was vice president of Sinn Féin until her murder, many men still were capable of seeing women only within the context of a traditional domestic sphere. Those women who see no contradiction between their feminism and their Republicanism certainly are not blind to the patriarchy historically endemic to Ireland and their own political movement. Alluding to the famous mural that read "You are now entering Free Derry," painted on the gable wall of a house in the Bogside, Bernadette Devlin-McAliskey once commented with characteristic wit, "Derry wasn't that free this side of the wall either."[16]

While undoubtedly there is much left to be done, important attempts have been made within Provisional Republicanism to address issues of gender, Sinn Féin's establishment of a women's department being only one example. It is also worth noting that in the last Assembly elections Sinn Féin elected the largest number of women of any party.[17] Though all of these battles—internal and external to Republicanism—are hard fought, in the film *Mother Ireland,* Devlin-McAliskey attributes these victories to the particular matrix in which Republican women are shaped, shape themselves, and in turn shape the world around them, claiming that "The best young women of the feminist movement are those who have come through the experience of the Republican movement—those who have come to an awareness of their oppression as women through a growing awareness of all other layers of oppression." The film's director, Anne Crilly, has remarked that Devlin-McAliskey's statement is the "most provocative" and "contentious" in the film, one obscured by the controversy over Mairead Farrell outlined below.[18] Writers such as Buchi Emecheta would likely disagree with Devlin-McAliskey's assessment, but nonetheless women such as her and Crilly demonstrate that debates regarding gender and nationalism remain vital within Republicanism today.

It is worth exploring the textual history of *Mother Ireland* as something of a preamble, for in addition to the film's exploration of disparate conceptions of feminism and Republicanism, the British government's censorship—both overt and subtle—of *Mother Ireland* echoes academia's anxieties about (and responses to) the writings of incarcerated Republican women activists and paramilitaries. Given that *Mother Ireland* is a feminist documentary focused on images of women in Irish history, in particular in the modern history of Irish nationalism, perhaps it is unsurprising that *Mother Ireland* was the first film to fall victim to the repressive atmosphere accompanying the 1988 broadcasting ban put in effect by the Thatcher administration.[19] The film was targeted in October of that year not only because of its images of Emma Groves—a woman shot in the face and blinded by a British soldier's plastic bullet—but also because of its interviews with Republicans such as Bernadette Devlin-McAliskey and IRA women such as Mairead Farrell.[20]

From the perspective of the British government, the footage of Farrell was particularly ill-timed, as she had been killed with two comrades in March 1988 in an SAS[21] shoot-to-kill operation in Gibraltar. This was not a firefight resulting in death, but rather a coldly planned execution. Coogan rightly places responsibility at the highest echelons of Westminster, relating that "at a cabinet level in Mrs. Thatcher's government, a judicial murder was decided upon. On March 2, 1988, an S.A.S. 'hit squad' was flown to Gibraltar with instructions to kill the I.R.A. party."[22] Farrell and Dan McCann were killed a short distance away from and a few moments before Seán Savage. All three were unarmed. In the documentary *Death on the Rock,* one key independent eyewitness told Thames Television that the SAS

> just went and shot these people. That's all. They didn't say anything, they didn't scream, they didn't shout, they didn't do anything. These people [Farrell and McCann] were turning their heads back to see what was happening, and when they saw these men had guns in their hands they put their hands up.[23]

Farrell and McCann were then shot repeatedly, even after their bodies hit the ground, an action duplicated during the killing of Savage who was struck by sixteen to eighteen bullets. One witness gave testimony that an SAS man actually stood on the fallen Savage and fired four shots into his head at pointblank range. This statement was borne out by Professor Watson, a pathologist who reviewed the forensic data during the later trial at the European Court of Human Rights.[24] With international attention focused on these killings, the political stakes were high and Westminster's actions with regard to this execution reveal the extent to which the control of discourse is a tool of counterinsurgency. *Death on the Rock* was broadcast on 5 May 1988, just five months prior to Thatcher's broadcasting ban. However, Foreign Secretary Geoffrey Howe had "asked" that the program not be aired.[25] Aired it was, but at a cost: in a move widely seen as punitive, the Independent Television Commission refused to renew Thames Television's franchise.[26]

Mother Ireland had been completed five days before Farrell's execution. In this tense atmosphere, Channel 4, the British television station that funded the production of the film, grew nervous. According to *Mother Ireland*'s director Anne Crilly, Channel 4 refused to show the documentary until the inquest into the shootings was complete; slowing matters further, the government body charged with approving television programming refused to either ban or approve the film. The delays continued until the British government introduced new broadcasting restrictions, ones that made large portions of *Mother Ireland* illegal to air because of the film's inclusion of interviews with Republican women such as Farrell: part of the legislation forbid the broadcast of footage containing the voices and images of members of "proscribed organizations" such as Sinn Féin, or even words spoken in support of such organizations. Regardless of the fact that Sinn Féin was at this stage considered a legal political party, its representation on the airwaves was nevertheless curtailed. Because of these broadcasting, the film was not screened until 1991, and even then only in edited form.[27] Like Republican women's prison writing, *Mother Ireland*, having been denied large-scale distribution, was forced to rely on localized distribution networks in order to disseminate its critiques. Crilly insists that smaller venues such as conferences and film festivals actually provided "a much better context because there was discussion,"[28] an ethos an alogous to prison writing's insistent drive away from the experience of a text in passive isolation. Localized networks such as these demonstrate the manner in which the state's imprimatur does not need to be sought, and demonstrates the way in which dominant forms of discourse might be circumvented in order to present "another knowledge."

Roseleen Walsh and Internment in Armagh

Though now sadly defunct, Glandore Press, located at the Springhill Community House, provided a fine model of the manner in which a local network can be set up to contest dominant discourse, for it involved the community in every aspect of writing its own stories and history, from the composition to the publication and distribution of text. The idea behind Springhill Community House's Heritage Series of publications was "to record for posterity the living memories of the people of West Belfast." The press actively solicited texts in any conceivable form including "oral or written memories, documents, artifacts, etc."[29] As part of these efforts to construct a counter-history, Glandore published the work of a number of Republican ex-prisoners, notable among them Jim McCann's series of Long Kesh memoirs, Brian Campbell's drama, as well as two volumes containing the poetry of Roseleen Walsh, an ex-internee in Armagh. Before her writings are examined, the physical conditions of Roseleen Walsh's incarceration should be touched upon. Until March 1986, when Maghaberry Prison replaced it, Armagh Gaol was the sole prison for women in the

Six Counties. Father Raymond Murray, chaplain of Armagh Gaol from 1971 to 1986 describes the layout as follows:

> There were two main cell wings emanating from a circle, one two-storeyed [*sic*] (A Wing) and the other three-storeyed (B Wing). These wings held 140 cells...In 1976 a small third cell block, known as C Wing, was opened in one of the prison yards. It was a two-storeyed concrete building with 30 cells.[30]

The effects of the resurgence of political conflict in the Six Counties and the British government's return to the tactic of internment without trial were as marked on this jail as in those prison compounds used exclusively to house males. The reason for Armagh's expansion can be seen in Murray's revelation that "the number of women political prisoners increased from 2 in 1971 to more than 100 in the 1972–76 period. Thirty-two of these women were imprisoned without trial."[31] In 1972, Special Category Status was won by political prisoners across Northern Ireland: in everything but name, the prison authorities treated the Republican women of Armagh as prisoners of war. Jim Challis describes dealing with the female POWs from his point of view as a former prison officer:

> They, as did their male counterparts, proved to be extremely difficult to handle. They mirrored the male internees in as much as they formed their own rank structure, both within the wing and in the jail as a whole...As with the men, they were constantly trying to disrupt the system.[32]

As a disciplined militant force, the women proved themselves every bit the equal of the males in various forms of prison protest. For instance, after the male internees of Long Kesh set fire to their prison compound in 1974, no news about casualties was permitted into Armagh. In protest, the Republican women took captive the governor of Armagh Prison and three female wardens, holding them hostage as leverage to gain information about the male prisoners. The officials were held for fourteen hours, during which time the POWs shouted their demands to and exchanged information with reporters who had gathered on the street. When the desired information was obtained, the prison officials were released and the prisoners returned voluntarily to their cells. Even Challis is forced to reveal that none of the officials were harmed in any way by this action.[33]

In this incident alone, the Republican women proved that they were able to achieve their goals as POWs in a disciplined manner, that is, able to be militant without inflicting injury. In fact, in his yearly report for 1974, Father Murray wrote that he had witnessed "good sense, good relations, and good leadership among all groups of prisoners," going on to say that "This high praise is not offset by the serious incident of 16 October 1974."[34] It is indeed interesting to note the way in which as time goes on Murray seems to grow more and more impressed with the political prisoners in his care. Writing in his Catholic Chaplain's Report in 1971, Murray expresses concern that the militarization of Armagh—the additional British Army presence, and the additional fortification of the prison itself—would have detrimental effects on the rehabilitation of "Ordinary Decent Criminals" (as they were classified by the British government).[35] His description of Internment in 1971 certainly lacks the fire of his later career: rather than unreservedly condemning the practice of imprisoning men and women indefinitely without charge or trial, Murray frames his discussion by revealing that the Republican prisoners view their detention "rightly or wrongly, as unfair."[36] Over the next decade, his views and the stridency with which he argues them in his reports change dramatically. In 1982, for instance, he contends,

> In the name of security the British government has committed the blunders of internment, the torture and brutality of Holywood and Girdwood,[37] the SAS, the Diplock courts, the Castlereagh beatings. This cruel will has spilled into prison affairs—condemnation of the innocent, excessive sentences, massive punishments during the prison protests, the debacle of letting the hunger strikers die...The political failures have insured the prison failures.[38]

In the 1971 report, it is almost as if it is the fault of the internees rather than the British government that Armagh Prison has turned into an armed camp. Eleven years later, Murray finds himself disabused of the notion, partly because of continued repression enacted by governmental authorities and partly because of the example of the disciplined courage of the Republican women of Armagh.

Nevertheless, a growing sense of admiration does not exclude a certain amount of apparent sexism from Murray's reports, particularly those from the earlier years of his chaplaincy. In 1972, for instance, the Republican women's political demands are portrayed as biological imperatives. He writes,

> There are a number of things that seem to cause constant irritation among the women prisoners, especially those special category who are

> sentenced. One of these is the cooking of food, perhaps because they are women. They always seem aggrieved at the cooking. Could they not be supplied with a hot plate? It would also keep them busy.[39]

One hopes that Murray is writing with a sexist governmental audience in mind, intending to manipulate the officials to whom these reports were initially addressed by tapping into their preconceptions. Certainly all of the women that I have interviewed in my research for this book have nothing but praise for Father Murray: Síle Darragh, the Republican OC during the time of Sands's hunger strike, describes him as "a great friend to the prisoners," one who frequently supplied them with tobacco and sweets.[40] This sexist phrasing may also have been deliberately intended to divert focus from the larger struggles related to Special Category Status in which both male and female POWs were engaged. After all, the male prisoners in Long Kesh made similar demands related to food, demands that derive not from the possession of two X chromosomes but rather from an insistence on political-prisoner status. As Challis reports, part of the terms of Special Category Status in the Cages of Long Kesh required that prison officers pass rations en masse to the prisoners through the "airlock" at each cage's entrance. The prisoners themselves then distributed the food amongst themselves.[41]

At issue, obviously, was not the mere distribution of prison food, but rather the reappropriation of agency through establishment of acceptable living conditions, particularly among those detained without charge or trial. While Challis argues later that "the food sent into the compounds very often came straight back out again, usually emptied over the staff sentry huts at the compound entrance for some trivial reason or other,"[42] the Republican POWs have a very different version of the story. Gerry Adams reports that "If the food is particularly gruesome it will be refused by the Camp or the Cage Staff."[43] To the Republicans, this is a decision made for political (and arguably *humanitarian*) reasons, and one that is formally executed by military chain of command. In addition, this refusal is related to the demands of the POWs that they be able to receive food parcels along with regular mail. Adams notes that those interned in Long Kesh "were permitted to receive a fairly wide selection of cooked food which was sent in from outside by our families or friends," but that those in the sentenced cages were more restricted in this regard.[44]

Like the men in Long Kesh, Roseleen Walsh considered herself a Republican prisoner of war. In 1973, she was interned in Armagh Prison along with twenty-three other women. In an interview she granted me in 1998, she related that "The basis for my imprisonment was—I was going to say evidence, but it wasn't evidence—lies told about me because I was a Republican by the RUC."[45] The hearing that put Walsh in prison was farcical. The commissioner hearing the case had, according to Walsh, been a commissioner in South Africa for years and had arrived in Northern Ireland just the week before. Indeed, to call the proceedings of internment a "trial" would be inaccurate, at least if one has in mind the standard of due process that normally are expected in modern democracies. Walsh points out,

> For most of the hearing I was put out of the room, so I don't really know what was said about me in my absence. My solicitor didn't know either; he was also asked to leave the room. But whatever was said, the commissioner found I should be interned in Armagh Prison.[46]

One part of the hearing that both Walsh and her solicitor were present for was the testimony of a member of the Security Forces[47] that a "friend" of Walsh's from the same area of West Belfast was already interned in Armagh, and he named this person.[48] Apparently, this testimony was intended to indicate guilt of some offense by association. However, Roseleen had never even heard of this woman and told her solicitor so. In fact, there was no such person in Armagh. The solicitor called one of the prison wardens to the stand. Walsh declares that the warden "got up, took the Bible, swore, and told that she was in Armagh twenty-three years and had never heard of this person. But that was overruled."[49] Subsequently, Walsh was officially interned.

While imprisoned, Walsh wrote constantly. As the back cover of her collection of short plays, *Sticks and Stones,* tells the reader, "she took great pride in covering her cell walls with her poetry. Eventually there was barely an inch of paint in any direction that hadn't one of her poems on it."[50] As it was for the men in the H Blocks, putting a poem up on the walls was a political act to Walsh, though not one driven by the same material conditions later endured by the Blanketmen. Protesting POWs in the H Blocks were forbidden writing material of any sort. In contrast, because she and the other women in Armagh had political status, Walsh acknowledges, "We weren't really restricted" with regard to access to the raw materials of literary production.[51] Writing on paper was acceptable to prison authorities at the time; technically, writing on the walls was a different matter, a breach of carceral—and domestic—discipline.[52] The relatively peaceful coexistence between POW and warder fostered by Special Category Status evinces itself in the fact that Walsh did not suffer harsh reprisals for her defiance. In fact, she recalls that "People of the community read different poems, even the 'screws' would come in to see what was wrote today."[53]

The poems that Walsh wrote in Armagh reflect the carceral space and regime in which they were composed. Unlike many poems smuggled out of the H Blocks during the height of the post–Special Category protests, these are not permeated by the immediate presence of incarceration. The horrors of the H Blocks and of Armagh during the No-Wash Protest are nearly inescapable: like Adams in the Cages of Long Kesh, prisoners with political status in Armagh have greater opportunity to momentarily transcend suffering, and Walsh's poem "Imprisoned Lovers" illustrates this. Walsh remembers the occasion of its writing, commenting that this poem was produced in 1973 in her cell in Armagh and that it was written "for an IRA prisoner in Long Kesh." Because, apart from its appearance on the Web site *Slí na mBán*, the poem has been published only by Glandore, it is here reproduced in full:

Imprisoned Lovers[54]
If I could wander
With the night
And
Be myself unseen
I'd travel to
Your place of sleep
And
Dream with you
Your dream.

But
I can't travel
With the night
Nor
Be myself unseen.
I can only in my sleep
Dream
Alone our dream.

The poem derives power from its economic phrasing, its delicate assonance, and its subtle consonance. Like it is to the speakers in Sands's H Block texts, sleep is a balm, a refuge in "Imprisoned Lovers." Indeed, the poem's accessibility and its reliance on repetition are reminiscent of a lullaby, certainly an appropriate move given the centrality of images of sleep, but even more so because the verse seems intended to soothe both speaker and her beloved. Isolation pervades the first stanza despite the drive toward physical reunion: the singular "I" seeks the singular "you." Even the dream is not strictly speaking a shared one in this stanza but is instead one the speaker desires to join, yet to which she does not seem to add. The dream is fashioned as one belonging to the auditor, a potentially problematic image when read with feminist sensibilities, nationalist or otherwise. However, the second stanza moves the poem away from this imbalance and does so in powerful ways. The wistful subjunctive mood of the first stanza must be tempered with the realities of her unspoken incarceration: the speaker cannot physically join her beloved. Nevertheless, the speaker takes consolation from her ability to merge with her lover on a mental and emotional level. The dream has become an equal partnership, a shared rather than joined experience.

The grim spatiality of the cell, so integral an element of Sands's work, is far less oppressively present in "Imprisoned Lovers," for concrete and mortar do not torture this speaker in the same way that the freezing walls and floors did the Blanketmen. The suffering endured in this Armagh cell is one proceeding more from physical and mental *absence* than from the physical penetration of the carceral space into body and mind. This, of course, would change later during the No-Wash Protests in Armagh, when the POWs were forced to live in their own feces, urine, and menstrual blood, conditions worsened by the prison officials' decision to board up the POWs' windows to prevent them from emptying their waste out of their cells. However, at this stage of the prison struggle, Special Category Status allows conditions tolerable enough that physical space retreats somewhat from consciousness. The cells are so ineffective in preventing the melding of the speaker with her listener as to not bear mentioning. Without the inclusion of the poem's title, a reader might never know the cause of the lovers' separation, a subtle and well-executed move on Walsh's part, on the one hand, and a tiny glimpse into the conditions of Armagh, on the other. *Any* separation might have prompted the meditation of the verse itself. There are enough precedents in canonical poetry: "Imprisoned Lovers" evokes the rhetorical move Donne makes in "Valediction Forbidding Mourning," for Walsh's poem likewise takes comfort in the elevated spiritual unity of the lovers that transcends their physical absence from one another. Solitude can be made a spiritual condition by those confronting it.

Yet, of course, in making this argument, I do not mean to imply that the experience of Armagh (or *any* other prison) was by any stretch of the imagination pleasant at any time. Any curtailment of freedom is difficult to bear even in the best of facilities, particularly when one is imprisoned without charge as Walsh was. It is worth recalling Gerry Adams's foreword to his own prison memoirs, where he stipulates that although many of his stories are humorous, it is only because those in prison kept their spirit and sense of humor against all odds.[55] Though the tone of "Imprisoned Lovers" is wistful rather than tragic—and ultimately triumphal in its union of dreams—the speaker would no doubt rather complement spiritual togetherness with the physical. Prison means love partially deferred, but the totality of this love makes incarceration bearable.

As evident in the capture of the prison governor in 1974 described above, the women of Armagh remained politically active during their incarceration—indeed, some became even more politicized in jail and encouraged others to do the same. This continued commitment is reflected in Walsh's poem "To My Silent Church." As background information to this poem, she told me,

> I was born a Catholic and I practice my religion. Now, myself and my husband go to daily mass. We receive the Eucharist daily. I fast one day a week and I'm a reader in the chapel, so I take my religion very seriously and I hold it very, very dear. I felt when I was in prison that we were—as a people—let down a lot by the Catholic Church. There were very few priests who spoke out about, for example, the injustice of Internment.[56]

Her frustration is readily apparent in the poem, a frustration that, as seen in Gerry Adams's story "Sláinte" and his essay "Christians for Freedom?" is shared by many Republicans who felt themselves deserted by the church hierarchy in their time of need. Again, the poem is reproduced in its entirety:

> To My Silent Church[57]
>
> Silence or Cell,
> Divided nations conquer well
> For imitation love of peace
> Give all up to the oppressor.
> Lose all, forget those who have given all
> So you can live in your imitation home
> Made of imitation security.
>
> Silence or Cell?
> I choose cell.
> My words were quiet
> But I was not silent.

I did not want the cell;
It came—because
I could not bare the Silence.
The Silence was imitation
Not truth.
Incomprehensible.

Christ died because he could
Not stand the Silence.
Because of your Silence
I am condemned
To be without freedom,
I am therefore dead!
Speak! Talk now![58]
Silent ones.

"To My Silent Church" evinces the same subtle technique witnessed in "Imprisoned Lovers": the repetition and development of a few key words and phrases whose meanings multiply and turn back on themselves as the poem progresses. The dramatic line "Silence or Cell" that begins the first and second stanzas exemplifies this, becoming a refrain that pushes the reader to consider the power of discourse and the nature of choice. In the first stanza, this line is observational—a declarative about the intersections of hegemonic discourse, the silence that perpetuates it, and the disciplinary regimes constructed by the state against counterdiscourse. The freedom meekly enjoyed by the populace in the first lines of the poem is illusory precisely because of its reliance on the whims of the state. Worse yet, no end to the injustice seems in sight, for, far from being temporary in the manner that their names imply, "emergency legislation" such as the Special Powers Act and the later Emergency Provisions Act have suspended basic rights of person and property in Northern Ireland for more than eighty years. A home that can be invaded and searched without warrant is indeed an "imitation home." Yet, "To My Silent Church" does not single out the British government for critique, for the poem suggests that repression of this nature can only exist when deliberately chosen. Silence and isolation are necessary conditions of state control, an image reinforced by the individual "you" holing up in her/his solitary "home," forgetting the collective sacrifices of "those who have given all" as they fought for more comprehensive rights. One of the most powerful institutions in Ireland, north or south, the Catholic Church, of course, has many members. That the poem can only liken it to a weak individual speaks volumes.

In its move to an interrogative mode at the beginning of the second stanza, the refrain "Silence or Cell?" unambiguously underscores that, from a Republican perspective, there is always a choice implied, a choice faced by all individuals forced by the historical circumstances surrounding them. That the choice is a Manichean one befits the postcolonial setting of the poem. The state has circumscribed all discourse in binary terms: "if you're not with us, you're against us." As the third line of the second stanza illustrates, even the most moderate displays of dissent result in incarceration. No counterdiscourse, even uttered softly, will be tolerated. Lest it be thought the poem overstates the case, consider the example of Rose McAllister who was arrested and imprisoned merely for wearing a combat jacket during a protest at a court in Belfast.[59] Like the speaker of "To My Silent Church," McAllister refused to be silent for the "Silence was imitation," a state of acquiescence alien to her very being. Colonial discipline fosters inauthentic existence on every level, especially in its denial of agency to those under its rule.[60]

The third stanza invokes Christ in order to critique the hypocrisy of those who claim to be followers of Jesus and yet who do not have the activist approach to faith that the speaker defines as the core of Christianity. Many Republicans such as Walsh felt that the Catholic Church as an institution had abandoned them, in particular the church hierarchy in Ireland. Individual clergymen did lend assistance: Walsh notes that in the absence of a true prison library, the aforementioned "Father Murray actually brought books to us."[61] However, in the final stanza, the speaker finds the church sharing equal blame with the British government, as it is "Because of your silence/ I am condemned." By refusing their own agency, their own sacred obligation, the church hierarchy actively assists in stripping agency from their flock. "To My Silent Church" suggests that it is those people who are nominally free who are truly incarcerated, their fear and silence their prison. Although their prison does not have physical walls as in Armagh, their timidity restricts their actions and confines their movements and minds as effectively as a cell. Only when injustices are truly addressed will there be true security. The final lines openly exhort both the church and the reader to act, to break the silence. The speaker equates lack of freedom with death, but, befitting the poet's own deep faith, the image of Christ makes one wonder whether this death has potential for glorious resurrection if the "silent ones" find their voices.

In a colonized society, silence is one of the greatest dangers. As such, poetry is one way to break the silence, to enable communication between people who the authorities try to isolate and thus more easily control. Similarly, it is a way in which bonds may be forged between those who on a surface level may not share similar experiences.

Metaphorically, an encounter with prison literature, whether as printed text or at a poetry reading, might collapse the boundaries between prisoner and nonprisoner. Speaking of her own experiences as a performer of her own poetry, Roseleen Walsh persuasively argues that "a lot of people who have heard the poetry have never been in prison, but they feel that they have experienced an imprisonment in their own lives—not necessarily the material prison. They've maybe had experience of mental and emotional prisons."[62] It must be remembered also that the experience of prison is rarely a completely unshared one: relatives, lovers, spouses, and children also must endure the incarceration in their own ways. As Roger Shaw wrote in *Children of Imprisoned Fathers*,

> As soon as the children of prisoners come into focus the major contradictions of a criminal system become glaringly obvious. When the legally-sanctioned punishment takes the form of incarceration the concept of individual punishment for individual law breaking collapses. Children become caught in the web of punishment.[63]

This situation is precisely that seen in Walsh's poem "To Aine." Aine is Walsh's youngest daughter, and the experience of her father's imprisonment had a marked impact upon her life as well as that of the family structure. Roseleen explains,

> Shortly after my husband and I were married he was arrested and before Aine was born he was sentenced to twelve years in the H Blocks. So that involved at the time one visit per month, which worked out in one year I saw him six hours. For Aine's first six months of life, she slept through the six visits, so she didn't see her father. And he was on protest,[64] so when she finally did see him he had long, scraggly hair, and a long beard, wearing horrible clothes. Aine wouldn't go near her father for exactly eighteen months. She wouldn't sit on his knee; she would've cried the whole visit up until this. And so Aine never bonded with her father until two or three years ago. She's twenty-one now [in 1998].[65]

I have included this final poem of Walsh to show precisely these far reaching effects of incarceration. Although "To Aine" is not prison writing according to the definition I have set up in the introduction—that is, it was not actually written during incarceration—given that it covers a topic so central to the experience of prison, it deserves inclusion.

> To Aine[66]
>
> Oh what wind blows thee so fair,

What peace of mind gives thee thy smile
And makes thee lovely like a child?
What hand outstretched doth show thee where
Love finds its rest in those who care
As doubt and hurt outside stir
While joy and song fill the air within.

Who put that courage in thy heart
And made it brave enough to start,
Who graced thy face in beauty's style
And give thee life for just a while?
Who so great gave these gifts to thee-
Daughter- was it only me?

In its formalism and its archaisms, "To Aine" evokes some of Yeats's work, perhaps not surprisingly as Walsh cites him as one of her primary influences along with Eliot. Given Yeats's dismissal of Republicanism, these influences may at first glance seem odd in a Republican poet, and Walsh is aware of the seeming contradiction. "I know his politics and sort of push it to the side," she says of Yeats, preferring to concentrate on the way in which he is able to "transport" the reader with the power of words.[67] Though she accurately notes that each of these poets were intellectuals, in her words, "removed from the masses of people," to Walsh it is their concern with "the ordinary things that most of us can identify with" that make their poems memorable.[68] In this, if not in the rest of their politics, Eliot and Yeats share a Republican concern with the everyday. It is the final line of "To Aine" that brings home the whole intent of the poem. This is not a work written just for a daughter; one senses that it is equally intended for the father, conspicuous in absence until that final moment. Poetry thus reconstitutes family ties temporarily broken by the experience of prison. It is as if the speaker takes the hand of the child and puts it in that of her father in those final syllables.

Walsh is a powerful reader, her forceful, measured delivery an integral part of the poetry itself. She asserts,

> If you read it well, you're actually conveying and communicating something to people that touches and wakens something in them. And though they mightn't understand the words, they mightn't identify with the words, they will identify with a tone. The reading of the poetry to me is as important as writing it. I don't like other people to read [aloud, publicly] my poetry. I like to read it myself.[69]

This is a reminder that rather than being the cold and solitary experience that it can become in isolation, poetry is best heard—literally—in a communal environment. This is especially important in a community that has experienced trauma. Walsh herself is a member of the Felons' Writers' Group, whose members are all former political prisoners. In such a setting, common experiences can be shared in a safe, group environment and as a result the isolation of both cell and counterinsurgency can be resisted, true histories related. Projects such as the Glandore's Heritage Series begin in such gatherings, and there is every hope that the history of communities such as West Belfast will soon be written by the residents themselves. Such counterdiscourse breaks the enforced silence of the official colonial archive, offering additional opportunities to contest patriarchal history.

Texts by Irish women remain in short supply, particularly prison memoirs written by the participants themselves. Walsh comments that "I think if men write they are definitely taken more seriously, but I don't really care. I just write because of something in me that tells me to write. I think generally I see the same things as men see."[70] This statement will be put to the test only when the stories of women are given equal attention as those of men. We must be given the opportunity to be able to see through the eyes of the women of Armagh, for it is only in this way—by becoming familiar with multiple perspectives—that healing will take place. Though Roseleen Walsh was released unconditionally, she, like other former prisoners, understandably still harbors bitterness. She confides, "When eventually I was released—I was interned for thirteen months and two weeks—no one apologized to me, no one said 'we're now sorry, we made a mistake.' I got no compensation, no apology, no nothing."[71] While an apology from the British government seems unlikely, perhaps in the telling of their stories the prisoners can reclaim a part of their lives forcibly taken from them.

After Internment: Gendered Discipline in Maghaberry and Durham

As it did in Long Kesh, 1 March 1976 wrought dramatic changes in Armagh Gaol. Apart from a continued tolerance of the wearing of civilian clothing rather than prison uniform, the ending of Special Category Status meant that the British government would no longer offer Republican women exemption from the full array of prison discipline. Yet, even this apparent flexibility with regard to clothing had very specific limits: under no circumstances were the women allowed to wear anything even vaguely resembling a paramilitary uniform.

The state's anxiety on this issue betrays the extent to which colonialism and patriarchy elide in carceral space. As individuals, the Armagh women could be more easily controlled; but in contrast to the individuation of the cell, the paramilitary uniform visually reinforces a dangerous group identity. As ex-POW Eileen Hickey comments, to the Armagh women the use of the uniform was crucial in reinforcing their collective identity, an identity that the British government sought to strip from them with the removal of Special Category Status: "It kept [the POWs] aware that they were soldiers. In Armagh you could feel so far removed from the movement, from the struggle outside."[72] In addition to reinforcing the political status of the POWs, the paramilitary uniform contests the legitimacy conferred by the state to the prison warders in the official signifier of their own military-style uniform. For the guards to derive any power from their uniform, they must be part of a monolithic disciplinary field. Alternative legitimacies such as that established by the paramilitary uniform cannot be tolerated. This alternative, politicized identity seems doubly threatening to prison officials because of the inmates' gender, for the paramilitary uniform's foregrounding of the subject position of "soldier" refuses the subordination to the domestic, to the unquestioned demands of the individual nuclear family on which capitalist patriarchy traditionally depends. Unsurprisingly, the disciplinary measures to which the prison regime turns to counteract such a dual threat proceed directly from the repressive gender norms central to patriarchal rule and seek to replicate that world order.

It is important at this point to recall again Harlow's previously quoted argument that part of the "historically dominant project of patriarchy" is "to maintain the self-interested conveniences of an unequal division of labor." As mentioned above in the context of Father Murray's 1972 report, the demands of the Armagh women for cooking facilities are likely to be misread by the prison administration as a biological imperative, not a desire for political status. Prison discipline echoes and consciously seeks to perpetuate these sex roles in more coercive fashion as part of a counterinsurgency effort, for prison officials attempt to impose work along gendered lines in political prisons both north and south of the border with the Six Counties, as well as in Britain. As Síle Darragh explains, the prison work that the administration unsuccessfully attempted to get the POWs in Armagh to accept consisted of doing laundry ("washing sheets and blankets") and sewing ("making prison uniforms").[73] The situation was similar south of the border. Councilor Chrissy McAuley, writer, Belfast City Council member (Sinn Féin, Lower Falls), and former Republican

POW, told me that during her incarceration in Mountjoy Prison the conditions for women were generally worse than those of the men as a result of this officiallyimposed division in labor. She reveals that in Mountjoy

> The main laundry for the whole prison, male and female, is situated in the female wing north. There was a small handful of women—the numbers could fluctuate. You could have a maximum of twenty-six, but you can have a minimum of six, and whatever the amount of women that was in the jail, they were expected to deal with the huge bulk of laundry—there were over four hundred men in the prison...The men don't take any part in the laundry because it's still deemed "women's work"...Then they had a sewing room. The women would make all the prison uniforms as well, because that was "women's work."[74]

As a Republican prisoner, McAuley normally refused to do officially imposed prison work of any sort, and in so doing simultaneously resisted both depoliticization as well as patriarchal gender roles. However, when the numbers of nonpolitical female prisoners dropped, she would voluntarily help out her fellow women to show her solidarity with them against the patriarchal regime. One must not misinterpret the nature of McAuley's protest or her apparent suspension of that protest: if her refusal to work had been motivated by sloth rather than by a higher political ideal, it certainly would not have been suspended during the periods when the greatest amount of work was required by the prison laundry. Her comrades regard her solidarity with the "ODC" women in this instance not as a retreat from Republican ideals, but rather as an affirmation of their most basic tenet: your actions should ultimately benefit the people of your community, whether they are Republican or not.

Irish Republican POWs in English prisons experienced similar gendered disparities in their conditions. As someone who served one of the longest prison terms ever handed out to a female Republican political prisoner, Martina Anderson was incarcerated in jails throughout Britain and the Six Counties and she reports that in the prisons women universally suffered greater deprivation than men. Durham, in England, was perhaps one of the most extreme examples. When Durham's sewer system got blocked—as it frequently did in the winter months—raw sewage flowed into the prisoners' dining area. Anderson angrily recalls that

> many of the [nonpolitical] prisoners, on their hands and knees—you weren't allowed a mop in Durham—without disinfectant, without

> gloves, would lift the urine and the excrement into buckets. And for their efforts they were rewarded with a Mars bar.[75] There was an ongoing battle between the rest of the women and us [Republican POWs] because for many of them they viewed their response to one similar to cleaning their homes.[76]

Outrages such as this illustrate once more the extent to which the carceral and the domestic share the same patriarchal disciplinary mechanisms. Perhaps most disturbing is the degree to which many of the "ODC" women have internalized and accepted their degraded status, to the point that they actively resist attempts by POWs such as Anderson to help them end such abuses. Like Bentham's Panopticon, the larger disciplinary system becomes effortlessly self-sustaining because the inmates police themselves, a process made easier because many of the women have been socialized to accept repressive gender norms long before they set foot in a prison. The horrific nature of the task and the insulting "reward" for which it is done seem second nature to those unwilling to question the dominant mode of society.

Republican women in later years and in different carceral spaces continued to resist confinement imposed by actual walls as well as by less tangible—but no less pervasive or dangerous—manifestations of patriarchy. Like Roseleen Walsh before them, these women continued to compose literature that interrogated all aspects of their confinement, not just the prison but the larger society that prison replicated in miniature. Nor is their analysis trapped in a Manichean model in which only British institutions are subject to interrogation: like Adams's Brownie articles, the prison literature of female Republican POWs casts a critical eye on their own political, military, and cultural traditions. In October 1991, Sinn Féin's Women's Department released a brief pamphlet entitled *Voices Against Oppression: A Collection of Poems,* authored by Republican women POWs in Maghaberry and Durham. In the introduction, Irene Sherry notes that "Some of the poems were written by individual prisoners, while others were collectively penned by women who participated in poetry workshops within the gaols."[77] At no point does the pamphlet specifically identify any of the poets involved in the project: the title provides the only clues to a reader fixated on traditional concepts of authorship.[78] In its deliberate anonymity, *Voices Against Oppression* echoes the writing that made its way out of the H Blocks a decade earlier. In this collection, however, the material conditions of incarceration allow more than a symbolic drive toward a collective voice. Groups of women actively worked together to create the verse and, just as importantly, the pamphlet makes no distinction among the single-authored texts and the collaborative poetry. Just as this rhetorical move blurs the lines between individuals, so it joins separate carceral spaces into a shared experience as incarcerated women Republicans—a drive for unity that the POWs sought on a physical level as evinced in the Durham women's battles to be repatriated to the North of Ireland to serve the remainder of their prison terms.

It is instructive to contrast *Voices Against Oppression* with poetry collections produced by male POWs of the same era. Indicative of the improved conditions for which the POWs had fought so hard to attain, poetry workshops had been established in the H Blocks in the autumn of 1988, and the first fruits of those labors were published in *Scairt Amach* (*Shout Out*), a series of stapled A5 pamphlets that first appeared in the spring of 1989. As one of the editors of *Scairt Amach* later reflected, "It was important for people's creative sense of worth that they could have something exposed to others in that way."[79] Unlike *Voices of Oppression*, in *Scairt Amach* each poem is accompanied by the name of its author: no pen-names appear.[80] In addition, there do not seem to be any collaborative texts in any editions of *Scairt Amach*: while they might have benefited from peer-group critiques, only single-author poetry appears in these pamphlets. In its emphasis on individual author and on *recognition* of that author, *Scairt Amach* evinces a more traditional notion of literary composition than the transgressive editorial ethos informing *Voices of Oppression*. Yet, to observe this is not to deny the importance of *Scairt Amach*, to minimize its revolutionary nature, or to fetishize the collaborative text. Instead, it seems likely that this continued reliance on anonymous collectivity is indicative of the carceral space inhabited by the women, one that still required "strength in numbers" with an urgency more insistent than was required in the H Blocks of the late 1980s. As evinced by the prison writing produced between 1976 and 1981 in the H Blocks, the utilization of anonymous collectivity in literature generally increased in proportion to the repression that the POWs suffered at the hands of their warders. Although in 1991 the women in Maghaberry and Durham were beginning to win back some of the benefits taken from them with the ending of Special Category Status, their smaller numbers and the patriarchy inherent to the system made at least some aspects of their struggle even more arduous than the cruel battles faced by male POWs.

Many of the poems in *Voices Against Oppression* reflect the editorial apparatus of the anthology. "Alone," for example, centers on the comradeship and defiance proceeding from the trauma of strip searching.

Though common to all experiences of political incarceration in Britain and the Six Counties, strip searching was a tactic directed with particular regularity and fury against women, and the technique was applied to POWs much more intensively and frequently than it was to "ODCs," a deliberate targeting that Republicans trace to protests against the practice in Armagh.[81] Because Republicans opposed it so vigorously, ex-POWs insist, prison officials turned to it all the more regularly for its punitive effect rather than its efficacy as a security measure. Government functionaries present strip searching merely as a security precaution, but in a political prison it is put into practice very much as an offensive weapon. The forcible removal of clothing extends the panoptic regime to near its furthest extreme, one exceeded only by the actual penetration of the body witnessed in the "mirror searches" of the H Blocks. Similar to the mirror searches, strip searches were intended both to degrade as well as to demonstrate the omnipotence of the state, for they were rituals meant to illustrate the POWs' lack of choice even with regard to their own bodies. Nothing can be kept private, not one's cell, not one's letters, not one's own skin. A Republican POW subject to literally hundreds of strip searches in Durham, Ella O'Dwyer asks, "how far more could [the prison regime] penetrate into one's system, into one's psyche than the constant awareness that you could be strip searched at any point in time?"[82]

In both form and function, strip searching and unprovoked physical violence by male riot squads must be seen as part of the same continuum that relegates women to the prison laundry room. If women refused their "place" as docile domestics, then the state responded with a punishment whose form proceeds directly from the darkest corners of patriarchy. As we will see below, one cannot help but be struck by the overtones of rape evident in the Republican women's descriptions of the punitive measures taken by their warders in response to the POWs' refusal to work in Armagh's prison laundry and to their wearing of paramilitary uniform.[83] Such symbolic rape perpetrated as part of the wider crackdown on protesting prisoners in Northern Irish jails prompted the Armagh women to begin their own No-Wash Protest. After first emptying the jail of potential witnesses such as religious officials and social workers, and subsequent to locking in all conforming prisoners, on 7 February 1980, under the pretext of a wing search a male riot squad brutalized the Republican women. The attack began when the POWs were out of their cells to serve themselves a meal. Síle Darragh relates how "there's a corridor that connects A and B wings which was always kept locked, and as we were lined up at the hotplate the door to this corridor opened. Thirty or forty male screws came out and formed a semi-circle across the wing, preventing access to the stairs that led up to the cells."[84] Mayhem ensued as, in Darragh's words, "the screws just went haywire,"[85] beating the women with batons. After about a half an hour, the POWs were locked into two double cells on the ground floor while the warders proceeded to search their cells, wrecking them in the process. For three days the male warders ran the wing, refusing the normal visits by Father Murray, Prison Welfare, or the Board of Visitors. During this time, the women were charged with assault against the guards. Darragh recalls, "The door opened and up to eight male screws piled in, pinned the women against the wall or their beds with riot shields—physically grabbed them and carried them to the prison governor."[86] The prison authorities refused women access to the toilets, and needless to say, their chamber pots soon were filled to overflowing. "That started the No-Wash protest [in Armagh]...There was no way of emptying chamber pots—we just told women to go ahead and empty the chamber pots out the window." As they did earlier in the H Block No-Wash Protest, the warders escalated the crisis. The prisoners were relocated, and "when we were moved into A Wing the windows had been blocked up."[87]

Until the beginning of the second hunger strike in the H Blocks, Republican women in Armagh were locked in their cells for twenty-three hours a day in their own feces, urine, and menstrual blood. The trauma of 7 February 1980 and endless other days identical to it is distilled into "Alone":

ALONE[88]

By yourself, alone with your dread
but not for long
you had the company
eight in all
held you down
we couldn't hear you
calling for us
each individually
but we share
we share your anger
although spared
the degradation
this time,
each of us
individually
comfort you
our comradeship
consoling you

each of our hands
make a fist
showing our white knuckles
our strength
and our sisterhood.

The overwhelming physicality of the state and the threat of isolation suffuse the first half of this poem, for the isolate individual cannot hope to fight against eight warders. Nonetheless, the poem counteracts the hands of the warders (implied by the woman's being "held down") with another image: the hands of her comrades. Her fellow POWs comfort the victim with comradeship but, working cleverly against the subject position of domestic caregiver into which the prison wants to discipline its victims, these fists also console in their embodiment of defiance. The anger common to all the women proceeds not just from the individual experience of "degradation" that all appear to have suffered, but from a recognition that all of the POWs are degraded as Republicans and as women by an action performed in this manner against one of their number. The cell walls may prevent the POWs from literally hearing the assault, but all share it. Indeed, this group trauma and collective resistance links POWs distant from one another in both time and space, connecting Armagh in 1980 with Durham of eleven years later, where women were strip-searched constantly as much to psychologically break them as to ensure security.

Like Roseleen Walsh's prison poetry, in subject the verse in *Voices Against Oppression* does not remain confined to a cell. Whereas Walsh's "To My Silent Church" critiques the inaction of the Catholic Church hierarchy, "From Eve" takes more direct aim on the patriarchy embedded in Judeo-Christian tradition itself.

FROM EVE[89]

From the rib of Adam she was formed
and from that hour she had but mourned
mourned the injustice in her life
made to accept the role of wife
man's object for him to abuse
never allowed to air her views
always expected to tend and care
would she rebel—should she dare
but new ideas were looming near
and misconceptions began to clear
"Woman you are no less than man
redeem your pride and make a stand"

so woman continues and still she fights
to gain her equality and assert her rights.

As uncomplicated as the poem may be with regard to rhyme and vocabulary, its sheer scope warrants scrutiny. Just as Adams and others in the Cages pushed Provisional Republicanism away from the conservative Catholic, physical force tradition of the early twentieth century, so we see here women writers challenging social, religious, and political orthodoxies. The first two lines of "From Eve" initially appear to reify the Christian origin myth, but by the poem's conclusion they are revealed to be ironic in intent, used to point out the historic subaltern status of women in Judeo-Christian theology and church hierarchy.[90] Simple as it may be, the rhyme scheme intensifies the linkage in the third and fourth lines—the "role of wife" becomes inherently unjust. Similarly, in lines five and six, denial of voice is revealed to be just another manifestation of abuse, one that is in its own way as appalling as physical battery.

Lines seven and eight are the fulcrum of the poem, the moment where hope emerges. Progress, "From Eve" suggests, can be made only if women cease to be defined (by others and *themselves*) only in terms of their capacity "to tend and care." The claustrophobic maternal imagery of the seventh line is underscored by its contrast with the subject position of "rebel" in the line that follows. In the Republican community, the word itself—whether noun or verb—indubitably brings with it positive connotations, which, of course, creates interesting tensions given the negative image of rebellion in the Christian tradition, that of Lucifer is only the most dramatic example.[91] Here the speaker reminds the reader that if political insurrection is permissible, if submission to the political status quo is not divinely ordained, so then must social activism be permissible, so then must gender roles be radically realigned to better serve the interests of justice and equality. The "misconceptions" that begin to clear are not just those of the women attaining a critical consciousness and leaving behind their acceptance of second-class status, they are also those of the men who must abandon their own sexist views. Equality must be gained and rights must be asserted both inside and outside the Republican movement. Writing from the perspective of a Provisional woman activist, Una Gillespe contends that

> while it may be said that the Republican Movement is perhaps one of the most progressive movements in regards to the equal rights of women, it is imperative that it develops sufficiently to challenge the

> sexist attitudes which constrain our women activists. This struggle for women's liberation must be ongoing with the struggle for national liberation, because the two cannot be separated. If we fail to realize this, we will only allow reactionary ideas to gain ground and put the struggle back years.[92]

To witness the danger of letting the national issue take precedence over all other forms of injustice, one need only recall the post-1922 history of the Twenty-Six Counties. Although the Easter Proclamation insisted on gender equality four years before women were given the vote in the United States, DeValera's new republic constitutionally consigned women to the home. Simultaneously, women such as Gillespie argue, colonial aggression cannot be ignored. Many Republican women activists in the Six Counties have been critical of what they see as a privileged middle-class feminism that ignores the reality of death at the hands of British security forces and Loyalist paramilitaries. Proponents of this position claim that despite the fact that both neighborhoods are within the city limits of Belfast, the psychic space permitted by the upper middle-class Malone Road and that which is possible in the working-class ghettos of the Falls Road are worlds apart due to the intensity of the everyday British military presence in the latter area and the relative absence of Army patrols in the former during the grimmest years of the conflict. Similarly they view as hypocritical an ideology that claims concern for and solidarity with all women that fails to come to the aid of women who are relegated to some of the worst prisons in Western Europe, many without charge or trial. As Liz Lagrua recounts, it should not come as a shock that in the early days of the contemporary conflict in the Six Counties many working-class women in the North of Ireland—especially Republican POWs—felt alienated by middle-class feminism: "They said that the men at the Kesh supported them and the women's movement didn't. The men in the Kesh wrote to them and the women's movement didn't."[93]

Naturally, while the sentiments in the quote above might have been heartfelt (at least on certain occasions) and are certainly a critique that feminist theorists have grappled with themselves, we might be suspicious of the binary suggested for a number of reasons. To begin with, although Lagrua was a devoted supporter of the Republican women in Armagh, as is incontestably evident in her choice to submit to the same two-month incarceration endured by Margaretta D'Arcy, like D'Arcy she herself was not Republican. In addition, Lagrua is English: one wonders how much of a self-consciously united front the

Republican women were putting up for the benefit of this university-educated, well-traveled foreign woman who they knew would be reporting their conditions and attitudes to the world. Although Republicans have always engaged in internal dialogue, during periods of particularly intense repression there have been attempts to keep the dialogue—and whatever disagreements might be present—internal so as not to appear weak or disunited to potential enemies.

It is worth returning to a woman with impeccable Republican credentials to evaluate some of the internal tensions with regard to gender in the Republican movement in the initial decade and a half of the contemporary conflict. Although history may remember Mairead Farrell best as the victim of the SAS, she is far more than that, for in addition to being a paramilitary she was also a creator of Republican policy and one of the central voices in Republican feminism in Armagh during the 1970s and the first couple years of the 1980s. Farrell was the officer commanding (OC) of the women in her prison and fought against the stereotype of the Irish woman as passive or subordinate to males, whether in the home, in prison, or in the IRA. In an interview in *Mother Ireland*, she mockingly summarized the conservative view that she fought even within her own politicomilitary organizations that held that "Women aren't supposed to be politically active; they're supposed to be looked after, taken care of and *definitely* not taking part in a No-Wash Protest, never mind being in prison. We even thought in the early days that we were an extension."[94] Farrell and the other female prisoners would soon prove to their critics—from inside and outside the Republican movement—that they were the equal of the men in endurance and in intellect, engaging in Blanket and No-Wash Protests, as well as in hunger strikes in order to achieve political status. On 22 November 1980, *An Phoblacht/Republican News* announced the looming hunger strike of Mary Doyle, Mairead Farrell, and Mairead Nugent, pointing out that

> the women's decision to hunger strike is not a solidarity action with the seven H-Block hunger strikers, nor a limited token gesture, but is being taken in their own right to political status, one which they have underpinned by resisting criminalization since the first prisoner to be sentenced after the withdrawal of political status, Mairead Farrell, went on protest on December 9th 1976.[95]

This insistence on the Armagh women's independence is echoed in the hunger strikers' own statement, which first outlines the demands specific to their own prison, only then adding that they "also fully support the demand of our H-Block comrades: the right not to wear prison uniform."[96] Nonetheless, despite the undeniable support of many of their progressive male comrades,[97] insidious, institutionalized sexism at times worked against the acknowledgment of the women's contribution to the strike. Often this bias evinced itself in subtle but telling ways. For example, *An Phoblacht/Republican News* ran featurettes on each of the men and women participating in the 1980 hunger strike, beginning each article with a small, frame-like icon that announced the article to be a "Portrait of a hunger striker [*sic*]," these words were printed to the left of a drawing of an anonymous, bearded, long-haired Blanketman: ironically, this male image introduced even the article about Mairead Nugent![98] Apparently realizing their mistake, when *An Phoblacht/ Republican News* subsequently published an article about Mary Doyle, the feature was foregrounded by the now-expected frame-like icon announcing the text to be a "Portrait of a hunger striker," but this time *sans* the Blanketman image, indeed, without any image at all in the headline.[99] Having myself worked in the production of a limited-budget periodical that always seemed to be racing against the clock when it came to layout, I can understand this error on a certain level: one's editorial attention is often focused on the text of the article rather than the artwork. However, what ultimately forces me to categorize this not as a minor oversight but as a telling Freudian slip is the fact that no other image is substituted when the error is finally caught. The archetypical image of the hunger striker remains gendered male, despite the three women on strike in Armagh, despite the historical precedent of Dolours and Marian Price in the mid-1970s, as well as Mary MacSwiney in 1922, to name just three.

By calling attention to the Armagh women's participation in physical resistance, I do not mean to reify physical force as the only or even the primary form of resistance in which the POWs engaged. Yet, some of the awe in which Farrell continues to be held seems to proceed solely from her physical sacrifices, with the unfortunate result that her intellectual prowess is frequently ignored. This is a regrettable state of affairs because by the late 1980s the POWs themselves—male and female—moved away from physical confrontation in their own struggles, relying more and more on the discursive practices they developed as they wrote to supporters or potential supporters *taoibh amuigh*, particularly during the Hunger Strikes of 1980 and 1981. As will be discussed in the next chapter, Republicans began to dismantle prison rules by drawing attention to those rules' own contradictions.[100] In a 1996 "Conditions Document," for example, Republican women prisoners in Maghaberry pointed out to the prison administration that although lock-ups had ended for the men in the H Blocks, this freedom "has not been extended to women even though there are no reasonable grounds for withholding this 'privilege.'"[101] This document also exposes the manner in which "educational facilities within the women's prison have always been inferior to those enjoyed on the male side [of Maghaberry]."[102] The Maghaberry women's ever-increasing trust in the power of their discursive abilities shines through in the confident, articulate prose of this document.

The women's discursive resistance is not directed simply against the dominant British disciplinary regime. In texts such as *Voices Against Oppression*, women Republican POWs held up a similar mirror to their own politicomilitary structures. How, for example, can one claim to fight for liberty and then refuse women equal status? Ann Marie Loughran remembers the irony of a Provisional social club that refused entry to women on Sundays, despite the fact that it was named in 1978 after one of Loughran's friends, an IRA woman who was crippled on active service.[103] These are issues at the heart of Gayatri Spivak's well-known essay "Can the Subaltern Speak?" when she contends that

> the question is not of female participation in insurgency, or the ground rules of the sexual division of labor, for both of which there is "evidence." It is, rather, that, both as object of colonialist historiography and as subject of insurgency, their ideological construction of gender keeps the male dominant. If, in the context of colonial production, the subaltern has no history and cannot speak, the subaltern as female is even more deeply in shadow...[104]

In order to be seen, Spivak suggests, one must be heard. However, like Parry, I insist on the need to pursue "another knowledge," one that does not necessarily play by the rules of the dominant discourse. As Councilor McAuley told me, part of the reason Republican prisoners write is to fight misrepresentations of history, "to record for others why we have a conflict here, why we need to address the causes of this conflict here. It's for others, so that others can't fall into the same silence."[105] One should not have a history passively experienced in traditional textuality but *live* a history that perhaps begins in text but ends in engagement in the world outside. The traditional role of the reader, like the traditional role of women, has been one limited by the imposition of passivity. This must end.

Chapter Five

"Captive Voices": Post-1981 Republican Prison Writing

The years following the Hunger Strikes proved to be an extremely fruitful period for Republican prison literature, though little of it was published by mainstream presses. Among the few texts that did receive widespread distribution were the works of Danny Morrison, one-time director of publicity for Sinn Féin, who produced the novel *On the Back of the Swallow* during his incarceration in the early 1990s and who later published some of his jail correspondence with his partner under the title *Then the Walls Came Down,* both books under the imprint of Mercier Press. Brian Campbell edited *H Block: A Selection of Poetry by Republican Prisoners*, published in 1991 by South Yorkshire Writers in 1991, an anthology of seven poets' work. In 1996, the *Journal of Prisoners on Prisons* devoted a special issue to Republican writing and included prose and poetry from the H Blocks, Maghaberry, Portlaoise, and Durham, all compiled by guest editor Micheál Mac Giolla Ghunna, a POW in Long Kesh.

The bulk of the POWs' writing, however, continued to be published only in Republican presses. In 1989, Sinn Féin released *Words from a Cell*, Gerry Kelly's collection of poetry. Writers such as Eoghan MacCormaic who composed texts during the worst years of the Blanket and No-Wash Protests in the H Blocks became all the more prolific as the prison conditions improved because of the POWs' continued activism. MacCormaic, one of the fiercest proponents of Gaeilge among the POWs, wrote in English as well and composed his epic verse drama *The Price of Freedom* in December 1983; published in the Sinn Féin magazine *Iris* in August 1984, MacCormaic's play is an extended meditation on what he sees as the lessons of the prison struggle, in particular the Hunger Strikes.[1] *The Price of Freedom* also marks the beginning of a remarkable era in which POWs literally rewrote the history of Provisional Republicanism in book-length tracts such as *Jail History* and *Questions of History*, published by Sinn Féin's Education Department. In particular, the engaged dialectic that Gerry Adams urged a decade earlier in his "Brownie" articles found some of its fullest expression in prisons in the Six Counties in the rise of a series of periodicals: *Scairt Amach*, *Iris Bheag*, and *An Glór Gafa/The Captive Voice*, all of which engaged the POWs in dialogue with one another and those *taoibh amuigh* (outside). One could devote a chapter to each of the publications that I have mentioned above; however, because of space limitations, I will focus primarily on *An Glór Gafa* not only because of its relatively large circulation, long print run, and its conscious attempts to represent inclusively the voices of Republican women and men held in prisons around the world but also because of how it typifies the often confrontational stance adopted by POWs in their writing. The dialogue in which the POWs participated (and often initiated) in *An Glór Gafa* would again have a marked impact on the Republican Movement, pushing it in yet more liberal directions.

We cannot speak of this unprecedented increase in the production of prison writing without considering the extent to which the POWs' own system of education encouraged it. In turn, the prisoners' growing confidence as writers encouraged further innovations in education, resulting in a vibrant circuit of "collective creative energy" as one ex-prisoner terms it.[2] As I outlined in previous chapters, incarcerated Republicans throughout history have always organized classes for themselves, though arguably this tradition found its most revolutionary expression in the post-1981 era. The creation in 1985 of a new position in the H Blocks camp command staff of vice officer commanding of education surely suggests the seriousness with which the POWs approached their studies there.[3] The seeds had been sown earlier, however, and much of what followed can be traced directly and indirectly to early 1982 when Jackie McMullan—a POW who would be one of the driving forces in structuring the educational program—received Paolo Freire's *Pedagogy of the Oppressed* from a supporter outside.

As those familiar with his approach might anticipate, Freire had great appeal to the men in the H Blocks who were most active in the creation of a revolutionary dialogue among the POWs and between *faoi ghlas* (those locked up) and *taoibh amuigh*. *Pedagogy of the Oppressed* outlines an activist approach to education, one which "denies that man is abstract, isolated, independent, and unattached to the world; it also denies that the world exists as a reality apart from people. Authentic reflection considers neither abstract man nor the world without people, but people in their relations with the world."[4] Freire observes that educational systems traditionally have sought to train students to "adapt" unquestioningly to the oppressive structures around them and to "accept the passive role imposed on them"[5] by a disciplinary regime that the POWs recognized as analogous to the one in Long Kesh that sought to individuate Republicans and thus depoliticize their struggle. The student-teacher hierarchy must be reworked so that learning is no longer an exercise in rote memorization without critical thought. Instead, praxis is key, a productive cycle of reflection, subsequent action, and then additional engaged reflection: a "problem-posing" dialogue that undermines the traditional lecture-based educational system and the vertical lines of power that such a system reinforces. Ultimately, Freire declares, "To exist, humanly, is to *name* the world, to change it. Once named, the world in its turn reappears to the namers as a problem and requires of them a new naming. Human beings are not built in silence, but in word, in work, in action-reflection."[6]

Freire's influence is clear in *Questions of History*, a 155-page book published by Sinn Féin's Education Department in 1987 that outlines the history of Irish Republicanism from 1782 to 1934. *Questions of History* traces its origins to a series of historical documents written by a number of men in the H Blocks, but with Anthony McIntyre especially involved.[7] Drafts of these documents were copied laboriously by hand and circulated among every wing in the H Blocks for group discussion. After discussion each group provided feedback and the documents were revised again.[8] Even in its final form, the collective authorship of *Questions of History* sought to avoid the monovocal form one normally expects in a history textbook. As its preface notes, the POWs originally intended the book to be printed using a four-color layout:

> The colour scheme involved is to try to throw up more clearly central themes and relevant points which need to be debated and discussed, not merely read or listened to. The mainstream of the paper is written in black, red is used for generative themes and special emphasis, green represents direct quotations, each of which has been carefully selected and inserted with the purpose of articulating an important point, blue is used for "problem posing" questions. Each 'generative' theme is designed to produce reflection on the part of the participants. Problem posing questions should be discussed at length and from constant familiarization with them, it is hoped to develop a critical and inquisitive approach to all study.[9]

Regrettably, the four-color layout proved to be too costly, and it was abandoned. To minimize the loss, the publisher italicized the "problem posing" questions in order to highlight visually their separation from other portions of the text. Although professional educators might fault the phrasing of some of the "problem posing" questions because they permit "yes or no" responses, presumably monosyllabic answers would be unlikely in the group discussions for which *Questions of History* was intended and facilitators could press the reticent. To emphasize the pragmatic value of the study of the past, many of the questions ask respondents to reevaluate historical events in context of contemporary conditions "on the ground," an exercise to promote critical thought common enough in university composition classrooms. Though revisionists might see this as another opportunity to reify an atavistic nationalism, by focusing on issues that expose, as one question phrases it, "the conservative nature of much republican [*sic*] thought," the authors' intent clearly seems to be the opposite.[10]

Another of the most emblematic educational developments in the H Blocks was the creation of a woman's studies course within the prison. In partnership with Joanna McMinn, an Open University tutor active in Long Kesh, Laurence McKeown and Jackie McMullan organized a class centered on issues of gender. Using "a group work approach," McMinn acted as facilitator; during a two-year period, over two hundred men in the H Blocks attended these classes.[11] McMinn later remarked that "Nowhere else, in my experience, have groups of men, working class men, participated in such large numbers in classes that sought to address feminist issues, with a feminist facilitator."[12] As McKeown writes in *Out of Time*, the reality of a couple of hundred POWs discussing feminist theory

> does not rest easily with the popular stereotype of the republican [*sic*] prisoner as "hardened terrorist" but once again it demonstrates how far removed those stereotypes are from the real people so-labeled. The prisoners were eager to pursue the type of discussions and debates that arose in the classes with Joanna because they were part of that ongoing process of challenging one's overall awareness and of implementing in practice the concept of self and mutual criticism which the prisoners advocated.[13]

These "feminist *ranganna* (classes)" had a profound impact on those who participated in them and inspired discussion that would continue for as long as the H Blocks existed as a functioning prison compound, as we will see manifest in *An Glór Gafa/The Captive Voice*.

Growing *conscientização* such as this lent itself well not only to the POWs' formal education, but also to their literary endeavors. When John Pickering and other Republican POWs in Long Kesh created their own poetry workshops beginning in the autumn of 1988, they made Freireian praxis an essential part of the structure. No spectators were allowed: everyone was expected to write, and everyone was expected to participate actively in constructive criticism of others' poetry. In the process, the workshops forced their participants to deal with a number of their own neuroses and prejudices. As the poet and hunger striker Gerry Kelly comments, in a macho environment such as the H Blocks, "poetry was still regarded as a fairly effeminate thing until Bobby (Sands) began writing and pouring his heart out and then it became very acceptable."[14] Written in the H Blocks in 1982, Kelly's poem "Tears" predicted the difficulties that many male POWs would have in overcoming their socialization to not display emotion. The subject of the poem is a young man who began life able to express sadness freely, but who as time goes on is forced by society to suppress outward displays of emotion. Later, as he engages in self-analysis, he finds it difficult to regain his lost connection with emotion: the poem mournfully concludes "Liberated man/Weep now/If you can."[15] The experience of a political prison only exacerbates preexisting societal pressure to remain impassive. One must remember that to survive the horrors of the Blanket and No-Wash Protests and the death of their comrades on hunger strike, many POWs needed to shut down emotionally, a difficult process to reverse. Even seven years after the Hunger Strikes, some prisoners found it easy to debate policy and politics, but difficult not to remain guarded about more personal forms of expression. Brian Campbell recalls that one of the most difficult obstacles facing him and the other workshop organizers

> was to create the culture that allowed people to turn the page over and show it to others. That's a major step because it has to be done in a way that people feel comfortable because your initial thoughts are "They'll laugh, people will ridicule me." To criticize and to take the criticism, to deal with criticism, neither to reject it nor just to react to it, that was the second major step. To be comfortable with that sort of process is a markedly important step.[16]

As those teachers who have incorporated peer groups into their classrooms will no doubt attest and as Campbell observes, such projects are difficult in that to function well they leave "no room for ego."[17] All involved must see the process of critique as constructive and must be willing to see writing as a continuing process involving "re-visioning" rather than surface-level revision or mere proofreading. The POWs rose to the challenge, and the writing groups became extremely popular. At their height there were seventy men participating in these workshops.[18]

In *Then the Walls Came Down*, we see Danny Morrison grappling with some of the same difficulties faced by the poetry workshop participants. At one stage, he argues that "It is difficult enough to expose one's inner depths even to the person we love, without going public with them,"[19] but considering that the book is comprised largely of a series of letters to his partner (now, his wife), written between 1990 and 1992, this fear must have been overcome. It is probably not by accident that immediately prior to this protestation he quotes Marcel Reich Ranicki, the author of a biography he is reading, whose philosophy is that "it is undoubtedly the right and duty of a serious writer to expose his inner depths, even at the risk of being accused of exhibitionism."[20] This does seem to be the governing policy of the book at times, for in some places a reader might feel unintentionally voyeuristic as the lovers' pet names for one another are revealed—variants of "Honey-Bunch" appear frequently, for example.[21]

In saying this I want to be clear that Morrison's narrative is far more than literary public display of affection, for it is precisely this emotional risk-taking that differentiates his work from many other prison writings and concomitantly allows us insight into the carceral regimes to which he was subject. When a reporter asks him in 1990 if he is "writing any Behanesque novels at the moment," Morrison's answer is a truthful no, for he has pushed the prison diary into a demonstrative realm that the genre seldom has the luxury to enter when actually composed *faoi ghlas*, allowing the reader to experience his doubts and depressions as well as his bright spots and moments of resistance with him.[22] Though, of course, any autobiographical or epistolary construction of the self is necessarily in part a fiction or a mask (a point that Morrison himself makes, stating "Whether or not all of this is accurate is moot"), one still gets the sense that he makes more than the usual prison writer's attempt to be present to himself as much as practicable.[23] As Morrison said to me in an interview about the correspondence that became *Then the Walls Came Down*, "It became obvious to me that I had an opportunity here to express myself in these letters to someone who was going to read them, one person—well, including the censor in the jail. It was an opportunity to say who I was, explain my past, and improve my writing."[24] In one respect, the letters are Morrison's attempt to regain agency and to remain connected to the world *taoibh amuigh*, but their unconcealed emotions also indicates something of a normalization of relations between Republican POWs and the prison administration. Gone are the days when POWs smuggled miniature cameras inside Long Kesh cells to document their brutalization: Morrison remarks in May 1991 that the jail actually provides a photography service to those receiving visits in the H Blocks. "It's a couple of quid[25] for three black and white shots," he reveals.[26]

Nevertheless, the prison still remains a prison, and the administration still sought in various ways to limit even discursive contact between the POWs and those outside. Morrison recounts that in his time in jail prisoners were forbidden to "rewrite letters, so you had to try to get them down as best you can" on the first attempt.[27] As Sands and his comrades demonstrated in dramatic fashion, Republicans generally found their way around such prohibitions but nonetheless, by impeding the ability to revise, the prison inscribes itself into the texts actually produced within its walls. As I argued with regard to the *téacs pluide* (blanket text) of the Blanket and No-Wash Protests, it is insufficient merely to distinguish prison writing produced during incarceration from that composed after incarceration ends. The conditions of possibility surrounding the composition and revision of a text meant for consumption on the outside necessitates a differentiation among types of *faoi ghlas* prison writing. At the time of the workshops, the prison administration apparently did not forbid the writing and revision of poetry, though political prose was another matter and it would be confiscated if found. This was part of the prison's continuing efforts to contain the POWs from those *taoibh amuigh*, for as Laurence McKeown recalls,

> The admin started from the position that [Republican prisoners] were not allowed to write to the media or at times even get in the *Irish News*. *The Andytown News* was banned for years until court cases were taken and thereafter was still stopped occasionally. The *An Phoblacht* was not allowed in until about 1990. So anything to do with the media they were going to stop—either in or out.[28]

Prison policy with regard to personal letters was only an extension of this containment. POWs in the H Blocks were allowed to write only two letters per week at this stage, though toward the end prisoners were allowed to purchase stamps in the prison and send out as many letters as they could afford (assuming these made it through the censor).

Given the restrictions described above, Morrison deserves a great deal of credit for keeping the prison in his prison writing. After all, as he acknowledges with regard to the transcription of his letters for publication in *Then the Walls Came Down,* "There's a big temptation to edit, which I resisted."[29] For instance, early in his incarceration, a song on the radio prompts Morrison to reminisce in one of his letters about the film *Reds*, though later he discovered that his recollection was faulty—the song does not appear in the film.[30] Yet, such imperfections only add to *faoi ghlas* prison narratives, for they profoundly demonstrate the extent to which carceral space compels the author to, as Morrison beautifully phrases it, "dig deep in memory" rather more than *taoibh amuigh*, to recognize that in writing "you not only recreate it, you *create* it."[31] If the act of textual creation sometimes requires vulnerability, it also offers powerful recompense in the ability to discursively shape the world—points that Republican POWs increasingly realized both on their own and in group efforts such as the poetry workshops.

The new willingness among POWs to open up had a number of unforeseen consequences. Initially the POWs saw the poetry workshops primarily as venues to polish their creative writing skills, but as time went on it became clear that participants were gaining confidence not just in their literary efforts but in themselves also. The self-assurance fostered in the act of writing encouraged each Republican to "see [her/himself] as an agent of change,"[32] one open to offering and receiving critique about the most personal matters and the most deeply held political beliefs. A culture of critique such as this always had the potential to create tensions with the leadership *taoibh amuigh*. After all, in any organization, particularly a revolutionary one, a balance must be struck between dynamic self-critique and the creation of a united front against those the organization sees as enemies, and Provisional Republicanism is no exception. In political prisons in the North of Ireland, the degree to which those *faoi ghlas* (imprisoned) dissent from the dictates of tradition—or whether dissent is pursued at all by them—seems to depend in part upon the material conditions of incarceration endured by prisoners. The implementation of Special Category Status created comparatively better conditions in the Cages of Long Kesh than were experienced by the POWs in the H Blocks, conditions that permitted greater freedom not only to write, but that also emboldened them to critique their own politicomilitary structures. Between 1976 and 1981, the abuses to which the Blanketmen were subject by the prison warders encouraged a closing of ranks among the POWs. As chapter three argues, the disparity between "Brownie's" discursive attacks on conservative Republicanism and the lack of overt critique of hierarchy in Bobby Sands's writings largely can be traced to the British government's brutal attempts to strip legitimacy from Republicans by individuating and depoliticizing them.

Adams's call for the implementation of such a dialectic within the Republican Movement appears to have been heeded by later Republican prisoners, as is evinced by the appearance of such formal publications as *Iris Bheag* in the later years of the H Blocks. *Iris Bheag* was a booklet produced monthly by Sinn Féin's Education Department between 1987 and 1990, and it established a direct dialogue between *taobh amuigh* and *faoi ghlas* that centered on critical reflection. The bulk of *Iris Bheag*'s content was comprised of (often heated) debates on such issues as socialism, the Irish language, and the future of Republicanism, all conducted by means of essays and letters responding to those essays. The epistolary nature of *Iris Bheag* in many ways prefigures today's Internet message boards, for in its pages a number of conversation threads continued over the course of several issues as (sometimes anonymous) writers *faoi ghlas* engaged in dialogue with one another and with writers *taoibh amuigh,* including such Republican leaders as Danny Morrison. No longer were POWs sending out "messages in bottles" that would be heard officially by the Republican Movement's leadership only once a year at the Ard Fheis: active dialogue regarding Republican policy was now being solicited from (and—if the numbers of entries by prisoners in *Iris Bheag* are any indication—even dominated by) incarcerated Republicans.

Some POWs, however, found themselves frustrated by what they saw as a lack of follow-through on the part of the leadership once the policy issues were discussed. As Morrison admits, "there may be some validity to the criticism from the people who wrote for it that it was a sop to them—that it was actively introduced in order to allow them to get this off their chest and that we [in the leadership *taoibh amuigh*] should have taken it more seriously."[33] Beyond this though, in hindsight it seems to me that in some measure the lack of traction for *Iris Bheag*'s proposals also proceeded from the limitations of the publication itself. After all, it was an internal, highly theoretical journal whose frequent use of Marxist terminology would not be out of place in a university classroom. As important a niche as *Iris Bheag* occupied, it was never intended to reach a general audience. Yet, as Freire would argue, one must not ignore the grass roots. Having identified such an absence, the POWs responded by creating *An Glór Gafa*.

The appearance of the first issue of *An Glór Gafa/The Captive Voice* in the autumn of 1989 marked another watershed moment in the history of Republican prison writing and in Provisional Republicanism itself. As Laurence McKeown, one of its founders, reveals, "at the start the magazine was smuggled out in its entirety, and it was only later that it was sent out via the censors, though a copy would have been simultaneously smuggled out."[34] While the editors and the majority of the contributors were incarcerated in the H Blocks, like *Iris Bheag*, this magazine solicited materials from a varied group of writers, and Republican POWs in the Six Counties, the Twenty-Six Counties, Britain, the United States, Belgium, and Germany all furnished texts. Women made important contributions to the content of *An Glór Gafa*, which provided a forum to attack patriarchy in all its manifestations, simultaneously affirming the equality of women in Maghaberry and Durham as comrades and writers. By so doing, *An Glór Gafa* inverts the deliberately gendered discipline that the British penal system seeks to impose. Indeed, every issue contained at least one text by a woman, a statistic particularly notable given the wide disparity in the numbers of female and male POWs, for, as the summer 1990 special issue on women POWs noted, there were seventeen Republican women incarcerated in the Six Counties in Maghaberry and three in Durham in England.[35] By contrast, in the H Blocks alone, at this point in time there were about four hundred Republican men. Indeed, given these numbers, a functional periodical could have been created merely by publishing the writers in Long Kesh. Yet, despite the H Blocks' prominence in world affairs and despite the disproportionate number of prisoners in the compound, texts from Maghaberry, Portlaoise, and elsewhere around the world are given equal representation in the magazine. In its insistence on the inclusion in each issue of a variety of experiences from multiple prisons and even from the occasional contributor *taoibh amuigh*, *An Glór Gafa* symbolically recovers a diverse nation from the fragmentation instigated by colonialism and reinforced by its judiciary. After all, the political prison gains much of its power though separation: the individual from the politicized group, men from women, *faoi ghlas* from *taoibh amuigh*. *An Glór Gafa* reunites these individual voices between its covers into, as the magazine's title itself insists, one collective voice, one that by 1991 was reaching 7,000 readers per issue.[36]

As I argued in the chapter centering on the H Blocks, there is a rough correlation in Republican prison writing between the excesses of the prison regime and the extent to which individual POWs choose to speak anonymously; thus, in *An Glór Gafa*'s bylines we can attain some sense of the material conditions in political prisons in the years after the Hunger Strikes. As will be addressed later in this chapter, the POWs frequently issued collective statements: for example, one encounters articles credited to "Republican POWs (Long Kesh)"[37] and "Women POWs (Maghaberry),"[38] as well as to smaller collectives such as "A Wing H5 (Long Kesh)"[39] or "POWs C2 (Maghaberry)."[40] However, unlike the deliberately anonymous individual writings from the H Blocks during the period 1976–1981 or the collection of Republican women's poetry in *Voices Against Oppression*, the overwhelming majority of texts in the later years of *An Glór Gafa* are credited to single authors with little use of an *ainm cleite* (pen-name). Interestingly, when an author utilizes an *ainm cleite* in the mid- and late 1990s, most often it is a choice made to protect the individual's identity from becoming known to the prisoner's *own* community, not to conceal it from prison authorities. Sometimes this "protection" was not truly in earnest, as in the case of the "Red Spider's" desire to slag his comrades unrevealed, which in the close-knit H Blocks could at best have been done only semianonymously in practice. On other occasions, however, the need was more serious, as seems to have been the case in "Marie's" frank discussion of the strains of separation from her POW husband in the article "A Fighting Battle" (discussed later in this chapter), or in the special issue focused on child abuse where a number of POWs spoke graphically of their past victimization. That women were far more likely to write anonymously and collectively (even producing a communally-written short story, "Big Pat")[41] speaks among other things to the disparity in prison conditions to which male and female POWs were subject and to the vulnerability inherent to the women's small numbers.

Diversity in general was another hallmark of *An Glór Gafa,* not only in the case of individual authors but also with regard to the texts themselves in both subject and form. One might expect writings centered on prison experience to appear regularly in the pages of the magazine, and so they did—but much less frequently than one might have anticipated. Less than half of the average issue of *An Glór Gafa* dealt with topics directly related to incarceration, and in some cases the editors emphatically looked outward from their cells, as evinced by the spring 1990 special issue focused on the environment and pollution.[42] The genres represented were as varied as the topics addressed, for while critical prose comprised the bulk of the periodical's content, poetry, creative prose, and art also appeared in its pages each time. In this respect, *An Glór Gafa* united the strengths of *Iris Bheag* and *Scairt Amach* (a series of stapled A5 booklets containing poetry written in the H Block workshops). Nor was humor absent from the magazine's pages. A series of comic strips such as Joe Corbett's "Blockheads" and Gerry Milligan's (later, Martin Gough's) "Chuckey" made lighthearted fun of the goings-on inside prison walls, as did

"The Red Spider" in his column. Furthermore, every issue contained at least one text *as Gaeilge* (in Irish Gaelic), a practice that sparked a characteristically energetic exchange between *taoibh amuigh* and *faoi ghlas* in the pages of *An Glór Gafa.*

In the first three issues of *An Glór Gafa*, Irish language texts appeared without translation. However, with the publication of Eoghan MacCormaic's essay "Ceachtanna Tíreolaíochta" in the summer 1990 issue, the editors announced that, "in response to numerous requests from non-Irish-speaking readers," the magazine would henceforth offer dual-language versions of articles originally written *as Gaeilge.*[43] Not all welcomed this change in policy. Among the readers dismayed by the dual-language texts was Máirtín Ó Muilleoir, a noted Irish language activist, Sinn Féin councilor for Belfast City Council (1987–97), and later the chief executive of the Andersontown News Group.[44] Ó Muilleoir's view is that "to translate the articles in *An Glór* [*sic*] into English makes the Irish redundant—a second class language which is only relevant if translated into the dominant language."[45] Anticipating those who would point out that Gaeilge is spoken by relatively few people even in Ireland, Ó Muilleoir calls attention to the publishing industry of Iceland. There, despite a population of only 250,000, more books are published annually in Icelandic than Ireland publishes books in English.[46] The speaking of Irish is a *right*, he concludes, and it is the "duty" of others to recognize this and respect *Gaeilgeoirí* (Irish speakers) as equal citizens.[47] The editors respond to Ó Muilleoir's letter apologetically, affirming that translations were added "as a courtesy" to readers unable to speak Irish, and that in so doing "It was not felt that the translations would detract from the Irish."[48] A call was made for arguments on both sides of the issue, and the invitation received responses from around the world.

In the summer 1991 issue, *An Glór Gafa* published representative letters from Ireland, the United States, England, Wales, and a Republican POW in Belgium addressing *An Glór Gafa*'s dual-language text policy. Of course, Wales faces similar language debates, and drawing on that experience the Welsh respondent's solution to the dilemma was to offer readers brief English abstracts of Irish-language articles, thus underscoring the primacy of Gaeilge without completely excluding readers without Irish. She anticipates that such an approach would have the added benefit of giving those interested in learning Irish "extra incentive" to do so.[49] In contrast, those who were in one way or another denied access to Irish language instruction argued for continued publication of dual-language texts: for example, one of only three Irish POWs in Antwerp Prison (none of whom was fluent in

Gaeilge), Kieran McCarthy was "very appreciative" of the translations, especially because he was "normally isolated" from his fellow Republicans in a jail where the vast majority of ordinary prisoners did not speak English.[50] Similarly, a reader in England found the translations helpful in her efforts to learn Irish, declaring, "I don't just go straight to the English, I always look to see how much of the text I can recognize and understand."[51] An Irish American urges translation for rather different (and disappointing) reasons and dismisses the importance of Irish-language texts, snorting that "we do not truly need another 'Tower of Babel' syndrome where everyone speaks a different language so none of us can talk."[52] Ultimately, *An Glór Gafa*'s editors decided to do away with dual-language texts, despite the fact that the majority of correspondents favored them. However, a suggestion made by two letter writers was adopted and henceforth a brief *foclóir* (glossary) of more difficult words and phrases accompanied articles written *as Gaeilge*. The editors conclude that this solution offers the most respect to the rights of *Gaeilgeoirí* "while at the same time making articles accessible to those not totally fluent. And for those of you with no Irish at all—perhaps you'll be spurred to learn by the thought of what you're missing!"[53]

I have outlined this debate in some detail because it speaks to so many of the larger issues of canonicity and power that Republican prison texts force us to confront. What becomes clear in the dialogue is that language and literature mean something quite different to Ó Muilleoir and the editors of *An Glór Gafa* than they do to many of the magazine's readers and, I assert, to many academics. In short, to Republican activists engaged directly in it, the production and study of writing cannot be separated from issues of human rights: the staff of *An Glór Gafa* initiated the dialectic to address equality of human representation, not to debate literary form in the abstract. Texts are not just objects to be transmitted and passively enjoyed: they do not merely communicate, but rather they urge a participatory act by the reader, an investment in a larger context. Such a view evokes the critique made by the Belfast Irish-language poet Gearóid MacLochlainn in "Aistriúcháin," an angry attack on an Irish audience who seems to believe that superficial familiarity with "café culture" and English-language writers such as "Séamus" merit the claim "go dtuigeann siad filíocht" (that they understand poetry).[54]

Such self-satisfaction as MacLochlainn describes is not limited to Irish monoglots, of course. Even a casual glance at some of the most prestigious academic conferences reveals how common a misconception this is: "Irish literature" appears to begin and end with Yeats and

Joyce in the eyes of many. Even more troubling are the moments when market forces and cultural imperialism unite in deliberate fashion to erase Gaeilge from academia, which likes to think itself beyond (or in active opposition to) such concerns. The editor of the *Oxford Anthology of Twentieth-Century British and Irish Poetry*, for instance, justifies his decision not to include any Celtic-language poetry of any sort in the collection because of "the fact that the bulk of this anthology's readers will be American" and that "these languages are simply not read in the United States, however influential they have been for particular British and Irish writers."[55] On the surface this editorial decision might appear to be motivated by a respect for Celtic languages and their speakers—a respect that initially seems similar to that of *An Glór Gafa*, for the inclusion of translations appears not to have been considered. Yet, in coming to terms with this absence we must consider the stark disparity in venue, for an academic anthology has a rather different purview than a magazine such as *An Glór Gafa*. The debate in *An Glór Gafa* centered on an intrusion, the imposition of a translation never intended by the writer. In the case of the anthology, however, we must ask why there was no consideration of poets whose works have appeared in translation with the blessing of the poets themselves (and sometimes with the poet actually involved in the translation): Gearóid MacLochlainn, Cathal ÓSearcaigh, and Nuala Ní Dhomhnaill are three obvious and influential examples from Ireland. In fact, I reckon that no one would benefit from a confrontation with alterity more than American readers.

The *Oxford Anthology of Twentieth-Century British and Irish Poetry*'s choice to exclude Celtic-language authors only provides more fodder to those concerned about the continued co-option of Irish studies by the United States. Indeed, it recalls one of the letters written by a reader of *An Glór Gafa* during the translation debate. This respondent insists that as an "international" publication *An Glór Gafa* has an obligation to provide dual-language texts, jokingly suggesting that they translate Gaeilge into "American!"[56] Bracketing for a moment the apparently common and rather chilling implication in both letter and anthology that the United States can stand unproblematically for the rest of the world (or that the limitations of its *readers* necessitates a revision of literary history), it is important to note that the international character of *An Glór Gafa* is itself a crucial factor in the editors' decision to reject dual-language texts. In so doing, they affirm on a global stage that *Gaeilgeoirí* will not accept second-class status or worse, total erasure.

To most of those who have themselves experienced postcolonial struggle, the necessity of an activist approach to literature seems self-evident. In the article "An Teanga," Eddie Seeley goes further, drawing a direct parallel between the Irish language and Republican POWs themselves. A POW in the H Blocks, Seeley links historical efforts to crush the language to attempts by the British government to strip a politicized identity from Republican POWs: "The failure of British policy on both counts can be seen from the fact that both the Irish language in the Six Counties and the POWs are in stronger positions than ever."[57] In both instances, survival was possible only through individual and collective resistance, Seeley declares. Moreover, the experience of and struggle against physical and linguistic oppression was constitutive to both language and POWs.

It is worth returning to Gearóid MacLochlainn to see the extent to which throughout the Six Counties collision with a colonialist presence reifies Seeley's conception of the link between a language, its speakers, and the politicized world around them. In the poem that concludes *Babylon Gaeilgeoir*, MacLochlainn's first book, the speaker describes his first experience being stopped by a British Army foot patrol, an event that the speaker initially welcomes, for in occupied West Belfast it signifies his entry into adulthood: soldiers do not regularly stop those they view as children. When one of the soldiers demands the speaker's name, the speaker insists on the spelling *as Gaeilge*, complete with *síneadh fada* (accent mark) on the vowels. As intended, this causes the soldier difficulty and, seeing the resistance for what it is, he orders the speaker to place his hands against a nearby wall. The speaker apparently had not considered how the situation might turn perilous, but this changes swiftly as other soldiers surround him. Standing helpless in search position, the speaker feels either a thumb or a gun pressed against his back as foreign hands roam his body, invading his pockets and socks. Eventually, having been cleared by a disembodied voice over the soldiers' radio, the squaddies allow him to go on his way. The poem's final lines remark that the experience was "an chéad uair/ a thuig mé an focal-/ ***Éireannach***" [emphasis in original]—translated literally, "the first time/ I understood the word-/ Irish person."[58] To be Irish, and in particular, a *Gaeilgeoir*, is to suffer various sorts of violence at the hands of foreign influence, a claim MacLochlainn forcefully makes in the poem's emphatically English title, "800 Years," with its invocation of the long history of the British colonization of Ireland.[59]

While other lines are altered, this vision remained the same when the poem was included in *Na Scéalaithe: Cnuasach Filíochta,*

MacLochlainn's next collection by the larger Irish-language press Coiscéim. However, when the first dual-language anthology of MacLochlainn's work appeared in 2002, interesting revisions are made to the poem, most notably in its title, which became "Teacht i Méadaíocht" (literally, "the coming of [self] importance") put into English by MacLochlainn as "Rite of Passage." Such a shift deemphasizes the larger historical valence set up in the original title, shrinking the scope of the experience into a more individualized one with less obvious postcolonial overtones. Similarly, MacLochlainn's translation of the final lines departs strikingly from the original *as Gaeilge*: he concludes with images of "the hypodermics / of military operations, / a first stab/ at translation."[60] Like the rest of the translations in *Sruth Teangachal Stream of Tongues,* this misdirection seems "a playful jibe thrown out at the monoglot who seeks truth in translation," as MacLochlainn himself describes it; but beyond this, it is perhaps fitting that such a translation also would be found more appealing by a bourgeois audience uncomfortable with anything that might be read as radical Irish nationalism.[61] In this respect there are resonances between MacLochlainn's trickster translations—which, to his ideal bilingual audience, certainly might not be viewed as concessions to English due to their subversive concealment of strongly nationalist views—and the progressive domestication of some of Bobby Sands's writings as they were published by successively larger or more expressly academic presses.

Must texts be radical in inverse proportion to the extent of their dissemination? The Republican POWs hoped not. Indubitably, unlike its predecessor *Iris Bheag*, which was a theory-heavy "internal publication" of Sinn Féin and thus not intended for consumption outside the formal boundaries of the Republican Movement, *An Glór Gafa* deliberately defined itself as a periodical for a general readership in Ireland and abroad. In the inaugural issue, the editors observe that "the media, the education system, and churchmen and politicians all play their part in guarding against the dissemination of revolutionary ideas": in contrast, *An Glór Gafa* was designed as an engine "to bring about change"[62] in the broadest arena. In a far more strident fashion than Adams's "Brownie" articles, Republican POWs now directly attacked social and political conservatism of all sorts, internal and external to Republicanism.

If the directness of the critique differed from Adams's more subtle approach, some of the targets of that critique remained unchanged from the times of the Cages. In part, the prisoners' internal "long war" against conservative Republicanism proceeded from the material conditions of the prison struggle itself. For instance, despite the drive toward praxis encouraged by Sands and others in the H Blocks, the extreme brutality endured by the POWs at the hands of the prison regime during the worst years of the protests at times threatened to disrupt Republican efforts at self-critique, encouraging an understandable "closing of ranks" on certain issues or a return to a "physical-force only" conception of resistance. It is not a coincidence that as a result of his hellish surroundings many of Bobby Sands's writings dwell on physicality—a preoccupation evident not only in his descriptions of his cell's impact on his body and mind, but also in images of armed struggle in such stories as "'Come on, You Wee Reds.'"[63] In fact, between 1976 and 1981, ex-POWs *taoibh amuigh* and POWs in the less brutal Cages were the ones who most vocally advocated the creation of what Adams terms "a broad-based action campaign"[64] that relies first and foremost on community mobilization, not paramilitary might. During the 1980 hunger strikes, Adams—then vice president of Sinn Féin—called for nonviolent demonstrations, adding that if marchers "are prepared to make their protests in a dignified and militant (although passive) manner, then this shows up who are the real aggressors."[65] Open, violent confrontation on the streets has the potential to isolate Republicans, he insists, making it easy for the British security forces simply to engage in a "mopping up" of resistance.[66] Although here Adams nominally addresses those involved in the anti–H Block/Armagh campaigns, the implications are clear with regard to Provisional Republicanism as a whole: with his usual tact the vice president of Sinn Féin is suggesting policies that run counter to the ideology of the then president Ruairi Ó Braidaigh, who would leave the Provisionals when Sinn Féin abandoned their policy of total electoral abstentionism.

In contrast, Sands's texts do not overtly critique Republican leadership: despite the heated debates on policy that Sands himself led, he and other Blanketmen seem to have decided—consciously or not—that, given the extremity of the crisis in the prisons, a united front on certain issues needed to be kept in the public venues in which their writings appeared. However, such unity should not be read as ideological inflexibility, but rather as a response to the uncompromising prison regime encountered by the POWs. As Sands himself frequently observes in his own work, it is perilous to exhibit even the appearance of weakness to prison authorities,[67] and in the symbolically loaded environment of the H Blocks, even a POW's request for toilet paper could be read by warders as evidence of vulnerability and trigger an attack on the defenseless prisoners.[68] Clearly, in the H Blocks of 1976–81, there is no Wordsworthian tranquility in which to reflect emotion.

Nor was this experience unique to Long Kesh, for the Republican women in Durham provide ample evidence that this repressive sort of disciplinary regime only emotionally and ideologically hardens the political prisoners subject to it. In 1993; subject to strip-searches every bit as brutal as—and even more frequent than—those the Blanketmen endured more than a decade earlier, Martina Anderson and Ella O'Dwyer realized that as a result of such abuse female POWs "over-censored what we wrote and said, we restricted conversation when screws were listening. The establishment was not allowed to see us cry and we seemed to care more about what the system thought of us than about the impression our loved ones were left with."[69] While arguably a temporary necessity *in extremis*, Anderson and O'Dwyer point out in their *An Glór Gafa* article "Let's Talk" that such survival techniques threaten to do more harm than good when not carefully monitored, potentially resulting in the stunting of the individual and collective ideological and emotional growth of the POWs.[70]

As the POWs in the H Blocks slowly won back conditions comparable to those allowed under Special Category Status, it is unsurprising that concomitantly they began more publicly to cast a critical eye back on their own sociopolitical structures in a fashion similar to Adams. The internal "culture of discussion" that flourished during the years of protest between 1976 and 1981 grew much stronger and more open in subsequent years and was further nurtured by Bobby Sands's hunger strike and election to the British parliament, events that prompted Republicans to radically reevaluate many of their traditional strategies. More forcefully than ever, progressive Republican POWs and like-minded others *taoibh amuigh* argued the necessity of continuing political analysis and engagement (even to the point of abandoning the tradition of abstentionism) in conjunction with the armed struggle, with the ultimate goal of rendering physical resistance unnecessary.

In order to build the "broad-based action campaign" of which Adams and other POWs spoke, the Provisionals needed to broaden long-held notions of militancy and also to provide practical advice for individuals interested in radical reform. Brian Campbell, one of *An Glór Gafa's* founders, suggests an activism that he terms "democratic confrontation," a strategy of publicly challenging politicians on their positions on important issues in a way that Republicans claim the mainstream media does not. Campbell explains that "this democratic confrontation doesn't require you to raise your voice or be aggressive in any way. Be polite but firm. It's a matter of asking the right questions."[71] The development of a critical consciousness is only the first step, the POWs urge. One can, *must*, individually and collectively intervene in the dominant discourse, and there are many forms that such intervention can take. One can be militant without military force.

Nowhere is this ideological shift more neatly symbolized than in the manner in which many of the Republican POWs in the H Blocks began to reassess the rituals of their Easter commemorations in the years immediately after the Hunger Strikes. In his *An Glór Gafa* article "Easter Renewed," Adrian Kelly outlines how in the first years of Long Kesh the POWs in the Cages honored the Republican dead with two minutes of silence and a reading of the Roll of Honor of the deceased, a ceremony preceded by a color party leading a disciplined parade in paramilitary uniform around the cage perimeter. By mirroring the commemorations taking place outside prison fences, inmates of the Cages not only honor fallen comrades but also symbolically disrupt the mechanisms—physical and otherwise—separating POWs from those *taoibh amuigh*: they are participating in a very real way with similar gatherings on the outside.[72] Such a semiotic move is crucial in many ways, especially given the place of such commemorations in Republican history. The ceremonies traditionally held at Bodenstown, for example, also are used as opportunities for Sinn Féin's leadership to reaffirm publicly their policy for the coming year. Past and future powerfully intersect in such moments. However, H Blocks *conscientização* prompted an even more revolutionary—and to conservative Republicans, transgressive—approach to Easter commemorations. No more would they begin and end with a militaristic march around the prison yard and an informal sing-song afterward. Rather, as Adrian Kelly relates, beginning in 1985, "in line with the new thinking it was suggested that we organise [*sic*] a pageant in each wing which would have an educational, as well as a commemorative value."[73] After much debate, this became general policy: the Role of Honor was still read, but henceforth the emphasis would be on active reflection. Individual wings would often follow such a reading with the prisoners' own literary and creative endeavors, including plays, poetry, and songs. No more could the occasion in prison be mistaken for a lecture centered on death or the reading of diktats from on high, but instead the commemorations became more expressly *conversations* centered on creation and participation, a much more rhizomatic redistribution of power than had existed previously.

The editors make no attempt to conceal their attack on an ideology focused solely on the removal of British security forces by physical force, acknowledging in the spring 1990 issue that "one of the aims of

An Glór Gafa is to challenge this exclusive view of struggle."[74] Yet, they observe, activists working to end "sexual oppression, oppression of the elderly, the sick, single parents, the destruction of the environment and so on [...] tend to view their struggles in isolation and not as part of a wider struggle."[75] The Republican Movement must reimagine itself as a group of activists united in struggle against *all* forms of inequality, embrace nontraditional tactics, and, most of all, be "subject to critical analysis [and] open to change."[76] *An Glór Gafa* grew more provocative the next year when it published an anonymous article coauthored by "a number of POWs in Long Kesh" who are unafraid to admit the extent to which paramilitary violence can be counterproductive to Republican interests. They claim that "the power of our armed struggle is that it forces the Brits to do something, but without necessarily guaranteeing that that something is what the armed struggle set out to achieve."[77] What is required is a mass movement in both the Six Counties and the Twenty-Six Counties, one that moves beyond a reliance on abstract nationalism. "It is not the armed struggle which has hampered our development in the 26 Counties," the authors conclude, "but our lack of a programme [*sic*] on everyday issues like housing, unemployment, health, etc."[78] This analysis is praised in the next issue by Maitiú Ó Treasaigh, a POW in Portlaoise. Like his comrades in the Six Counties, Ó Treasaigh warns, "the main lesson for ourselves now must be that unless we can combine a radical social and economic programme with the demand for national freedom we too, like the Republicans of the past, will be pushed aside."[79]

The irrelevancy feared by Ó Treasaigh would only be avoided by direct intervention to change aspects of the party's own ideology, and the POWs made sure that their voices were heard by leadership outside.[80] This was especially true at crucial moments such as the advent of the Downing Street Declaration in 1993, where Republican POWs produced the "H-Block Submission to Sinn Féin Peace Commission."[81] Nor was this input limited to momentous occasions such as Downing Street: then as now[82] Sinn Féin's yearly Ard Fheis is the locale where major policy is decided. Republican POWs added their input to these annual debates through such writings as the "Prisoners' Address to Sinn Féin Ard Fheis."[83] In later years when prerelease paroles were offered to prisoners, Republican POWs utilized them to physically attend this national convention, where they proposed and voted on party policy motions. *An Glór Gafa* provided an outlet both to report the result of such votes as well as to encourage further debate on motions that failed. In "Sinn Féin 90th Ard Fheis: A POW Delegate's

View," Mairtín Óg Meehan outlines his participation as a representative of the H Block Sinn Féin *cumann* (chapter), noting with pride that the party accepted without amendment all six of the motions from the POWs in the H Blocks that year.[84] Meehan's article also provides fascinating insight into the deliberations over social issues under formal discussion in 1996. In particular, Meehan is distressed at the failure of a policy motion centered on women's right to choose, a motion proposed by the Republican women in Maghaberry Jail. Meehan himself voted for the resolution, believing "simply that women in Ireland should have the right to take decisions which affect their own bodies, i.e. self-determination."[85] In contrast, a document focused on protecting the rights of gays and lesbians was adopted, Meehan remarking that "it was simply a matter of common sense and compassion."[86]

Indeed, *An Glór Gafa*'s authors regularly proved themselves to be at the vanguard of the nationalist community's drive for social change. For example, the fearlessness with which the magazine approached the issue of gay rights in its 1991 publication of Brendí McClenaghan's article "Invisible Comrades: Gays and Lesbians in the Struggle" is evident not only in the content of McClenaghan's essay, but in its physical layout as well: a large photo of two men kissing is a focal point of the article's headline.[87] In a statement reminiscent of Ngũgĩ wa Thiong'o's contention that there can be no real postcolonial independence without true equality for women, McClenaghan insists that "national liberation by its very nature incorporates gay/lesbian liberation as an integral part, and it is only through open debate leading to an understanding of gay/lesbian experience that our equality in struggle can be made a reality."[88] Unlike Ngũgĩ, however, McClenaghan speaks from within the subject position he describes as "doubly oppressed"[89] for he himself is gay, a point that he makes clear in the article. Such a public admission was risky on a number of levels, a point not lost on the magazine's editors who offered to publish the article anonymously—an offer that McClenaghan refused.[90] After all, discrimination against gays and lesbians was a policy on which conservative Catholicism and conservative elements of Republicanism often could agree, as evident in the initially fearful reaction to the article by some in the movement outside and the appearance of bigoted graffiti on the walls of McCleneghan's home district. In fact, McClenaghan's essay was one of only two texts in the magazine's history that the Republican leadership *taoibh amuigh* threatened to censor.[91] Certainly not all of the leadership had such reservations, as Danny Morrison's novel *On the Back of the Swallow* demonstrates. In creating its gay protagonist, Morrison was motivated in part "to defend an oppressed minority," to add his voice to those speaking out against the "deeply homophobic" society in Ireland.[92] Yet, despite continued objections from those involved with the magazine and other progressive Republicans, McClenaghan's essay was partially censored. It appeared in *An Glór Gafa*, but not in the issues published in the United States, where it was replaced by an article by Gerry Adams soliciting funds for Sinn Féin.

This particular substitution speaks volumes about the vexed relationship between the Provisionals and many of their supporters in Irish America. Those who argued—disingenuously or not—for the excision of the article on the pragmatic grounds that it would alienate support in the United States would only have to cite the continuing controversy surrounding the local government's refusal to allow gays and lesbians to march in New York City's Saint Patrick's Day Parade as powerful evidence of continued conservatism across the Atlantic. Yet, though intolerance of this sort continues in the United States, Republicans in Ireland seem to be progressively less willing to engage in its appeasement. In 1996, five years after McClenaghan's article appeared in *An Glór Gafa*, as he marched in New York City's Saint Patrick's Day celebration parade with the United Irish Counties Association, Gerry Adams himself critiqued the barring of gay and lesbian participation in the parade. When confronted by a member of the Irish Lesbian and Gay Organization in the audience of a March 12 speech during this 1996 visit, Adams called for the crowd to allow the woman to speak, reminding some booing auditors that the Easter Proclamation insists that "all the children of the nation" must be cherished.[93] Adams then asserted that "As someone who has been excluded from many places, I would like to think that we're big enough to be inclusive."[94] At another event, Adams added that he "would like to think St. Patrick's Day is a celebration of the diversity of Irishness," a pointed commentary on the controversy.[95] Later in the 1996 visit, to the dismay of gay rights groups, Adams would retreat somewhat from his attack, declaring that he "would like to see [the parade controversy] resolved to the satisfaction of all, and in a manner which accords to everyone the respect which is our due"; nevertheless this was an important and public turning point in Provisional policy.[96] At the Sinn Féin Ard Fheis that same year the party approved a policy statement protecting the rights of gays and lesbians. The statement insists that

> Self-determination is our core demand, not only as a nation, but also as diverse communities within that nation. When confronted with

> experiences which are similar to our own (such as those of ethnic minorities, Travellers, women etc) it should be automatic for us, as republicans [*sic*], to understand and actively express that understanding through solidarity. The denial of justice from one section of this nation is a denial of the rights of us all.[97]

Some observers like Agnès Maillot consider this perspective "problematic, since minorities do not necessarily share the same experience when it comes to discrimination."[98] While Maillot is correct to insist that we should not elide individual experiences too easily, she reads this statement rather too unkindly. Note that the policy focuses on "similarity": it certainly does not posit a one-to-one correspondence between subalternities. Instead the statement calls for solidarity amidst apparent differences on issues of social justice, certainly a strong indication of the manner in which Provisional Republicanism has, since the mid-1970s, steadily moved away from an exclusive focus on "the national question." While slow in coming and undoubtedly with more yet to do, such change has begun to evince itself within Provisional Republicanism, with regard to gay and lesbian rights. 2002 witnessed Adams publicly voicing his support for the right of same-sex couples to marry, adopt, and to have the legal status as heterosexual couples do with regard to property rights and insurance.[99] It seems obvious today that McClenaghan's article assisted this reform of Provisional policy with regard to the rights of same-sex couples. In 2001, Brian Campbell reflected that "the article on gay rights was a very good example of the value of the *Glór Gafa* [*sic*]. I don't want to exaggerate, but in terms of opening up the whole debate it prompted all sorts of responses."[100] In their direct challenge to conservative Republican values of the past, the writers and editors of *An Glór Gafa* are the direct descendants of Adams and his "Brownie" articles, and their writings, like those of their predecessor, had a positive shaping influence on the Republican Movement's official policies.

An Glór Gafa courted controversy again with a series of texts exploring the impact of political incarceration on couples, in particular on the partner left outside. Laurence McKeown's 1990 short story "The Visit" initiated[101] the discussion in earnest: told from the perspective of a nameless wife waiting for a visit with her imprisoned husband, the narrative gives voice to the isolation endured by many prisoners' partners.[102] The protagonist finds herself disowned by her family because of her husband's incarceration, and worse yet, her relationship with him has been reduced to small talk over the past seven years of visits. Embittered by his lack of interest in her emotional well-being, she has decided to force a conversation, one in which "she was going to battle for what she wanted . . . for herself, for him, for the both of them."[103] In the final lines of the story, she smiles as she walks toward the visiting area, a smile that "came from the sudden sensation of movement deep within her body. It lasted only an instant but was no less real for that. She felt exhilarated at the thought of this 'company,' this 'new life'—which was, at the same time, the source of all her troubles."[104] It is obvious that we are to read the "movement" in her body as a literal quickening, a pregnancy from an extramarital affair,[105] but this "new life" is also her own, a metaphoric representation of the woman's desire to live a life not centered exclusively on her husband's needs.

McKeown's decision to end the story before the conversation between the husband and wife takes place is a wise one in a number of ways. Certainly, such a lack of specific resolution begs further discussion among readers: what happened subsequent to this visit and why? What exactly is it that the wife "wanted" the outcome of her revelation to be? Indeed, McKeown told me that this is the aspect of his story that readers were most curious about.[106] McKeown's story deliberately provokes, its contextualization of the woman's actions a call to reevaluate judgmental attitudes toward those facing similar dilemmas. Such a critique gains power in that it comes from a male POW doing time in the H Blocks: because McKeown creates such a sympathetic vision of the prisoner's wife, the story thus becomes resistant to attacks from those who would argue that such an open dialogue about prison relationships would damage the morale of POWs. But beyond this, "The Visit" also begins a conversation about the patriarchal elision of female independence with infidelity, an elision all too common in Republican areas as will be outlined below.

A few years after McKeown's story, *An Glór Gafa* returned to the topic of prisoners' relationships, making it the central theme of the spring 1993 issue: in it, five texts dealt directly with the dilemma faced by POWs and their partners outside. Eschewing the relative safety of creative writing and the plausible deniability that it licenses, three of these texts are explicitly autobiographical prose; one essay from a female POW, one from a male POW, and one representing the point of view of a POW's wife. Building on McKeown's story, the editors foreground not just their desire to illustrate the internal strains on the family unit itself, but also their intentions to discuss the impact of the "unrealistic expectations imposed by people in the republican [*sic*] and wider community" on prisoners' partners, the overwhelming majority of whom are female, very often with young children.[107] In

"Love Is...," Jim McCann provides insight into the "born again" husband/boyfriend that he and his comrades encounter occasionally in the H Blocks, observing that while the wife or girlfriend may have been "a mere appendage" to the "born again's" life outside, subsequent to incarceration the woman becomes an all-consuming obsession.[108] McCann reckons that because this "born again" often has a long history of cheating on his partner, he assumes that his partner is now two-timing *him*, and worse yet, "that everyone knows and that he's being laughed at, derided, or pitied. With suspicion gnawing at his fevered imagination, he turns into a real hate-the-world."[109] The boringly predictable male preoccupations parading through the "born again's" mind are intensified in carceral space, precisely because prison discipline itself attempts to individuate the POW, transforming him into a powerless object of ridicule. Given that the H Block prison warders played the song "Torn between Two Lovers" on the public address system during visits "rather too often" according to one POW, there can be no doubt that male insecurity not only reinforces an unjust patriarchy, it also can quite literally be appropriated as a tool of counterinsurgency.[110] By addressing their own sexist behavior and anxieties, McCann implies, the POWs can build trust within their own relationships, help create a more equitable society, and simultaneously render ineffective one more psychological weapon in their warders' arsenal.

To ensure that the conversation represented as many perspectives as possible, in addition to including an essay by a woman who had to leave her husband and children behind when she was incarcerated in Maghaberry,[111] the editors solicited the thoughts of a POW's partner. Those familiar with Anne Devlin's play *Ourselves Alone* will recognize many of the complaints voiced by "Marie," the pseudonym given to the woman interviewed in the pages of the article "A Fighting Battle." Like Donna in *Ourselves Alone*, both times that her husband was arrested "Marie" was left to provide for her children and her husband as well, for he needed to be supplied with clothing (in addition to whatever extras she could afford to send up in parcels) during his first incarceration as a Republican POW with Special Category Status.

The most difficult stresses were not financial, however, but emotional. Like a great many POWs and their partners, in their decision to remain together "Marie" and her husband faced more than a decade of separation from one another. In the introduction to "A Fighting Battle," the editors note that, given her husband's release date, "Marie" expected to spend fourteen of her twenty years of marriage alone before being reunited with him.[112] She encountered all of the trials facing single parents everywhere, yet the nationalist community's expectations surrounding the "proper behavior" of a POW's wife exacerbated the situation further, intensifying the feelings of loneliness and isolation that at times plagued her. "Marie" complains,

> If you did go out with a few friends and were enjoying yourself people would look at you, you're supposed to sit there nice and quiet and not make any noise. Every time you'd move you'd see the eyes following you ... you stand by your husband, go up and visit him—and yet you're not supposed to show any feelings that it's getting to you. At times I feel mad, they wouldn't even ask how are you keeping, it's always "How is he?"[113]

Like the prisoners themselves, partners on the outside often felt a duty—imposed from within and without—to dwell behind an emotionless facade. Republicans both *taoibh amuigh* and *faoi ghlas* at times fashioned this mask as an attempt at self-preservation, a denial of their own grief, but seemingly even more frequently than the POWs (who used it also as a weapon against their captors), the partners' facade was constructed for others' *benefit*, a sacrifice meant to comfort their loved ones and comrades.[114] Falling on this emotional sword has its costs, of course, not least in that it typically impedes real communication and, by extension, real development as an individual, as a couple, and, *An Glór Gafa* argues, as a community. "Marie" reveals that her relationship with her husband began "blooming" as the couple "started to talk more and more openly with one another," directly addressing issues that were previously left unsaid or that were denied, not least of which was the fear of infidelity.[115] In "Marie's" experience, conversations about this emotionally laden topic led to greater trust.

A flurry of responses followed the publication of "A Fighting Battle," perhaps the most radical of which appeared in the next issue of *An Glór Gafa*, an article penned by two Republican women incarcerated in Maghaberry. In "How Free Are Prisoners' Partners?" Mary McArdle and Ailish Carroll point out the sexism at the root of some of the difficulties faced by women such as "Marie": for instance, patriarchal anxiety about female sexuality certainly informs the unwarranted suspicions of "Marie's" infidelity. These anxieties prompt the creation of the omnipresent community surveillance to which she is subject, a panoptic disciplinary field as coercive in its way as the manipulations of visibility inside prison walls. Like the panopticon's victims, "Marie" has internalized some of this discipline and at times polices her own behavior, a response that McArdle and Carroll find understandable but misguided.[116] Making the situation even more frustrating to the women experiencing it are the double standards applied to masculine desire, for, McArdle and Carroll assert, the nationalist community tends to expect and even to excuse male infidelity because males commonly are thought to desire sex more than women. McArdle and Carroll dismiss both the concept of men possessing a naturally greater libido than women as well as the community's acceptance of male infidelity, claiming that

> because sex is predominantly a physical function some people may feel that in order to fulfill a physical need, it can be separated from emotional ties. In Marie's case it may have been possible for her to gain physical comfort and pleasure without threatening the stability of her relationship with Seán. Indeed, by fulfilling her sexual needs, Marie might well have overcome much of the frustration and anger pent up inside her, and so her relationship with Seán could have benefited as a result.[117]

Although unapologetic in putting it forth, McArdle and Carroll stress that the solution outlined above is but one of many options that couples might consider. Yet "How Free Are Prisoners' Partners?" generated fearful and angry responses from some in the Republican community, many of whom appear to have misread the article as a call to reckless "free love" in all instances. Undoubtedly some of this reaction originated in a horror not of infidelity in general, but of *female* infidelity in particular, a sexism firmly embedded in the conservative nationalist archetype of the revolutionary's woman, passively and chastely waiting for her man's return from battle or prison. Critics of the image of the passive female point out its origin in archetypes like the Virgin Mary and Mother Ireland, often deeply rooted in the Irish psyche. Indeed, Mairead Farrell once commented that the Republican women in Armagh Gaol frequently grumbled "Mother Ireland, get off our backs!" when confronted with such sexist presumptions about women and their own participation in the struggle.[118]

While some outside reacted to McArdle and Carroll's article with invective, within the magazine's pages, Paddy Devenny offers a somewhat more balanced critique of "How Free Are Prisoners' Partners?" in his own article "An Encouraging Concept?" which appears in the winter 1993 issue of *An Glór Gafa*. Although Devenny presents himself as one who is willing to entertain and even "accept" McArdle and Carroll's suggestion, he ultimately finds it on pragmatic grounds unlikely to move out of the realm of theory into practice, countering that it requires extraordinary maturity and a complete absence of jealousy on the part of the POW—conditions that in his view may not be possible.[119] More interesting than his skepticism is Devenny's choice of imagery when he anticipates the reaction of the community outside to the suggestion that sex could be separated from emotional ties: such a proposal, he imagines, would draw as much approval "as would a call on the IRA to declare an unconditional and unilateral cease-fire and hand in all its weapons, and for Sinn Féin to submit for a 20-year period of quarantine before even being given a voice in negotiations."[120] In making this statement, Devenny contends that he does not seek to belittle McArdle and Carroll, but rather he merely wishes to point out the extent of "sexual jealousy in society in general."[121] While a subsequent contributor to *An Glór Gafa* criticizes Devenny's comment as a "sarcastic jibe [that] adds nothing to a very worthy debate and simply appears to be included in the absence of constructive criticism,"[122] Devenny's choice of simile at least is useful to remind readers of the extent to which the armed struggle and the "waiting woman" continue to share a history.

POWs continued to educate one another about this issue, as revealed in the final issue of *An Glór Gafa*, which appeared in the summer of 1999. In the last year that the H Blocks functioned as a prison, Republican POWs were able to view the play *Just a Prisoner's Wife*, an all-female community production first shown in March 1996 in the Felon's Club in the heart of Republican West Belfast. *Just a Prisoner's Wife* dramatizes the struggles faced by women whose partners are incarcerated in political prisons in the Six Counties: similar to McKeown's short story "The Visit," this play includes a scene in which a woman reveals to her friends her romantic involvement with someone other than her husband. Crucially, her companions do not condemn her for her actions: an understanding reaction shared by the male POW who coauthored with a cast member (and former POW) an article about the performance of the play in B Wing H5. The coauthorship of the article "Just a Prisoner's Wife" exemplifies yet again *An Glór Gafa*'s commitment to the crossing of borders, to the reuniting of *faoi ghlas* and *taoibh amuigh*.[123]

Like contemporary Provisional Republicanism itself, Provisional prison writing at times evinces continuities with traditional Republican ideology, while at other times departing radically from those traditions. As incarcerated Republican authors knew, prison writing can assist not only in healing a traumatized history (whether personal, local, national, or international), but also in constructing new identities for the future. The progressive strides evident in the pages of *An Glór Gafa* show us that Provisionals are not merely interested in some mythic past (as some writers have mischaracterized them); more frequently, tangible issues of social justice form the core of these writings. Indeed, the Provisionals' progressive public stance on many of these concerns, including gender equality and gay rights, puts that of many—if not most—politicians in the United States to shame, even among the so-called liberal Democrats. Similarly, the POWs' drive towards Freirean praxis mirrors (and in some cases, predates) recent attempts in academia to eliminate what Freire terms the "banking system of education" that is based on learning by rote as opposed to critical thinking and engagement with the world.

Literature is not a mere pastime to prisoners like Bobby Sands, but frequently a means to survive the often brutal environment that surrounds them. Writing provides an opportunity for POWs to regain agency through discourse, not only allowing prisoners to reassert control over the way in which they are represented, but also inspiring active solidarity among the population outside when their texts are smuggled out and published. Texts by Republican POWs can provide a lesson to all that the composition and study of literature need not be viewed as passive activities. As these prison authors knew, our own lives and the world surrounding us are shaped by the texts we read, by *how* we read them, as well as by our own discursive skills: a lesson that everyone, not just university students, should learn. As the Republican POWs discovered, the ability to read and write critically contains within it a power that can be put to use in everyday settings to shape our lives in positive ways. Writing itself can be resistance.

Chapter Six

Postscript: "You Look Like Jesus Christ": Images of Republican POWs in Contemporary Cinema

Midway through the film *Some Mother's Son*, Gerard—a newly incarcerated Irish Republican Army prisoner—is shocked at Bobby Sands' appearance. It is 1980—the height of the Blanket and No-Wash Protests for political status in the H Blocks. Though his reputation precedes him as officer commanding (OC) of the Republican prisoners in the H Blocks, Sands's scraggly beard and long hair make him unrecognizable to Gerard. "Do I look that bad?" Sands asks his new cellmate with a chuckle. "You look like Jesus Christ!" replies Gerard, only half-joking, his smile dissolving into a look of startled concern.[1]

In this moment, *Some Mother's Son* enters the debate surrounding the contested iconography of the Troubles at one of its most volatile flashpoints—the representation of Republican prisoners. In large part, the conflict in contemporary Irish prisons such as Long Kesh was (and is) one of definition: are Republican paramilitary prisoners religious zealots, common criminals, terrorists, prisoners of war, holy martyrs, or some uncomfortable combination of these identities? A number of recent films have grappled with this topic and come to very different conclusions about how Republican paramilitary prisoners should be defined. For example, the Irish prison experience occupies a central position in two of Jim Sheridan's films, the aforementioned *Some Mothers' Son* as well as *In the Name of the Father*,[2] two films that sparked international controversy in their treatment of issues related to the contemporary conflict in Ireland.

It is primarily through the key figure of the Irish Republican Army leader—the officer commanding—that these two films articulate their stance regarding Republican prisoners, and by extension, Republicanism in general. What is surprising about the films' representations of IRA prisoners is the degree to which they fetishize and in some cases *glorify* Republican POWs even as they simultaneously remain hostile to Republican ideology. Although both films indict

Republicanism for being more akin to a theology than a political ideology, ironically each does so by depicting IRA OCs using overtly Christian signifiers. Moreover, when the two cinematic IRA leaders are examined side by side, the strikingly self-contradictory nature of the films' use of Christian iconography is evident: the peculiar hagiography of Bobby Sands in *Some Mother*'s *Son* stands in diametric opposition to *In the Name of the Father's* demonization of Joe McAndrews, the IRA OC possessed by a paradoxically passionless bloodlust.

On the surface, it seems puzzling that *In the Name of the Father* and *Some Mother's Son*—two films whose screenplays were authored in whole or in part by the same Irish filmmaker[3]—present such contradictory visions of Republican prisoners; however, I argue that such contradictory images in Sheridan's films offer a telling glimpse into contemporary Ireland's schizophrenia with regard to the national question in general and Republicanism in particular. In the minds of many observers—particularly writers and artists from the Twenty-Six Counties—it is not that Republican prisoners are either holy martyrs or cold-blooded killers: paradoxically, Republicans often seem to be envisioned as occupying *both* identities simultaneously.

In Ireland, jail semiotics have far-reaching consequences, as the Republican prison struggle is an extension of the wider politicomilitary struggle. Legitimacy conferred to Republican prisoners will be by extension conferred also to Republican groups outside jail walls (and vice-versa), and it was precisely this realization that prompted the British government's ending of Special Category Status in 1976. As outlined in detail in chapters two and three, Special Category Status granted prisoner-of-war status in all but name to those inmates who had been detained for political offences (or suspected political offenses)[4] committed prior to 1 March 1976. Prior to this date, in the North of Ireland, the vast majority of male political prisoners were incarcerated in the Cages of Long Kesh, a prison compound whose watchtowers and barbed-wire-surrounded Nissen huts were reminiscent of the prisoner-of-war camps of World War II. POWs incarcerated in the Republican Cages followed a military chain of command, each led by an officer commanding. In the short story "Early Risers,"[5] Gerry Adams (who before his rise to prominence as president of Sinn Féin served time in Long Kesh as both an internee and a sentenced prisoner) elaborates on this command structure in the Cages, noting that it was "very formal and militaristic, but that's the way prison camp is. We elect an OC and he selects a staff that includes an adjutant, an

IO [Intelligence Officer] a quartermaster and various other dignitaries."[6] Within the confines of the Cages, the prisoners were responsible as individuals only to their officers, not to individual "screws" (warders): relations between prison officials and POWs were negotiated only through the camp or individual Cage OC. Another of the most important components of Special Category Status was that prisoners were granted the right to wear their own clothes rather than the prison uniform, an act that to the Republicans symbolized institutional recognition of the political—rather than the criminal—nature of their confinement.

The elimination of Special Category Status reveals the extent to which both insurrection and counterinsurgency are as much semiotic as military in nature: by redefining Republican prisoners as criminals rather than guerillas, the British government sought to contain dissent by controlling discourse. Offenders sentenced for offenses committed after 1 March 1976 would no longer be allowed to wear their own clothes but would instead be required to wear prison uniform. Similarly, prison officers in the H Blocks refused to recognize Republican command structures and dealt with prisoners on an individual basis, without regard to paramilitary affiliation (if any). After the communal imprisonment of the Cages—where as many as thirty men would share a single hut—ended, prisoners were incarcerated individually or in pairs in the cells of the H Blocks, cells constructed specifically for the purpose. The spatial organization of the H Blocks reflected the new stance of the government: Republicans became individual felons by this definition (or at best, members of a criminal conspiracy), not members of guerilla armies. Such individuation also was part of another counterinsurgency strategy, for, by cutting off contact in panoptic fashion with other members of the group (either specifically paramilitary or broadly Republican), the prison authorities sought to break individual resistance to the system through the despair of isolation.

In response, Republicans began what came to be known as the Blanket Protest: refusing the prison uniform and the criminality that it embodied to them, Republican POWs clad themselves only in prison-issued blankets. Eventually the situation would intensify into the No-Wash Protest, where, in response to increased brutality by their warders, the Republicans first refused to clean out their cells and then to leave the cells to use shower facilities; finally, after being "denied access to the toilet"[7] by the guards, the POWs resorted to pouring their urine on the floor and smearing their excrement on the walls.[8]

Ultimately, the Republicans escalated their protest to the extremity of two hunger strikes, the second of which ended in 1981 with Bobby Sands and nine other Republican POWs fasting to death in an attempt to regain the political status that ended in 1976. It is this period, culminating in the fatal hunger strike of 1981, that continues to be the fulcrum on which opposing discourses regarding Irish Republican prisoners are levered.

Some Mother's Son (1996) is one of the very few feature-length films released internationally in which the narrative centers on the H Block prison struggle.[9] On one level, *Some Mother's Son* is a study of the relationship between two women of dramatically different backgrounds and ideologies thrown together by their sons' imprisonment for IRA activities; however, like the H Block protests that provide a backdrop for its narrative, *Some Mother's Son* at its heart is an examination of Republican legitimacy seen through prison bars. In large part, the film articulates its view of Republicans through its construction of Bobby Sands.

The Bobby Sands we encounter in *Some Mother's Son* is more nuanced than the figure Ruth Barton describes as the "classic psychopath" typical of most cinematic depictions of IRA leaders.[10] As the film accurately dramatizes, Bobby Sands was the officer commanding of the IRA prisoners in the H Blocks of Long Kesh immediately prior to the 1981 hunger strikes. The historical Sands had been sentenced to fourteen years in September 1977, and because his arrest and sentencing took place after 1 March 1976, he was not given Special Category Status in the Cages. Instead, Sands was incarcerated in the H Blocks where the Blanket Protest was well underway. In the H Blocks, Sands proved an even more prolific writer than he had been during an earlier imprisonment in the Cages, penning poems, short stories, and political essays that were smuggled out of prison and printed in Republican newspapers.[11] Just as he did during his prior incarceration, Sands continued to contribute to the development of Republican dialectics in the H Blocks.[12] By all accounts, Sands was at the forefront of creating a formal system of education in the Republican wings that centered on "a culture of discussion," to utilize the words of Dr. Laurence McKeown who was himself on the 1981 hunger strike with Sands.[13]

This pedagogy had lasting effects on the vertical hierarchy and exclusively military focus that had been present in older Republican command structures in Long Kesh: many Republican POWs had found these earlier structures excessively rigid and had argued that they discouraged innovation. For instance, inmates such as Gerry

Kelly—who became a Republican leader both during and after incarceration—questioned the compulsory nature of physical exercise in the Republican Cages:

> People can get in the doldrums so there was the belief that there was a responsibility to keep people in trim. But these things go in phases. If someone is doing a life sentence you can depress them by making them train two or three times a week. When we eventually stopped compulsory training we found most people continued with it anyhow.[14]

Similarly, Brendan Hughes, who would later be OC of the H Blocks and leader of the 1980 hunger strike, points out that some important IRA officers in the Cages actually "came from a British Army background and they used to send round these wee manuals. I couldn't stick all that stuff, being trained as non-thinking combatants. You weren't allowed to think."[15] In contrast, Sands's fellow POWs note that, as a result of the policies that Sands and others implemented, prisoners in the H Blocks "openly debated policies and orthodox republican beliefs," noting that "men were not prepared to just blindly 'follow a leader' or meekly 'obey orders.' They were going to question what they did not agree with or what had not been fully explained to them."[16] As OC of the H Blocks, Sands continued to redefine the role of OC into one of "first among equals."

Disregarding completely the accounts of those actually incarcerated with Bobby Sands, *Some Mother*'s *Son*'s fictitious Bobby Sands is wedded to a hierarchical command rooted in the physical. One scene depicts Sands rising at dawn to lead the POWs under his command in a series of calisthenics, his subordinates groaning as he announces each new exercise. "Jesus," moans one Republican, "[Sands] takes this prisoner-of-war stuff very serious." Despite his small frame, Sands is physically unstoppable, a quality brought into sharp relief by the complaints of his noticeably more muscular comrades. "What's the fuckin' point? We're not going anywhere," questions Gerard as they exercise. "We have to keep our discipline," replies Sands quietly, "Come on, stop talking and do the dips."

Screenwriters Jim Sheridan and Terry George may have intended this scene to be a sympathetic portrayal of Sands and the Republican POWs—after all, George himself was a Republican prisoner in the Cages in the early 1970s. By leading his comrades in the calisthenics, Sands is shown not as a common criminal content to meekly serve his time via the path of least resistance, but rather as a leader who is indeed committed to a continuation of the Republican struggle within jail walls, if only in symbolic military fashion. Yet, I maintain that however well-intentioned the characterization of Bobby Sands in *Some Mother's Son* may be, in this "calisthenics scene," the film perpetuates one of the most commonplace stereotypes about Republicans that remain in currency: the erroneous belief that contemporary Republicanism never proceeds beyond a military, physical-force tradition. As the previous quotes from Sands's comrades (and the third and fifth chapter of this book) underscore, the historical Bobby Sands had a rather vexed relationship with the sort of conservative Republicanism that *Some Mother's Son* depicts him as spearheading. However benevolently enforced, both the compulsory training and the order to "be quiet and do the dips" fashion the cinematic Sands into exactly the sort of OC that the historical Sands and his comrades had begun, in private, to deconstruct.[17]

The "calisthenics scene" is symptomatic of *Some Mother's Son*'s wider preoccupation with the corporeal: whatever limited legitimacy the film accords to Republicans proceeds not primarily from the POWs' ideals, but rather from a respect for their physical prowess, their ability to endure. It is not the POWs' intellect or political acumen that is valued but their physical presence, or rather their ability to transcend the brute matter of their bodies. For instance, despite Sands's extensive corpus of prison writing, *Some Mother's Son* never provides a glimpse of Sands in the act of writing. One scene does represent Sands as author of a communiqué to the Republican leadership outside; tellingly however, this is not one of his literary works but rather a utilitarian message warning of the impending hunger strike. In this moment *Some Mother's Son* again fashions Bobby Sands solely in a physical-force military role, not as a Republican poet and prison intellectual.

In its dramatization of the 1981 hunger strike, *Some Mother's Son* again fetishizes the physical, though interesting tensions surface in these scenes as a result of the use of Christological motifs. As the scene with which I open this chapter demonstrates, the film constructs Sands as a Christ-figure from his first appearance, and in fairness, the long hair and beards of the Blanketmen are reminiscent of traditional representations of Christ. Yet, the fact that Sheridan and George consciously, and without a trace of irony, invoke Christian iconography in the dialogue cannot be ignored, particularly given that, as the historical Sands reveals in the diary he kept on his hunger strike, on 17 March 1981, "mo chuid gruaige gearrtha agam níos gaire, agus é i bfhad níos fearr freisin"[18]: as the anonymous editor translates it, Sands relates that he had "my hair cut shorter and much better also."[19] Despite

Sands's own testimony that he received a haircut, *Some Mother's Son* insists on constructing a shaggy-haired OC, an attempt to recruit sympathy on a human—not a political or ideological—level for the Republican POWs by eliding the physical appearance of Sands with traditional images of the tortured Christ.[20]

While the film categorically rejects violence of any sort (and indeed frequently calls into question the legitimacy of Republican ideology), it doggedly insists on the essential humanity of those who have engaged in political violence. *Some Mother's Son* emphasizes the sufferings that those on hunger strike endured, dramatizing Sands's physical decline in horrifying detail: first, we are shown Sands sleeping on his prison bed, his livid skin and labored breathing the first symptoms of his deterioration. In a subsequent scene, Sands is transferred to the prison hospital. Though Sands must be carried from his bed into a wheelchair, his cellmate Gerard refuses to let the prison orderly touch Sands and as Gerard labors to lift the incapacitated man Sands cries out in agony, his head lolling on Gerard's shoulder. Even the hardened prison officer who had previously threatened the POWs with his nightstick is moved by Sands's anguish, the camera moving briefly to a close-up of the guard's sympathetic expression as Gerard struggles with his task. Despite his obvious torment, Sands remains firm: his eyes clear and focused, Sands whispers, "I won't let you down," as he is wheeled backward out of the cell. Both Gerard and Bobby know that it is the last time they will see one another.

The sheer magnitude of the suffering Sands must have endured in his final weeks is represented in several brief scenes: when a visiting priest brings Sands news that he has been elected to British parliament, Sands has lost his vision, his milky eyes searching in vain for the source of the voice addressing him. Upon hearing the news that the British government will make no concessions to the prisoners despite his victory, Sands rasps, "I will see this through—to the end." In an extended scene of Sands on his death-bed surrounded by vulture-like priests in black—the camera lingering over his emaciated corpse as it is given extreme unction—and in the dramatization of the horrifying seizures another hunger striker endures immediately prior to death, *Some Mother's Son* again foregrounds Sands's physicality. Sands is indeed a secular Christ in *Some Mother's Son*, a point driven home by Harrington, a British Home Office official, who reflects on "the role of Irish martyrs in history," commenting that in allowing Sands to die the intransigent Thatcher regime has "created another one," a statement that echoes the iconography of a political mural seen in the background of an earlier scene. In the mural, a long-haired, bearded POW hangs crucified on the bars of a Union Jack.

Some Mother's Son's Bobby Sands exposes some of the contradictions in popular images of Republicans. On the one hand, the film critiques the presumed inability of Republicans to engage in anything but physical resistance: the executions of two prison officers (one in front of his wife and son) are presented in garish detail, and the horrors and hopelessness of the hunger strikers' declines are catalogued in near-voyeuristic detail. Yet, the film is unable to completely dismiss the sacrifice made by the hunger strikers, and it is precisely the graphic depiction of the grim physicality of the hunger strike that evokes sympathy for the suffering POWs. Instead of creating a sympathetic Sands by foregrounding his progressive leadership or his literary activity, ironically in order to provide evidence of Sands's praiseworthiness, the film ultimately turns to the paramilitary activity that it has condemned—the hunger strike, after all was considered a weapon by those who engaged in it. Even more, *Some Mother's Son* fashions Sands as much more of a religious—rather than political—martyr than most contemporary Republicans themselves would claim.

In sharp contrast to the relatively sympathetic portrayal of Bobby Sands in *Some Mother's Son*, *In the Name of the Father*'s vision of an IRA OC is one that seems to owe much to the official line of the British government regarding Republicans after 1 March 1976. As Liz Curtis notes in *Ireland: The Propaganda War*, after the removal of Special Category Status, Republicans and Republican paramilitaries alike were termed common criminals both by the British government as well as by the press. Curtis maintains,

> The word "godfathers" entered the lexicon of reporters describing the IRA in the mid-seventies. This mafia metaphor gained currency during the term of office of Labour Northern Ireland Secretary Roy Mason, whose strategy was to deal with the IRA revolt as if it were a purely criminal matter.[21]

This vocabulary invoking images of organized crime—rather than groups with primarily political motivation—is one insistently present in the iconography of *In the Name of the Father.* Likewise, never do we hear the use of Republican paramilitary terminology regarding command structures, even by IRA men: there are no OCs anywhere in this film, only bullying gang leaders. From the first moment that the IRA leader Joe McAndrews enters *In the Name of the Father,* this Mafioso stereotype is invoked, though with interesting variations.

We initially encounter McAndrews in police custody, as he listens impassively to the long list of violent offences with which he is being charged, staring steely-eyed and unflinchingly at his captors. Unlike Gerry and Guiseppe Conlon (the son and father on whom the film centers), he is unambiguously guilty of the crimes of which he is accused. Indeed, in this scene, we discover that it is McAndrews's actions that have caused the Conlons all their grief, for when the police officer finishes reading the charges, McAndrews adds one more to the list: "And the Guilford pub bombings. You've innocent people in jail for that." These are the very attacks for which the Conlons have been wrongfully imprisoned, yet McAndrews's statement is not a confession in the psychological sense of the term. Clearly McAndrews feels no remorse for his actions in Guilford, for in his view, as he later tells Gerry and Guiseppe, "it was a military target: a soldiers' pub." The larger cinematic narrative presented by the film pushes the audience to disagree through a recurring image of one of the last people to enter the pub prior to the explosion: a young, clearly civilian woman, whose purse we later see amid the scattered, flaming debris of the bombed pub. Similarly, when detectives toss crime-scene and autopsy photos in front of Gerry Conlon in their early attempts to force a confession from him, like the detectives, director Sheridan has chosen to display pictures of dead women to drive home the depravity of McAndrews's act, depravity made all the more reprehensible by McAndrews's refusal to see the bombing as anything but a military action.

While such visuals are none-too-subtle indictments of McAndrews, one of the most explicit rejections of the IRA prisoner comes from Guiseppe Conlon, the moral centre of *In the Name of the Father*, who replies fiercely that the victims of the bombing were "innocent people—God's children," subsequently demanding that McAndrews not speak with him again. This word choice is crucial for, as Martin McLoone correctly argues, *In the Name of the Father* "is one of the most overtly Christian films to emerge in popular [Irish] cinema in recent years."[22] If there is a Christ-figure in the film who though innocent of any crime suffers persecution it is certainly Guiseppe, whose immense patience and pacifism stand in stark contrast to McAndrews's violence. Guiseppe's suffering is both psychological and physical, for his incarceration dramatically worsens his preexisting health problems. The prison authorities refuse to give Guiseppe compassionate parole despite his obvious physical deterioration, and he eventually dies in prison as a result. Indeed, in the prisoners' view, the authorities bear direct responsibility for Guiseppe's demise, one prisoner shouting, "Guiseppe is dead! They killed Guiseppe!" as the prison wing pays tribute by tossing lit papers from their cell windows, one of the most striking visuals of the film.

In diametric opposition to Guiseppe, Sheridan constructs McAndrews as an archetypal gangster, as much motivated by personal vendettas as he is by militant Republicanism. McAndrews's criminal pathology is written even in his physical appearance: like the audience, the prisoners note the cold cruelty inscribed on his face. Upon McAndrews's first appearance in the prison, a Caribbean inmate points him out to the younger Conlon. As McAndrews pauses at the top of a prison landing to survey the common room with, to borrow Yeats's phrasing, "a gaze as blank and pitiless as the sun," the Caribbean prisoner remarks, "Him look like the real thing": that is, unlike the innocent Conlons, McAndrews, by his very physicality, is self-evidently an Irish terrorist.

There is, of course, a great deal of irony in the fact that this line is spoken by Benjamin Bailey, a man of Afro-Caribbean descent, especially as in other moments in the film he is used to signify the oppressed postcolonial "other" in solidarity with the Irish colonial experience. Sheridan creates this inmate as a prototypically postcolonial subject almost from his initial overtures to Gerry. Recognizing that anti-Irish prejudice isolates Gerry from almost everyone in the prison, Bailey extends a helping, similarly subaltern hand and strikes up a conversation with the young Conlon. His friendship also integrates Gerry into a small network of like-minded Rasta-types. Though Sheridan presents Gerry's new friends primarily as escapist drug-users, the humorous irony in their method of intoxication reveals at least a degree of political awareness on their part: they ingest pieces of a jigsaw-puzzle map of the British Empire that has been dipped in LSD. In the words of Conlon's new-found friend, the Rastas have been "dropping the British Empire for the last six months." Similar postcolonial critique occurs elsewhere in the film. For instance, during the prison protest described above, another black inmate covers himself with white paint, and on a towel around his waist he paints the words "I demand white man's justice."

I find it puzzling that *In the Name of the Father* critiques prejudice originating in physical appearance in this case but ignores the visible essentialism inherent in the creation of the character of McAndrews. We might expect more care with regard to essentialist statements about physical appearance from a character who suffers at the hands of a prejudiced institution. Unfortunately, however, by reinscribing moral characteristics in physical ones, *In the Name of the Father* unwittingly perpetuates bigoted visual stereotypes of the Irish that trace their origin to nineteenth-century images of violent, simian Hibernians, perhaps most famously disseminated by the magazine *Punch*. By deliberately calling attention to McAndrews's villainous phrenology, the film moves well beyond the tired trope of casting a sinister-looking actor to play a sinister role and dangerously near to essentialism, if not racism. Of course, those prejudices are precisely the ones that the British government exploited during the "criminalization" campaign following the revocation of Special Category Status: if a certain misguided minority of the British population already believed that the Irish are physically predisposed to violence, it is that much easier to recast a guerilla campaign as an apolitical criminal conspiracy.

Though, as McLoone argues, the film does paint a more complex view of Republican paramilitaries than is often discerned by critics,[23] I must disagree with his claim that *In the Name of the Father* rejects the IRA prisoner McAndrews "not on the grounds of his criminality" but rather as a result of "his chilling and uncompromising politics."[24] I concur in part that "McAndrew's [*sic*] political acumen is well established...when he effectively organizes the disparate prisoners into collective action to protest prison conditions":[25] *In the Name of the Father* does indeed present McAndrews as someone with *some* politics. However, the film suggests that McAndrews undermines such potentially constructive passive resistance with his pathological need for bloodshed, a psychosis that moves well beyond militant politics into criminal insanity. We witness such behavior from McAndrews on many occasions. For instance, criticizing the sit-in, Guiseppe warns McAndrews that "It will end in violence," to which the IRA prisoner responds impassively, "Good." Blood-lust of this nature hardly demonstrates real political acumen: McAndrews is a sadist, not someone engaged in uncompromising *realpolitik*.

Indeed, I maintain that via McAndrews *In the Name of the Father* represents Republicans as ultimately motivated by personal grudges rather than by political analysis. Simply put, the demonic presence of McAndrews completely effaces the more nuanced image of Republican paramilitaries the film presents in its opening sequences. McAndrews is at his most violently evil in those moments when he uses politics as a cover for personal vendettas, and *In the Name of the Father* reserves its harshest criticism for the IRA prisoner when he acts accordingly. To illustrate, when the peaceful sit-in does indeed elicit a heavy-handed response from the authorities, in a voice-over Gerry tells us that McAndrews "never forgave" the chief prison officer for calling in the riot squad, a personal blood feud that McLoone ignores. The cinematic

Conlon's word-choice is revealing: no hint of Christ-like—or even human—capacity for forgiveness evinces itself in McAndrews. Immediately after the protest is squashed the IRA man hatches a plan to exact revenge on the warder, an attack that tellingly takes place in the prison common room during a screening of the film *The Godfather*. In perhaps the most horrifying visual sequence of the film, the chief prison officer—with whom the audience develops sympathy through his genial interactions with Guiseppe, and who we learn is a father of two—is set alight by McAndrews's improvised blowtorch. Engulfed in fire, the prison officer rushes about the room; the audience is shown a terrifying close-up of his face, panicked and blistering in the flames. Gerry Conlon eventually smothers the fire with a blanket and the camera lingers over the smoldering figure of the prison officer, twitching as he goes into shock. As the smoke literally clears, McAndrews is rejected by both Gerry Conlon and—just as importantly in terms of the wider postcolonial implications—immediately afterward by Gerry's friend, the Caribbean subaltern Benjamin Bailey. *In the Name of the Father* thus implicitly dismisses any claims the IRA might have to solidarity with other postcolonial groups elsewhere in the world.

Even having observed a scene as horrific as this, one can only perceive the extent to which *In the Name of the Father* perpetuates the image of the psychopathic IRA godfather by turning to Gerry Conlon's autobiography. In it, Conlon presents the reader with an image of actual IRA prisoners in diametric opposition to that of the cinematic McAndrews. Conlon writes,

> Republican prisoners are different from other prisoners, because they are not there for personal gain and they are not freaks. That sets them apart from everyone else. They are generally very disciplined. They don't involve themselves in the pettiness of much of prison life, such as setting up complicated attacks on the nonces [sexual offenders], and grudge attacks on the screws [warders] or other prisoners.[26]

Indeed, the brutal attack on the prison officer so powerfully depicted in the film never actually occurred. Sheridan must construct a fictional attack, not reenact one taken from actual events in Conlon's life[27]: in fact, McAndrews is a Frankenstein composite of the propaganda accompanying the British government's ending of Special Category Status in British prisons. In the creation of such a monster, Sheridan perhaps attempted to preclude accusations that his film was somehow "pro-IRA," a ridiculous claim that some critics—notable among them, Conor Cruise O'Brien—still made despite the clear dismissal of McAndrews by all of the central characters. McAndrews proves to be a gangster rather than a guerilla, and worse: like Yeats's slouching beast, he is not a messiah but an anti-Christ, filling the prison with the prideful flames of his own hell on earth.

Yet despite their apparent dissimilarities, I argue that Joe McAndrews and the cinematic Bobby Sands in fact are *not* two separate characters proceeding from two disparate areas of Ireland's filmic unconscious. The fixation of both films on the physicality of the IRA OC suggests a certain weariness of the complex horrors of the conflict in Ireland, a longing for a certainty mapped out in the corporeal: good or evil defined materially, easily recognized by visual signs. Yet within this desire lurks the uncomfortable knowledge that all human nature is capable at turns of violence and transcendence, all cartography is limited. To Sheridan and George, the Provisionals in *Some Mother's Son* and *In the Name of the Father* ultimately represent the provisional and the contingent, the fearful uncertainty of nation.

Notes

Chapter One Introduction: *Taoibh Amuigh agus Faoi Ghlas:* The Counter-aesthetics of Republican Prison Writing

1. Gerry Adams, "The Fire," *Cage Eleven* (Dingle: Brandon, 1990) 37.
2. Ibid., 46.
3. Pat Magee, *Gangsters or Guerillas?* (Belfast: Beyond the Pale, 2001) v.
4. David Pierce, ed., Introduction, *Irish Writing in the Twentieth Century: A Reader* (Cork: Cork University Press, 2000) xl.
5. Ibid.
6. Shiela Roberts, "South African Prison Literature," *Ariel* 16.2 (Apr. 1985): 61.
7. Michel Foucault, "Power and Strategies," *Power/Knowledge: Selected Interviews and Other Writings, 1972–1977*, ed. Colin Gordon (New York: Pantheon, 1980) 141–2.
8. In "The Eye of Power," for instance, Foucault argues, "The tendency of Bentham's thought [in designing prisons such as the famed Panopticon] is archaic in the importance it gives to the gaze." In *Power/ Knowledge* 160.
9. Breyten Breytenbach, *The True Confessions of an Albino Terrorist* (New York: Farrar, Straus & Giroux, 1983) 147.
10. Ioan Davies, *Writers in Prison* (Cambridge, MA: Blackwell, 1990) 4.
11. Ibid.
12. William Wordsworth, "Preface to Lyrical Ballads," *The Norton Anthology of English Literature* vol. 2A, 7th edition, ed. M. H. Abrams et al. (New York: W. W. Norton, 2000) 250.
13. Gerry Adams, "Inside Story," *Republican News* 16 Aug. 1975: 6.
14. Gerry Adams, "Cage Eleven," *Cage Eleven* (Dingle: Brandon, 1990) 20.
15. Wordsworth, "Preface" 249.
16. Ibid., 250.
17. Ibid.
18. Terry Eagleton, *The Ideology of the Aesthetic* (Cambridge, MA: Blackwell, 1990) 27.
19. W. B. Yeats, *Essays and Introductions* (New York: Macmillan, 1961) 521–2.
20. Bobby Sands, *One Day in My Life* (Dublin and Cork: Mercier, 1983) 98.

21. Certainly others may edit such work. However, I have found few examples of what textual scholars such as G. Thomas Tanselle term "substantive" changes (word-level, as opposed to "accidentals," punctuation, capitalization, and spelling) made between the initial, anonymous publication of Sands's texts in *An Phoblacht/Republican News* and the versions that were published after his death. [G. Thomas Tanselle, *Textual Criticism and Scholarly Editing* (University Press of Virginia, 1990) 191.] A more detailed examination of the textual history of Sands's prison writing takes place in chapter three.
22. W. B. Yeats, "Introduction," *The Oxford Book of Modern Verse* (New York: Oxford University Press, 1937) xxxiv.
23. Ibid.
24. Ibid.
25. Wordsworth, "Preface" 246.
26. Edna Longley, "From *Poetry in the Wars*," *The Field Day Anthology of Irish Writing*. vol. 3, ed. Seamus Deane (Derry: Field Day, 1991) 648.
27. Edna Longley, *The Living Stream* (London: Bloodaxe, 1993) 9.
28. Ibid.
29. Longley, "From *Poetry*" 648.
30. Terry Eagleton, "Nationalism: Irony and Commitment," *Nationalism, Colonialism, and Literature* (Minneapolis: Minnesota University Press, 1990) 33.
31. Frank Ormsby, "Introduction," *Poets from the North of Ireland* (Belfast: Blackstaff Press, 1990) 20.
32. Gerry Adams, "Inside Story," *Republican News* 16 Aug. 1975: 6.
33. Section 31 was repressive legislation passed in the Twenty-Six Counties to censor points of view that the government found dangerous.
34. Tim Pat Coogan, *The IRA* (Niwot, CO: Roberts Rinehart, 1994): 238.
35. While perhaps this nomenclature might evoke a chuckle, interstices of neoconservative political and literary interests such as Ireland's Section 31 continue to threaten academic freedom elsewhere, including the United States. The International Studies in Higher Education Act, for instance, which was approved by the U.S. House of Representatives in 2004, calls for the establishment of what it terms an "International Education Advisory Board," two members of which would be agents of, to quote the act itself, "federal agencies that have national security responsibilities." This board would recommend to the federal government, again in the words of the act, ways "to improve the [university] programs under this Title to better reflect the national needs related to homeland security." [Qtd. in Laurie King-Irani, "We Aren't the World," *In These Times*. 28: 3 2004: par. 7.] Does the wording of this act not threaten an iron fist in a velvet literary canon?
36. Anthony McIntyre, for example, has termed himself a "dissident Provisional republican [*sic*]," and has been sharply critical of Sinn Féin and the Provisional IRA. [Anthony McIntyre, "Provisional Republicanism: Internal Politics, Inequities and Modes of Repression," *Republicanism*

in Modern Ireland, ed. Fearghal McGarry (Dublin: University College Dublin Press, 2003) 181.] McIntyre left the Provisionals after they accepted the Good Friday Agreement.

37. Other Republican groups also wrote while in prison, though their literary output seems to have been more limited. In the Cages of Long Kesh in the mid-1970s, the Officials produced a publication entirely by prisoners called *An Eochair*.
38. Anthony McIntyre, Laurence McKeown, Pat Magee, and Ella O'Dwyer all have doctorates.

Chapter Two "Our Barbed Wire Ivory Tower": The Cages of Long Kesh

1. Speakers of Irish Gaelic will immediately note the grammatical error in the magazine's title: in standard Irish "glas" should be affected by *séimhiú* (lenition). The error might trace its origin to a misreading of older Irish typescripts that indicate *séimhiú* with a diacritical mark: "ġlas" in the old typescript = "ghlas" in the modernized orthography.
2. Colm Keena, *A Biography of Gerry Adams* (Dublin and Cork: Mercier, 1990) 64.
3. "Out of the Ashes," *An Phoblacht/Republican News* 27 Jan. 1979: 1.
4. Keena, *Biography* 65.
5. This overcrowding is predictable given the sheer number of people interned. On the first day internment was reintroduced in the north (9 Aug. 1971), 342 men were arrested, all from a Nationalist/Catholic background [Raymond Murray, *State Violence: Northern Ireland 1969–1997* (Cork and Dublin: Mercier, 1998) 41]. By Mar. 1972 the number of internees had reached 2,357, again the vast majority of whom were Catholic/Nationalist [Allen Feldman, *Formations of Violence* (Chicago: University of Chicago Press, 1991) 86].
6. "Brownie" (Gerry Adams), "Inside Story," *Republican News* 16 Aug. 1975: 6.
7. Michel Foucault, *Discipline and Punish* (New York: Vintage, 1979) 202.
8. Although most of Adams's writings in *Cage Eleven* are near-verbatim reproductions of the *Republican News* articles, some of the stories contained in this anthology evince much editing. For instance, the bulk of "Cage Eleven" is drawn word-for-word from "Inside Story," though in its brief description of the shooting of an inmate it alludes to topics dealt with in greater depth in "Out There on the Motorway," the second article by "Brownie." *Cage Eleven* also includes several texts that did not appear in *Republican News*.
9. Gerry Adams, Foreword, *Cage Eleven* (Dingle: Brandon, 1990) 10–11.
10. Laurence McKeown, *Out of Time: Irish Republican Prisoners Long Kesh 1972–2000* (Belfast: Beyond the Pale, 2001) 177.

11. Adams, foreword, *Cage Eleven* 13.
12. Ciaran Carson, "Question Time," *Belfast Confetti* (Winston-Salem: Wake Forest University Press, 1989) 63.
13. Ibid.
14. Adams, foreword, *Cage Eleven* 13.
15. Liz Curtis, *Ireland: The Propaganda War* (Belfast: Sásta, 1998) 289–90.
16. Ibid.
17. Adams, "Cage Eleven" 16.
18. The word "screw" is derogatory prison slang for a warder. A prison historian and a former H Block guard himself, Jim Challis traces the term's origin to Pentonville Prison in the 1840s where a machine called "the Crank" was put to penal use. It was precisely what its name implied: "a handle attached to a gear and counting mechanism. The handle had to be turned 20 times a minute—10,000 times a day—and, if the going got too easy, a screw could be tightened to control the pressure to make it harder to turn." Jim Challis, *The Northern Ireland Prison Service 1920–1990: A History* (Belfast: The Northern Ireland Prison Service, 1999) 123. It is not surprising that Republican prisoners would readily incorporate this clever metonymy into their everyday vocabulary. This is yet another example of how Republican POWs view prison officers as almost literally a part of a larger disciplinary machine.
19. Qtd. in personal email to author.
20. Kieran McEvoy, *Paramilitary Imprisonment in Northern Ireland* (New York: Oxford University Press, 2001) 219.
21. Henri Lefebvre, *The Production of Space* (Cambridge: Blackwell, 1991) 165.
22. Ibid., 374.
23. Indeed, the move from the "Cage" system to individual cellular incarceration in the H Blocks in 1976 demonstrates the shift by the British government to a more explicitly panoptic regime of the sort theorized by Bentham. Such a move was motivated in part by a desire to break and delegitimize Republican solidarity, both in terms of command structure as well as morale. When Foucault writes that in panoptic disciplinary structures "The crowd, a compact mass, a locus of mutual exchanges, individualities merging together, a collective effect, is abolished and replaced by a collection of separated individualities" [Foucault, *Discipline* 201], it is difficult not to think of the cells of the H Blocks and the move to "criminalize" political offenders when Special Category Status is no longer given to those sentenced after 1 Mar. 1976.

    Unlike the communal Cages, POWs in the H Blocks were subject to cellular confinement, either alone or at most with one cellmate. In addition, the policy of "criminalization" introduced in March 1976 ended the de facto recognition of paramilitary command structures by prison authorities: warders were to deal with POWs on an individual basis rather than through their OCs. Perhaps worst of all to the incarcerated Republicans, the new prison regime in the H Blocks required the wearing of official prison uniform by all prisoners. This reversal of British policy prompted Republican POWs to embark first on the Blanket Protest, where prisoners refused official prison clothing and wore only the blankets from their beds. Because of increased abuse of prisoners by the warders, this protest eventually escalated into the No-Wash Protest in 1978 where POWs resorted to smearing their excrement on the walls [McKeown, *Out of Time* 56]. Faced with continued British intransigence, in 1980 and 1981 the POWs embarked on hunger strikes and Bobby Sands was the first of ten men to die on the 1981 strike. The H Blocks are dealt with in greater detail in chapter four.

24. Gerry Adams, "Sláinte," *Cage Eleven* (Dingle: Brandon, 1990) 52.
25. Ibid., 55.
26. Lefebvre 43–4. As Adams points out, such bootlegging began in earnest after 1661 when a tax was levied on local distilleries. Adams declares that "Nobody in South Derry, North Antrim, South Armagh or Tyrone paid [the tax], nor would they drink the new 'parliamentary whiskey'" [Adams, "Sláinte," *Cage Eleven* 42]. Perhaps it is not surprising that areas known for armed struggle also are known for subversive gestures in the form of *poitín* stills. Lest it be thought I overstate the case, I invite the reader to recall the so-called Whiskey Rebellion of the nascent republic in the United States, a near civil war sparked by the imposition of a tax on alcohol that was only quelled by an extended military campaign led by George Washington himself. I wonder if it is no coincidence that the areas where the rebellion was fiercest were those settled in largest numbers by immigrants from Ulster.
27. Michel deCerteau, *The Practice of Everyday Life* (Berkeley: University of California Press, 1984) xiii.
28. In the version of the story that appears in *Cage Eleven*, this sentence is revised to describe the warder as "a remarkable piece of humankind, a right pockel" (27). A "pockel" is defined later in the American version of *Cage Eleven's* glossary as an "awkward person" [Gerry Adams, *Cage Eleven* (New York: Sheridan Square, 1990) 145]. Similarly, "sleekitly" is defined as "cunningly, slyly" (145). There is no glossary in the original Brandon Books version, which also appeared in 1990.
29. "Brownie" (Gerry Adams), "Screws," *Republican News* 10 Apr. 1976: 7. In *Cage Eleven* a paragraph break appears at this point. Similarly, in the original *Republican News* version of this story the idiosyncratic punctuation is standardized: the underscoring separating the parallel activities of warder and prisoner is replaced by semicolons. Similarly, a comma is added after the "Like" that begins the last sentence of the quoted section.
30. It also is hard not to see a variant of Hegel's Master/Slave relationship being enacted in moments such as this. Just as the Master has seemingly

assumed a position of superiority through force of arms, the ascendancy proves itself unstable. For, Hegel writes,

> It is not an independent, but rather a dependent consciousness that he [the Master] has achieved. He is thus not assured of self-existence as truth; he finds that his truth is rather the unessential consciousness, and the fortuitous unessential action of that consciousness...But just as the position of the master showed itself to be the reverse of what it wants to be, so, too, the position of servant will, when completed, pass into the opposite of what it immediately is: being a consciousness repressed within itself, it will enter into itself, and change around into real and true independence. [Georg Wilhelm Hegel, *The Philosophy of Hegel* (New York: Random House, 1954) 406–7.]

Unlike the POWs, the warders who guard the wire of Long Kesh in "Screws" can only ever be a reactionary force. Their function is to keep the situation safely in the confines of the status quo; a mastery based on military prowess alone.

31. Hegel, *Philosophy of Hegel* 406.
32. Adams, "Screws" 8.
33. For example, the model of discipline Foucault elaborates in his best-known work often disregards human agency, for as Felix Driver accurately observes "there is little evidence in *Discipline and Punish* of Foucault's concern with resistance and struggle." ["Bodies in Space: Foucault's Account of Disciplinary Power," *Reassessing Foucault: Power, Medicine, and the Body,* ed. Colin Jones and Roy Porter (New York: Routledge, 1999)121.] In other, more neglected texts Foucault does acknowledge the limits of panoptic power: for instance, Foucault faults Bentham in "The Eye of Power" for not taking into account "the effective resistance of the people." [*Power/Knowledge: Selected Interviews and Other Writings*, ed. Colin Gordon (New York: Pantheon, 1980) 162.] However, although the latter argument may be implicit in the discussion of power in *Discipline and Punish,* it is not framed in such potentially emancipatory terms.
34. McEvoy, *Paramilitary Imprisonment* 42.
35. The translator of Paolo Freire's *Pedagogy of the Oppressed* glosses this term as "learning to perceive social, political, and economic contradictions and to take action against oppressive elements of reality." Qtd. in Paolo Freire, *Pedagogy of the Oppressed*, trans. Myra Bergman Ramos (New York: Continuum, 1993) 17.
36. Gerry Adams, *Before the Dawn: An Autobiography* (New York: William Morrow & Co., 1996) 245.
37. Gerry Adams, "Only Joking," *Cage Eleven* (Dingle: Brandon, 1990) 141.
38. Dr. Laurence McKeown, who was on the 1981 hunger strike for 70 days, denounces members of the church hierarchy such as Fr. Faul, who (in McKeown's words) engaged in an "anti-hunger strike campaign of vilification of the Republican Movement and its leadership" (Campbell, McKeown, and O'Hagan 210).

39. In many Native American nations, tricksters and contraries perform their vital and sacred function through reversal of expected roles and by the laughter resulting from their unexpected, often obscene behavior. In the words of anthropologist Barbara Tedlock,

> The [Native American sacred] clown's mystical liberation from ultimate cosmic fears brings with it a liberation from conventional notions of what is dangerous or sacred in the religious ceremonies of men... Although the clown, by causing people to laugh at shamans and other religious authorities, might appear to weaken the very fabric of his society's religion, he might actually revitalize it by revealing higher truths. ["The Clown's Way," *Teachings from the American Earth: Indian Religion and Philosophy,* ed. Dennis and Barbara Tedlock (New York: Liveright, 1992) 108–9.]

Although tricksters may seem humorous or even worthy of ridicule, in fact they are endowed with great powers. Paradoxically, they encourage critical detachment from the surrounding world while simultaneously showing the way toward integration within that world. Readers might make comparisons between the contrary and Bahktin's notion of the carnivalesque; however, I maintain that important distinctions need to be made not only because of the explicitly sacred place accorded to the contrary in many Native American nations, but also because the contrary's function is not merely parodic or antagonistic. Contraries do not just mock official discourse, but rather they simultaneously reinforce aspects of it.

40. Barbara Harlow, *Resistance Literature* (New York: Meuthen, 1987) 16.
41. "Brownie" (Gerry Adams), "Christians for Freedom?" *Republican News* 22 Jan. 1977: 2. The *Cage Eleven* version notes that the assistant "peeked out at them from behind the Bishop's door." [Adams, "Christians" 100.]
42. Adams, "Christians" 2.
43. "Brownie" (Gerry Adams), "Frank Stagg," *Republican News* 10 Jan. 1976: 4.
44. While literary scholars have ignored the Brownie columns, British journalists have caused controversy in their investigations of Adams's collaborations with other writers with whom he shared the Cages. For example, in *Man of War, Man of Peace: The Unauthorized Biography of Gerry Adams* (London: Pan, 1997), David Sharrock and Mark Devenport have suggested that because some of the speakers in the Brownie columns identify themselves as paramilitaries the articles provide evidence of Adams's IRA membership, a claim that the British security forces themselves have not been able to prove. According to Sharrock and Devenport, Adams "maintained that the Brownie articles were not written solely by him, but were the work of a number of prisoners. Asked if he therefore wrote the articles which contained no damaging admissions, but not those which did, he replied yes." For their part, Sharrock and Devenport conclude that "the Brownie columns are clearly the work of an individual rather than a committee" (132).

It may be that political expediency prevents Adams from claiming sole authorship of some or all of the controversial articles. After all, although figures such as Nelson Mandela and former Israeli Prime Minister Menachem Begin (who, as leader of the resistance movement Irgun was responsible for the bombing of the King David Hotel in July 1946, an attack that killed 92 people) might be lionized today, it is largely because their links to armed struggle have been conveniently—sometimes deliberately—forgotten. However, unlike Sharrock and Devenport, I have no particular investment in proving (or disproving) Adams's alleged connections with the IRA. It is perhaps telling that, despite an apparently thorough familiarity with the Brownie columns, Sharrock and Devenport refuse to even mention an article such as "Frank Stagg" that overtly foregrounds Adams as coauthor. This omission is particularly problematic given that Gerry Kelly, one of the coauthors in question, was imprisoned for IRA activity, a detail that supports Adams's assertions that such joint literary ventures with avowed paramilitaries occurred in some of the Brownie columns.

Finally, one must also remain aware of the manner in which Adams may at times utilize a persona not necessarily his own. Furthermore we must also remember that, as recent autobiographical theory has explored, texts are necessarily constructs even when they attempt to represent autobiographical experience objectively. In the foreword to *Cage Eleven* Adams explains that "In this book the main characters are fictional, but they and their escapades are my way of representing life as it was in Long Kesh" [Adams, foreword, *Cage Eleven* (Dingle: Brandon, 1990) 14]. Some, perhaps even the majority, of Long Kesh's literary denizens seem carefully modeled after actual personages (including, as Bobby Devlin attests in his memoirs of Long Kesh [8] the loony Cratur—originally identified by his nickname "Thumper or Tumper" in the Brownie column of the same name [Gerry Adams, "'Thumper' or 'Tumper'" *Republican News* 8 Nov. 1975: 5]. However, we must consider the possibility that others, including at times Brownie himself, are composite characters, who, as Adams suggests above, might come as close to an accurate representation of life in the Cages as one could expect from a work of "nonfiction," a sentiment shared by his comrade Jim McCann, who reveals in his own account of imprisonment in the Cages that his "recollections are 80 percent true and 90 percent as close to the truth as my aging memory permits." Jim McCann, *The Night the Kesh Went Up* (Belfast: Glandore, 1998) 3.

45. Adams, "Frank Stagg" (*RN*) 4.
46. It is worth noting that while it similarly notes that Adams "used [Feeney's and Kelly's accounts]... almost as they were written," the *taoibh amuigh* version of "Frank Stagg" does not place quotation marks around the passages in question [Gerry Adams, "Frank Stagg" (*RN*: 5; *CE* 117)].
47. The *Cage Eleven* version omits this word. Adams, "Frank Stagg, 1976" (*CE*) 119.

48. Adams, "Frank Stagg, 1976" (*CE*) 4.
49. In the *Republican News* version this paragraph reads as follows: "Only the Irish people can guarantee those rights [of Republicans in English jails to be treated as POWs] and they can do this by opposing the Brit presence in Ireland and the injustices and tortures meted out to Irish prisoners" (5). It makes no mention of the "Dublin government."
50. Adams, "Frank Stagg, 1976" (*CE*) 124.
51. Adams, "Frank Stagg, 1976" (*RN*) 5.
52. Adams, "Frank Stagg, 1976" (*CE*) 124.
53. I do not mean to denigrate the past and present efforts of those at *An Phoblacht/Republican News,* which I think is an outstanding example of grassroots journalism. However, as the title announces, the paper reports news from a Provisional Republican perspective, a perspective sadly, though unsurprisingly, absent in papers such as the *Belfast Telegraph* that enjoy greater circulation in the north (and that make more frequent claims of journalistic objectivity despite a decidedly Unionist slant).
54. In making this claim I do not dispute the need for libel laws properly applied. However, when attempting to make sense of a situation as vexed as that of Ireland, readers must avail themselves of a variety of perspectives. The need for the sort of accountability called for in the Brownie articles is all the more pressing when one considers the degree to which the "mainstream" media has historically been manipulated by British military intelligence. According to Colin Wallace, a British Army press officer during the early 1970s, "We had Information Policy, which was the psychological warfare team hidden in the press office" (qtd. in Sharrock and Devenport, *Man of War* 118), and by this conduit MI6 fed information directly to the media, including names and photos of Republican activists and people they alleged were members of the IRA (Adams numbered among these). As Sharrock and Devenport—two reporters generally hostile to Republicanism—confirm, in 1974 such media plants were "part of an overall strategy to soften up the Provisionals in advance of negotiating a new ceasefire with them" (119).
55. The term "Free State" is used pejoratively in this fashion by northern nationalists with regard to the Twenty-Six Counties to point out what they view as the Republic's abandonment of the Six Counties.
56. McKeown, *Out of Time* 176.
57. Adams, *Before* 319.
58. Ibid., 317.
59. McEvoy, *Paramilitary Imprisonment* 204.
60. "Brownie" (Gerry Adams), "A Week in the Life," *Republican News* 29 May 1976: 3.
61. Ibid.
62. McEvoy, *Paramilitary Imprisonment* 206.
63. Dennis Faul and Raymond Murray, *The Hooded Men: British Torture in Ireland August, October 1971* (Dungannon: Fr. Faul, 1974) 1.
64. Qtd. in Faul and Murray, *Hooded Men* 40.

65. Ibid., 23.
66. Ibid., 27.
67. Indeed, the attempts by the Security Forces to sever POWs from temporality mirrors their attempts to forcibly decontextualize Republicans in other ways, for instance in the repeated attempts by the British to deny or remove Special Category Status.
68. Qtd. in Faul and Murray, *Hooded Men* 41.
69. Ibid.
70. Adams, *Before* 189.
71. Ibid.
72. Ibid., 222.
73. Ibid., 245–6.
74. "Brownie" (Gerry Adams), "Belfast: 1913 or 1976?" *Republican News* 13 Nov. 1976: 2.
75. "Brownie" (Gerry Adams), "The Republic: A Reality," *Republican News* 29 Nov. 1975: 4.
76. Adams, "Republic" 4.
77. Richard English, *Armed Struggle: The History of the IRA* (New York: Oxford University Press, 2003) 166.
78. This term derives from the Officials' use of Easter lily badges with sticky adhesive backing as opposed to the Provisionals' badges which utilized a pin.
79. "Brownie" (Gerry Adams), "Out There on the Motorway..." *Republican News* 23 Aug. 1975: 7.
80. This critique of the Officials is similarly evident in "The Awakening," which, apart from the farewell that appeared on the same pages below it, was the last of the regular Brownie columns. In "The Awakening" the protagonist, a horse trader described as "a Stick by persuasion" (4), discovers the legendary hero Malachi and his band of warriors in an enchanted slumber in a cavern near Dundalk. An archetypal warrior-king such as Arthur, according to folklore Malachi will drive the English from Ireland when he is awoken, yet the Official wastes his chance to free his country. When one of the warriors stirs and asks him "Is it time yet?" the Stick replies "No, not yet, but it won't be long now" (4) and the warriors remain asleep.

    In "Such a Yarn," the *Cage Eleven* version of this story, the horse trader is not an Official but a "Fianna Fail minister" [Gerry Adams, "Such a Yarn," *Cage Eleven* (Dingle: Brandon, 1990) 66]. This change is more than a simple reflection of the fact that by 1990 the Officials had ceased to exist. As was the case with the revisions to "Frank Stagg," Adams keeps the article relevant to the particular moment of publication by refocusing his critique on the Dublin government. In Adams's analysis, through their anti-interventionist policies and their hostility to Sinn Féin, Fianna Fail were virtual collaborators in continued British dominance of Ireland.
81. Adams, "Motorway" 7.

82. Ibid.
83. Ibid.
84. I of course recognize that Republican paramilitaries are not averse to hijacking cars if no other option presents itself.
85. I use this term deliberately, for in fact the British first invented such prison compounds in South Africa during the Boer War. While today—for obvious, tragic reasons—the term "concentration camp" carries with it associations with Nazi Germany, we must still recognize the distinction between the concentration camps of the early years of the Nazi regime (whose primary function, like the South African camps, was to confine political dissenters such as communists) and the death camps of later years, whose purpose was industrialized slaughter of human life.
86. Adams, "Motorway" 7.
87. Ibid.
88. McEvoy, *Paramilitary Imprisonment* 67.
89. Adams, foreword, *Cage Eleven* 12.
90. Ibid.
91. Adams may or may not have been aware that the Officials had their own tradition of prison writing in the Cages, their typed and mimeographed periodical entitled *An Eochair.*
92. Qtd. in English, *Armed Struggle* 225.
93. Dave Morley, "Simplicity," *Faoi Glas* Aug. 1975: 3.
94. Ibid.
95. Tim Pat Coogan, *The IRA* (Niwot, CO: Roberts Rinehart, 1994) 255. In this otherwise excellent book Coogan claims that political and literary texts "are not important to Republicans of the 'physical force' school. Deaths, commemorations, holding firm with the past—these are and will be the preoccupations that nourish the IRA" (255). Although this may be true of some Republicans and Republican paramilitaries, I insist that in such a statement Coogan is wildly inaccurate in that it simply does not take into account the radical fashion in which many prisoners embraced literature and political theory on their own, first during incarceration as well as subsequent to release. A glance at the books that comprised the library of the Republican H Blocks—whose holdings include writers from Paolo Friere to W.B. Yeats—should disabuse one of the notion that Republicans, whether paramilitary or otherwise—cannot be simultaneously intellectual and of the "physical force school." This collection is currently held in the offices of Coiste na nIarchimí in Belfast.
96. *Faoi Glas* No. 1 Aug. 1975: 1.
97. This partition remains today, certainly in the minds of revisionist critics such as Edna Longley who attacked *The Field Day Anthology of Irish Writing* not just for what they perceived as a nationalist bias, but also for the apparent crime of placing other forms of writing on an equal footing with "Literature."

98. Derec MacThomais, "Greetings from the Kesh," *Faoi Glas* No.1 Aug. 1975: 3.
99. Harlow, *Resistance Literature* 120.
100. Qtd. in McKeown, *Out of Time* 38.
101. Ibid.
102. Gerry Adams, "The Night Andy Warhol Was Banned," *Cage Eleven* (Dingle: Brandon, 1990) 131.
103. Ibid., 132.
104. Ibid., 133.
105. Ibid.
106. Ibid.
107. The reader must keep in mind the fact that although the young Adams was indeed a rising star in Provisional Republicanism in the mid-1970s, other—mainly older—figures occupied the highest positions of power in both Sinn Féin and the IRA Army Council.
108. Alexandre Kojéve, *Introduction to the Reading of Hegel* (New York: Basic, 1969) 51.
109. In this crucial respect Adams's texts differ from the best-known prison writings of Bobby Sands. Generally Sands's work does not engage in the unconcealed subversion of Republican hierarchies that we see in the Brownie articles and *Cage Eleven*. For a thorough analysis of the factors that contributed to this disparity, see my discussion of Sands's writings in chapter three of this book.
110. McKeown, *Out of Time* 39.
111. This would change in later years in the H Blocks, when "anyone in the wing" could take up positions in the leadership [McKeown, *Out of Time* 245], regardless of affiliation with the PIRA.
112. McKeown, *Out of Time* 24.
113. A derogatory term in Northern Ireland for a Catholic.
114. Qtd. in Martin Dillon, *The Shankill Butchers* (New York: Routledge, 1989) xxiii.
115. Dillon xxi.
116. Adams, "Inside Story" 6.
117. Qtd. in McKeown, *Out of Time* 43.
118. McKeown, email to author.
119. "Brownie" (Gerry Adams), "The National Alternative," *Republican News* 3 Apr. 1976: 7.
120. Adams, "Alternative" 7.
121. Ibid.
122. See also the works of Campbell et al., McKeown, Feldman, and Coogan for detailed discussion of the H Block struggle.
123. The burning of the Cages by POWs in October 1974, and the riot immediately afterward in Belfast's Crumlin Road Prison to express solidarity with "the men behind the wire."
124. McKeown, *Out of Time* 176.
125. Adams, foreword, *Cage Eleven* 13.

126. McKeown, *Out of Time* 180.
127. "Brownie" (Gerry Adams), "An Ard Fheis," *Republican News* 18 Sept. 1976: 2. The *Cage Eleven* version alters the original phrasing, combining the first and second sentence, correcting the spelling of the Irish words, and does not italicize any words: "In an exclusive interview the Cage O.C. and Adjutant told me that they considered the Árd Fheis to have been a great success and hoped Sinn Féin *cumainn* outside would give a favourable reception to proposals sent out to them... They would wait with interest a report from the Árd Fheis outside and promised, somewhat pessimistically that the Cage would probably have another Árd Fheis next year." Adams, "An Árd Fheis," *Cage Eleven* 76.
128. Caroline Kennedy-Pipe, *The Origins of the Present Troubles in Northern Ireland* (New York: Longman, 1997) 71.
129. Tim Pat Coogan, *The Troubles* (New York: Palgrave, 2002) 203.
130. Ibid., 333.
131. Dillon 21.
132. Coogan, *Troubles* 337.
133. English, *Armed Struggle* 173.
134. David Lowry, "The English System of Judicial Injustice," *Catholic League Newsletter* 7.11 (1980): 2.
135. Kennedy-Pipe, *Origins of the Present Troubles* 51–2.

Chapter Three "Comrades in the Dark": Writing in the H Blocks, 1976–1981

1. Bobby Sands, "Trilogy" *Skylark Sing Your Lonely Song: An Anthology of the Writings of Bobby Sands* (Dublin and Cork: Mercier Press, 1982) 57–8.
2. W. B. Yeats, "The Tower," *Oxford Anthology of British and Irish Poetry*, ed. Keith Tuma (New York: Oxford University Press, 2001) 47.
3. Ibid.
4. Allen Feldman, *Formations of Violence* (Chicago: University of Chicago Press, 1991) 148.
5. Similar legislation went into effect in Britain: the Prevention of Terrorism Act (PTA) established juridical procedures identical to those of the EPA. Perhaps the most famous contemporary victims of miscarriages of justice, the Guilford Four and the Birmingham Six were arrested and unfairly imprisoned under the PTA. The case of the Guilford Four received much publicity as a result of the film *In the Name of the Father*: for more analysis of this film see the final chapter of this book.
6. This "emergency" legislation was renewed by Westminster every time that it came up for review, even after the PIRA and other paramilitary groups called ceasefires in 1997 and the Good Friday Agreement was

ratified in 1998. The recent attacks in London by militant Islamists make it unlikely that such legislation will disappear any time soon—indeed, many MPs have argued to broaden the powers of such "antiterrorist" legislation. Likewise, these issues have become all too familiar in post–September 11 America as illustrated by the U.S.A. Patriot Act, the "illegal combatants" denied protection under the Geneva Conventions in Guantanamo Bay, and the National Security Agency's warrentless wiretapping scandals among others. Interestingly, many of the Irish Americans who spoke out so vociferously against British suspension of Irish rights aggressively defend similar legislation enacted in America's so-called war on terror.

7. David Lowry, "The English System of Judicial Injustice," *Catholic League Newsletter* 7.11 (1980): 3.
8. Pat Magee, *Gangsters or Guerillas?* (Belfast: Beyond the Pale, 2001).
9. Tim Pat Coogan, *The IRA* (Boulder: Roberts Rinehart, 1994) 368.
10. Feldman, *Formations of Violence* 152.
11. See *Nor Meekly Serve My Time* or a more complete history of the H Block protest; for a history of both the Cages and the H Blocks, see *Out of Time*. These books are the definitive works on the topic, as they both utilize the testimony of those incarcerated in Long Kesh.
12. Denis O'Hearn, *Nothing but an Unfinished Song: Bobby Sands, the Hunger Striker Who Ignited a Generation* (New York: Nation, 2006) 185–6.
13. Qtd. in Feldman, *Formations of Violence* 191.
14. As Danny Devenny revealed in his *AP/RN* eulogy, Sands was an active author during his earlier incarceration in the Cages; "Life in the cages of the Kesh," *An Phoblacht/Republican News* 9 May 1981: 22. O'Hearne claims the earliest known text by Sands is a short story in Gaeilge written in late 1975 during his incarceration in Cage Eleven (O'Hearn, *Nothing but an Unfinished Song* 90).
15. Feldman, *Formations of Violence* 166.
16. Gerry Adams, "Inside Story," *Republican News* 16 Aug. 1975: 6.
17. Eileen Fairweather, Roisin McDonough, and Melanie Mc Fadyean *Only the Rivers Run Free, Northern Ireland: The Women's War* (London: Pluto, 1984) 57.
18. O'Hearn, *Nothing but an Unfinished Song* 213.
19. Ibid., 215.
20. David Lloyd, *Anomalous States* (Durham: Duke University Press, 1993) 47.
21. Sands, *Skylark* 20.
22. Ibid., 14.
23. Ibid., 8.
24. Bobby Sands *One Day in My Life* (Dublin and Cork: Mercier, 1983) 25.
25. Gerry Adams, "Cage Eleven," *Cage Eleven* (Dingle: Brandon, 1990) 16.
26. Bobby Sands, "I Once Had a Life," *An Phoblacht/Republican News* 17 Mar. 1979: 2.

27. Roy Mason, Secretary of State during the late Seventies.
28. Bobby Sands, "Christmas Eve," *Skylark Sing Your Lonely Song* (Dublin and Cork: Mercier Press, 1982) 99.
29. Irish Gaelic, meaning "Our day will come." Sands is credited with politicizing this phrase (Coogan, *The IRA* 380), and one sees it replicated in the discourse of graffiti and wall murals in nationalist areas of the Six Counties, as well as in that of Republican writing.
30. Sands *One Day* 117–8.
31. Bobby Sands, "The harvest Britain has sown" [*sic*], *Republican News* 16 Sept. 1978: 8.
32. Elaine Scarry, *The Body in Pain.* (New York: Oxford University Press, 1985) 4–6.
33. Sands "Harvest" 8.
34. Bobby Sands "Teach Your Children" *Skylark Sing Your Lonely Song* (Dublin and Cork: Mercier Press, 1982) 113.
35. Laurence McKeown, *Out of Time: Irish Republican Prisoners Long Kesh 1972–2000* (Belfast: Beyond the Pale, 2001) 70.
36. Devenny 22.
37. The prison writings of Thomas Clarke, the first signatory of the Easter Proclamation, are but one example, though unlike the work of Sands and Adams's "Brownie" columns Clarke's reminiscences were written *taoibh amuigh*. First published in 1912–13 in *Irish Freedom*, they were later collected and published in 1922 as *Glimpses of an Irish Felon's Life.*
38. Sands, *Writings* (Dublin) 37.
39. Bobby Sands, "How Much More?" and "I fought a monster today" [*sic*], *Republican News* 7 Oct. 1978: 9.
40. Bill Ashcroft, *Post-Colonial Transformation* (New York: Routledge, 2001) 168.
41. Bobby Sands "On the Blanket," *Republican News* 1 Apr. 1978: 2.
42. Adams, "Cage Eleven," *Cage Eleven* 16.
43. Such valences remain even in post–Good Friday Agreement Belfast. Tired of the yearly strife resulting from contentious Orange parades, a Republican friend of the author who moved with his family from the Ormeau Road to Andersontown in West Belfast related how his former neighbors envied his relocation to, in their words, "Disneyland."
44. Variants include "a young West Belfast fellow" (7 Jan. 1978), "OUR YOUNG COMRADE FROM WEST BELFAST ON THE BLANKET" (21 Jan. 1978), "OUR YOUNG COMRADE FROM WEST BELFAST PRESENTLY ON THE 'BLANKET PROTEST'" (1 Apr. 1978), before stabilizing as "A YOUNG WEST BELFAST REPUBLICAN" for three more articles (3 June, 10 June, and 1 July 1978).
45. Ashcroft's observations regarding the *testimonio* are worth remembering when examining the writings of Republican POWs such as Sands, for they also are marked by a "communal subject position" in which "self-identity . . . is inseparable from the oppressed group or class" (114). Yet, unlike the *testimonio*, the *téacs pluide* does not rely in as complete

(and as problematic) a fashion on an academic interlocutor to reach an audience. For this reason alone Sands's writings are less mediated than those of individuals from the *testimonio* tradition such as Rigoberta Menchu.

46. Sands, "Harvest" 8.
47. Michel Foucault, *Discipline and Punish,* trans. Alan Sheridan (New York: Vintage, 1977) 201.
48. Sands, "Harvest" 8.
49. Ibid.
50. Bobby Sands, "The window of my mind" [*sic*], *Republican News* 25 Nov. 1978: 7.
51. O'Hearn, *Nothing but an Unfinished Song* 206, 209.
52. Ibid., 206.
53. Bobby Sands, "The Gloves Have Been Removed," *Republican News* 16 Sept. 1978: 8; Sands, "Harvest" 8.
54. Bobby Sands, "I fought a monster today" [*sic*] and "How Much More" *Republican News* 7 Oct. 1978: 9.
55. Bobby Sands, "The Birth of a Republican," *Republican News* 16 Dec 1978: 6.
56. O'Hearn, *Nothing but an Unfinished Song* 346.
57. Ibid., 183.
58. Earlier visions of such an ideology of course might be traced to Republican theorists such as James Connolly. However, as discussed in detail in the previous chapter, post-1922 mainstream Republicanism was notable for its conservatism and hostility to anything resembling radical socialism. Mickey McMullan, imprisoned in the Cages, remembers that in 1976 the OC of his Cage forbid the POWs to watch television programs about the Cuban revolution, Mao Tse Tung, or Vietnam because the OC deemed them "about communism and therefore not educational" (qtd. in McKeown, *Out of Time* 38). It was not until the rise to prominence in the mid-1970s of theorists such as Gerry Adams and Bobby Sands that Provisionals gave broad support to this blend of the physical force tradition with a socialist politicization of the rank and file.
59. The manuscript of the first stanza of Sands's epic poem "Trilogy" provides a fascinating visual representation of this deliberate deferral of individuality. As evident in *Skylark Sing Your Lonely Song's* photoreproduction of the *teachtaireacht* (message) itself, although the third line of the poem depicts the speaker as inscribing "B.S. was here" on the wall of his cell, next to the title of this first section of the poem Sands signs his name as "Marcella POW." Sands, *Skylark* 2.
60. Laurence McKeown, manuscript letter to *Irish Press*, c. 1980.
61. Bobby Sands, "On the Blanket," *Republican News* 7 Jan. 1978: 6.
62. Bobby Sands, "Poetic Justice," *Republican News* 2 Dec. 1978: 5.
63. "Poems from the H Blocks," *Republican News* 9 Sept. 1978: 10.

64. Qtd. in McKeown, *Out of Time* 64.
65. Danny Morrison, "Introduction," in Bobby Sands, *Prison Poems* (Dublin: Sinn Féin Publicity Department, Oct. 1981) 10.
66. The degree to which this ideal has been put into practice is at present largely unknowable. Unfortunately, the vast majority of Sands's manuscripts have been locked away in the National Archives in Dublin by the Bobby Sands Trust, and will be unavailable to the public until, at earliest, the end of 2007, months after I am contractually obligated to deliver this manuscript to the publisher. As a result, I have only been able to study those *teachtaireachtaí* that have either remained in the hands of his comrades or that have been photoreproduced in works such as *Skylark Sing Your Lonely Song* and *Nothing but an Unfinished Song.* This, I admit is a serious—but sadly, unavoidable—absence in the present study, and one that I will address as the manuscripts become available. I take some solace in the fact that according to Danny Morrison in an interview he gave me in 2003, even he and Gerry Adams are unable to access these manuscripts—particularly notable because Morrison is the director of the Bobby Sands Trust. In fact, Morrison and Adams have a running bet on whether or not a particular line in the published version of one of Sands's poems mirrors the original wording. It is a bet that will be settled only when the manuscripts are made available again. Danny Morrison, interview, July 2003.
67. Roibeard O Seachnasaigh (Bobby Sands), "An scéal" [*sic*], *An Phoblacht/ Republican News* 10 Dec. 1981: 10.
68. Elsewhere in *The Living Stream* Longley defines true poetry as something that, "feeling its way through form" exhibits a "utopian pull against the biases of society." Longley, *The Living Stream* (London: Bloodaxe, 1993) 221. The perils of such a mystification evince themselves when they lead to similar confusion about the neutrality of participants in the conflict in Ireland. Unbelievably, earlier in *The Living Stream* Longley praises the "hands-off stance of the UK government" towards the Six Counties! Longley, *Stream* 193. Such a misguided claim is all the more maddening when it is made shortly after the 1992 trial of Brian Nelson, a former Loyalist paramilitary who was put to work as an undercover British intelligence agent in the Ulster Defense Association (UDA), a loyalist paramilitary group. Coogan reveals that Nelson's handlers in British intelligence did nothing as in 1988, under Nelson's guidance, the UDA imported weapons from South Africa. Between 1985 and 1988 the UDA killed three people: in the five years subsequent to the shipment, the UDA killed 160 people with their South African weapons. Coogan, *Troubles* 310. In 1992, a BBC exposé insisted that Nelson himself "had been involved in ten murders or murder plots carried out by the UDA with the knowledge of the [British] army." Coogan, *Troubles* 311. A hands-off approach by the U.K. government indeed, but only as a form of brutal counterinsurgency.

69. Sands, *Skylark* 167–8.
70. O'Hearn, *Nothing but an Unfinished Song* 415.
71. Ibid., 333–4.
72. Revenge is a complicated concept in Sands's writings. Although in this moment the poem seems to suggest a physical-force response, readers should recall that elsewhere Sands uses the term to contrast the brutality of the state with the United Ireland that he imagines, claiming in his hunger strike diary for example that the Provisionals' "revenge will be liberation of all." [Sands, *Skylark* 166.] In an even more forgiving moment he predicts that "the laughter of our children" will be the only revenge.
73. Roibeard Ó Seachnasaigh (Bobby Sands), "An Mhaidin," *Faoi Ghlas ag Gaill* (Belfast: Gaeil Bheal Feirste in Eadan H-Bloc agus Ard Mhacha, 1981): no page numbers, but appears on 19th page. I have reproduced the song exactly as it appears in *Faoi Ghlas ag Gaill*, making no attempt to allow the longer lines prevented by the limited space of the collection's page.
74. In the same issue of *An Phoblacht/Republican News* that first published Bobby Sands's hunger strike diary, Deasun Breatnach claims that "Up to the time of the *amhrán* (popular song), Irish poetry largely was aristocratic. The *amhrán* marks the proletariatization of song and poetry in Irish. It also marks the beginning of the powerful national song, one no longer confined to one class, family or province, but one which covers the entire Irish people, one such as Róisín Dubh [*sic*]." Though perhaps an oversimplification of the origins of contemporary poetry in Druidic tradition, Breathnach's article rightly urges us to ponder the intersections of class and poetic aesthetics. Similarly, he also reminds us that ancient Irish poetic tradition is steeped in the politics of the day as evident in what today might be termed "nationalistic" historic lays, druidic satires intended to effect change, and poems in praise of rulers. "The druid and the poet." *An Phoblacht/Republican News* 13 June 1981: 15. Whatever one thinks of his claims, Breatnach's article merits study because of the insights it gives us to Provisional Republican poetic models.
75. Ó Seachnasaigh (Sands), "Mhaidin" 19.
76. Sands, *Skylark* 168.
77. It is unclear to what degree succeeding editors of Sands's work were aware that other versions of the song exist, let alone that a specific decision was made to privilege the version in the hunger strike diary. Such is the difficulty of oral tradition.
78. Jerome McGann, *A Critique of Modern Textual Criticism* (Chicago: University of Chicago Press, 1983) 8.
79. Ibid., 7.
80. O'Hearn, *Nothing but an Unfinished Song* 197.
81. Ibid., 220.
82. Ibid., 264.
83. G. Thomas Tanselle, *Textual Criticism and Scholarly Editing* (University of Virginia Press, 1990) 187.

84. Qtd. in Tanselle 193.
85. Sands, *Skylark* 172.
86. Bobby Sands, "The Diary of Bobby Sands," special supplement, *An Phoblacht/Republican News* 13 June 1981: vii.
87. Bobby Sands, *The Diary of Bobby Sands* (Dublin: Sinn Féin Publicity Department, June 1981) 42. Bobby Sands, *The Diary of Bobby Sands* (Dublin: Republican Publications, May 1990) 53.
88. Sands, *Skylark* 173.
89. Ibid.,172.
90. Ibid.,172–3.
91. Ibid.,172.
92. It does, however, raise the question as to why so few of Sands's Irish-language texts have made it into widespread publication. *Nothing but an Unfinished Song* has given the world an invaluable gift in its photo-reproduction of a portion of the manuscript of Sands's first-known prison writing in Irish or English, "Ag bunadh gaeltachta." However, I am aware of at least four other texts *as Gaeilge* by Sands that have not yet been anthologized, or indeed appeared in print since their publication in local Republican pamphlets or newspapers: the poem "An Choir inár gCionne" and the prose pieces "An Scéal," "Easbaidh Gaeilge ar Raidio agus Teilifis Eireann" [*sic*] and "Coiscéim Amháin ón Uaigh."
93. Sands, *One Day* 23.
94. Sands, "Diary" iii.
95. Sands, *Skylark* 171, 172.
96. Sands, "Diary" vi.
97. Bobby Sands, "The Writings of Bobby Sands," *An Phoblacht/Republican News* 21 Mar. 1981: 6–7.
98. Ibid., 7.
99. Qtd. in Brian Campbell, Laurence McKeown, and Felim O'Hagan, *Nor Meekly Serve My Time* (Belfast: Beyond the Pale, 1994) 104.
100. Qtd. in Campbell, McKeown, and O'Hagan 107.
101. Sands, "Birth" 6–7.
102. Bobby Sands, "The Birth of a Republican," *An Phoblacht/Republican News* 4 Apr. 1981: 7.
103. Bobby Sands, "The rhythm of time" [*sic*], *An Phoblacht/Republican News* 29 June 1981: 16.
104. Bobby Sands, "The Captain and the Cowards" and "All God's Children," *An Phoblacht/Republican News* 19 Sept. 1981: 8–10.
105. O'Hearn, *Nothing but an Unfinished Song* 353.
106. Gerry Adams, "Introduction," in Bobby Sands, *The Writings of Bobby Sands* (Belfast?: Sinn Féin, Mar. 1981).
107. Adams, *Writings* intro.
108. The prose pieces are: "I Once Had a Life," "I Fought a Monster Today," "I Am Sir, You Are 1066!", "A Thought in the Night," "The Window of My Mind," "Alone and Condemned," and "The Lark and the

Freedom Fighter." The poems are "Modern Times" and "And the Woman Cried."

109. Adams, *Writings* intro.
110. "A Mouse-Eye View," *An Phoblacht/Republican News* 17 Mar. 1979: 2.
111. The cover's main semiotic strategy—to humanize, to connect a face to a name—also, of course, fits well with the larger stratagem by which Sands's supporters hoped to save his life through widespread political pressure, a tactic that reached its zenith in the campaign to elect him to the British parliament. The sadly mistaken theory was that the British government would not allow an MP to die on hunger strike. All involved knew that the election would be bitterly contested, one necessitating maximum voter turnout: Sands's bid as an "anti–H Block political prisoner" courted voters outside the Republican core who required some convincing that Sands was human first, Republican second. It's likely that the affable, grinning image of Sands used on placards helped in this goal.
112. "Thoughts from H Block by a Blanket Man's Brother" [*sic*], *Republican News* 10 June 1978: 3.
113. When first published in *Republican News* on 1 July 1978 "I Am Sir, Your [*sic*] Are 1066!" is accompanied by a similar drawing of a fist, though *sans* barbed wire.
114. Such an image does not accompany the initial publication of the story in *An Phoblacht/Republican News*.
115. Bobby Sands, "The Lark and the Freedom Fighter," *The Writings of Bobby Sands*, (Belfast?: Sinn Féin, Mar. 1981). No pagination.
116. Ibid.
117. Ibid.
118. Feldman, *Formations of Violence* 160.
119. Sands's *Republican News* articles "On the Blanket" (7 Jan. 1978), "The Agony of It All," and "One of Those Days That Never Ends" all are accompanied by the same portrait of a generic, bearded Blanketman viewed face-on. Starting on 20 January 1979 all of Sands's "Marcella" articles are accompanied by a "logo" consisting of a bust of a bearded POW seen in profile as if on a coin, superimposed over the backdrop of a large "H," with the cursive signature indicating that the article is "by Marcella, H Block, Long Kesh." An earlier version of this logo makes its appearance alongside the first appearance of Sands's article "The Birth of a Republican" on 16 December 1978, though the image itself assigns no authorship.
120. Gerry Adams, "Introduction," in Bobby Sands, *The Writings of Bobby Sands* (Dublin: Sinn Féin POW Department, Apr. 1981) 5–6.
121. Despite the fact that the later American version of this pamphlet reproduces the identical introduction as accompanies the Dublin edition, I say this with some confidence. The American edition, published in New York by the "I.P.O.W. Committee" of Irish Northern Aid in "May 1981" is decidedly more funereal in layout. The cover, for example, is

overwhelmingly black, with the title, the "lark and barbed wire" icon, and—like a gravestone—Sands's birth and death years inscribed in purple.

122. At least two other versions based upon the Dublin edition are extant. The first is a Canadian version, which seems only a photocopy of the original using 8 ½ by 11" paper folded in half with a heavy white paper cover. The only difference between this edition and the Dublin one is the addition of two lines at the bottom of the title page, immediately beneath the bibliographic information that identify the pamphlet as being the work of the Sinn Fein POW Department in Dublin: "IRISH PRSONER OF WAR COMMITTEE/BOX 5085, STATION E, HAMILTON, ONTARIO" (1). As noted above, the American version of *The Writings of Bobby Sands* differs in layout. The same ten stories and two poems appear in it. The texts appear in the same order with one exception: "A break in the monotony" precedes "The woman cried" in the Dublin edition, vice versa in the American. Similarly, the American edition uses exactly the same illustrations and photographs, which appear in the same order apart from those that accompany "I am Sir, you are 1066." In both editions the story's text is divided by a drawing of an H Block warder looming in silhouette over a crouched, near-naked Blanketman, the same drawing that appeared next to the story in its reprint in *An Phoblacht/Republican News* on 21 Mar. 1981. However, in the American edition, an image of an excrement-smeared cell window acts almost as a introduction to the story, unlike the Dublin version where the photo follows this story and performs the same function for "I fought a monster today" (30). The American edition boasts only twenty-eight pages in contrast to the thirty-six of the Dublin edition, this condensation providing one possible explanation for the reversals described above. Although the New York editors apparently desired the illustrations to retain connection to the stories that they originally accompanied, sometimes space limitations required minor reformatting. A more substantial shift in focus manifests itself in the change in the inside back cover. In the Dublin and Canadian edition it is a photographic advertisement for *An Phoblacht/Republican News*, Sands's "publicity photo" a central feature of the newspaper issue depicted. In contrast, the inside cover of the American edition advertises the Irish American newspaper *The Irish People*, with an accompanying invitation to join Irish Northern Aid, which it describes as "an American based non-profit organization formed to alleviate the sufferings of the dependents of Irish political prisoners through An Cumman Cabrach in Dublin and affiliates such as Green Cross in Belfast" (29).
123. Sands, *Writings* (Dublin) 32.
124. Ibid., 15.
125. Ibid., 16.
126. O'Hearn, *Nothing but an Unfinished Song* 1.
127. Sands, *Skylark* 154.

128. Sands, *Writings* (Dublin) 22.
129. Ibid., 21.
130. Ibid., 4.
131. One wonders how this image might be used today in the post–Good Friday Agreement era. Marcella Sands has made no secret of her dissatisfaction with the direction that Sinn Féin and the Provisional IRA have taken. Adams, of course has always been a strong proponent of the Agreement, and the Independent Monitoring Commission has recently verified the PIRA's total decommissioning of weapons. In the absence of Sands's own analysis of the present situation this photo might easily be used to gain support among potentially dissident Republicans, for it visually creates a connection between Sands and one of the architects of the Agreement.
132. Sands, "rhythm" 16.
133. Other poems credited to Sands ran in *An Phoblacht/Republican News* only subsequent to the release of *Prison Poems*: "The jail tunnel" [*sic*], 17 Dec. 1981: 11; "Dreamers" and "Stars of freedom" [*sic*], 31 Dec. 1981: 7. These three poems do not appear in *Prison Poems*, but do appear in *Skylark Sing Your Lonely Song.*
134. Marcella, H6 (Bobby Sands), "... and the woman cried" [*sic*], *An Phoblacht/Republican News* 24 Mar. 1979: 11.
135. Roibeard, H5 Block (Bobby Sands), "Poetic Justice," *Republican News* 2 Dec. 1978: 5.
136. Sands, "The Rhythm of Time," *Prison Poems* (Dublin: Sinn Féin Publicity Department, Oct. 1981) 81.
137. Sands, "Rhythm" (*PP*) 82.
138. Gerry Adams, "Real poetry" [*sic*], *An Phoblacht/Republican News* 17 Dec. 1981: 9.
139. Adams, "Real poetry" 9.
140. Wordsworth 250.
141. Percy Bysshe Shelley, "From A Defence of Poetry," *The Norton Anthology of English Literature.* Vol. 2A. 7th edition, ed. M.H. Abrams et al. (New York: W.W. Norton, 2000) 796. On the other hand, in poems such as "Ozymandias" and "England in 1819" Shelley might be accused of failing to heed his own advice, for in the latter poem in particular he all but directly calls for armed insurrection against a tyrannical regime in a very specific historical moment. Perhaps it is asking too much for poets—and literary critics such as myself—to remain consistent.
142. Sands, *Skylark.*
143. Foucault, *Discipline* 202.
144. Longley, "From *Poetry*" 648.
145. Sands, *Skylark.*
146. Ibid., 153.
147. Bobby Sands, *Writings from Prison* (Boulder: Roberts Rinehart, 1997) 3, 24.
148. Ibid., 82.

Chapter Four "Silence Or Cell?": Women Writing in Armagh, Maghaberry, and Durham

1. A staunchly Republican area of Belfast.
2. Margaretta D'Arcy, *Tell Them Everything* (London: Pluto, 1981) 15.
3. Barbara Harlow, *Barred: Women, Writing, and Political Detention* (Hanover: Weslyan University Press, 1992) 96.
4. Certainly, there is no lack of courage or political commitment in many instances of voluntary incarceration: conscientious objection, for instance. In addition, many fine literary works have been produced by those willingly serving jail time for their refusal to pay government offices: Thoreau's "Civil Disobedience" ranking highly among them.
5. D'Arcy, *Tell Them Everything* 68.
6. Harlow, *Barred* 83.
7. Mary Corcoran, *Out_of Order: The Political Imprisonment of Women in Northern Ireland 1972–1998* (Devon: Willan, 2006) 17.
8. Harlow, *Barred* 4.
9. Benita Parry, "Problems of Current Theories of Colonial Discourse," *The Post-Colonial Studies Reader*, 1st edition, ed. Bill Ashcroft, Gareth Griffiths, and Helen Tiffin (New York: Routledge, 1995) 43.
10. Gayatri Spivak, "Can the Subaltern Speak?" *The Post-Colonial Studies Reader*, 1st edition, ed. Bill Ashcroft, Gareth Griffiths, and Helen Tiffin (New York: Routledge, 1995) 28.
11. Kristin Holst Petersen, "First Things First," *The Post-Colonial Studies Reader* 2nd edition, ed. Bill Ashcroft, Gareth Griffiths, and Helen Tiffin (New York: Routledge, 2006) 237.
12. Ibid., 238.
13. Chandra Talpade Mohante "Under Western Eyes," *The Post-Colonial Studies Reader* 2nd edition, ed. Bill Ashcroft, Gareth Griffiths, and Helen Tiffin (New York: Routledge, 2006) 242.
14. Nell McCafferty, *The Armagh Women* (Dublin: Co-Op, 1981) 66.
15. *Mother Ireland*, dir. Anne Crilly, Derry Film and Video, 1988.
16. Ibid.
17. "Interview with Mary Nelis," *Slí na mBán*, ed. Melissa Thompson, 1999, accessed 29 Sept. 2006 <http://www.tallgirlshorts.net/marymary/marynelis.html>
18. "Interview with Anne Crilly," *Slí na mBán*, ed. Melissa Thompson, 1999, accessed 29 Sept. 2006 <http://www.tallgirlshorts.net/marymary/anne.html>
19. This ban is discussed in this book in greater depth in the chapter dealing with Gerry Adams.
20. Liz Curtis, *Ireland: The Propaganda War* (Belfast: Sásta, 1998) 291.
21. An elite British commando group, comparable to the American Delta Force or the Special Forces.

22. Coogan, *IRA* 440.
23. Qtd. in Raymond Murray, *State Violence: Northern Ireland 1969–1997* (Cork and Dublin: Mercier, 1998) 193.
24. Ibid.,195.
25. Westminster's apprehension with regard to this documentary proved to be well-founded. On 27 September 1995, the British government was found guilty of breaching Article Two of the European Convention of Human Rights, the Right to Life. The British government simply ignored the verdict. In fact, the Deputy Prime Minister, Michael Heseltine, boldly stated that if given the choice "the same decisions would be made again" to kill the three unarmed people. Qtd. in Murray, *State* 192.
26. Curtis, *Ireland* 288.
27. "Anne Crilly," *Slí na mBán.*
28. Ibid.
29. Qtd. in Roseleen Walsh, *Sticks and Stones* (Belfast: Glandore, 1999) 40.
30. Raymond Murray *Hard Time: Armagh Gaol, 1971–1986* (Cork and Dublin: Mercier, 1998) 8.
31. Murray, *Hard Time* 10. The sharp division in the great numbers of men interned compared to what may seem to be a small number of women in 1972 is actually somewhat misleading. During the height of the Anglo-Irish War in 1920–21, although there were 4,000 men interned throughout the whole of Ireland, according to Challis, "The Government felt it unnecessary to intern women, as they felt it was sufficient to curb terrorist activity [*sic*] by the internment of males." Jim Challis, *The Northern Ireland Prison System 1920–1990: A History* (Belfast: The Northern Ireland Prison Service, 1999) 25. The proportionately small area and population of the Six Counties (as opposed to all thirty-two in 1920–21) must also be taken into account.
32. Challis, *Northern Ireland Prison Service* 30.
33. Ibid.
34. Murray, *Hard Time* 36–7.
35. Ibid., 15–6.
36. Ibid., 18.
37. British Army barracks where brutal interrogations took place during Internment. In 1972 and 1978 Amnesty International accused Britain of human rights abuses at interrogation centers such as these and Castlereagh. Responding to these substantiated reports, in 1976, the European Commission of Human Rights found Britain guilty of torture for the treatment of detainees. In 1978 the European Court of Human Rights found Britain guilty of "inhuman and degrading treatment."
38. Murray, *Hard Time* 87.
39. Ibid., 26–7.
40. Síle Darragh, personal interview, 7 June 2004. Eileen Hillen (nee Morgan) also termed him "a friend to the [Armagh] women" and described him also as a "great singer" who did his best to entertain the POWs in their difficult hours. Eileen Hillen, personal interview, 5 June 2004.

41. Challis, *Northern Ireland Prison Service* 59.
42. Ibid., 60.
43. Gerry Adams, "Cage Eleven," *Cage Eleven* (Dingle: Brandon, 1990) 18–19.
44. Ibid., 19.
45. Roseleen Walsh, interview, Andersontown, 1998.
46. Ibid.
47. Walsh and her solicitor were told that this was a member of the RUC, but this remains unverified as all testimony was given from behind a screen.
48. Walsh stated the name during my interview with her, and though it is clear the member of the Security Forces was fabricating the woman's imprisonment as well as Roseleen's association with her, I have decided not to print the name in case the person herself actually exists.
49. Walsh, interview.
50. Walsh, *Sticks and Stones*.
51. Walsh, interview.
52. "Interview with Roseleen Walsh," *Slí na mBán*, ed. Melissa Thompson, 6 Oct. 1999, accessed 29 Sept. 2006 <http://www.tallgirlshorts.net/marymary/roseleen.html> As outlined at the beginning of this chapter, this is the same "offence" that eventually landed Margaretta D'Arcy in Armagh. Although transgressive enough to merit three months in Armagh on the outside when directed against the official repository of state-sanctioned culture as embodied in the Ulster Museum's walls on which D'Arcy wrote "H Block," such defiance is all the more courageous when already inside the disciplinary mechanism. The reprisals threaten to be worse, not only because punishment would be concealed from public gaze, but also because a prisoner refusing discipline is doubly defiant in the eyes of the state, having already been judged deviant enough to merit incarceration.
53. "Roseleen" *Slí na mBán*.
54. Roseleen Walsh, "Imprisoned Lovers," *Aiming Higher*...(Belfast: Glandore, 2001) 32.
55. Adams, foreword, *Cage Eleven* (Dingle: Brandon, 1990) 13.
56. Walsh, interview.
57. Walsh, "To My Silent Church," *Aiming Higher*. . .(Belfast: Glandore, 1999) 33.
58. In a reading of this poem that she did for the interview on 24 July 1998, this line was read: "Speak! Play now!" This is also the wording in the earliest published version of this poem that I have been able to uncover, one titled "To You," which appeared in *Republican News* in 1974. The poem was used to conclude "Ireland's Valiant Women," an essay about Republican women's activism. Interestingly, the article's introduction to the poem tries to suggest that the verse is directed at Walsh's "fellow Irish women, particularly in Southern Ireland where so many have their heads buried in the sands of apathy and indifference." Qtd. in Michael Tobin, "Ireland's Valiant Women," *Republican News* 31 Aug. 1974: 4.

The altered title certainly might push the poem toward such a reading; one wonders if the changes were made by editors afraid of alienating devout Catholics. At no stage in my interview with Walsh, in other interviews with her that I have read, or in the prefatory remarks in the Glandore Press version have I encountered any suggestion that the poem was not specifically directed at the Catholic Church hierarchy. While certainly "To My Silent Church" might be read as a critique of all those silent in the face of oppression, its present title makes it a more transgressive work in nationalist circles than the version in *Republican News*.

59. McCafferty, *Armagh Women* 18.
60. The draconian nature of the Special Powers Act was so complete as to forbid the possession of phonograph records deemed subversive by the state.
61. Walsh, interview.
62. Ibid.
63. Qtd. in Carol Coulter, *Web of Punishment* (Dublin: Attic, 1991) 21.
64. The Blanket and No-Wash Protests are explained in greater depth in the preceding chapter covering Bobby Sands.
65. Walsh, interview.
66. Roseleen Walsh "To Aine" *Aiming Higher*...(Belfast: Glandore, 1999) 37.
67. Walsh, interview.
68. Ibid., Walsh cites "The Journey of the Magi" and "The Lake Isle of Inisfree" as examples of this.
69. Walsh, interview.
70. Ibid.
71. Ibid.
72. Qtd. in "1969–1994 Women in a War Zone," *Women in Struggle/Mna I Streachailt* Autumn 1994: 12.
73. Síle Darragh, interview.
74. Chrissy McAuley, interview, Belfast City Hall, Aug. 1998.
75. A small candy bar, known as a "Milky Way" in the United States.
76. "Interview with Martina Anderson," *Slí na mBán,* ed. Melissa Thompson, Oct. 1999, accessed 29 Sept. 2006 <http://www.tallgirlshorts.net/marymary/martina.html>
77. The Republican Women Prisoners, Maghaberry and Durham, *Voices against Oppression: A Collection of Poems* (Dublin: Sinn Féin Women's Department, 1991).
78. Unlike the work of Sands, the poetry in this collection remains anonymous for years afterward. For example, the poems "Who Is Free?" and "Resistance" appear on page 25 of the Aug. 1994 edition of the Republican periodical *Women in Struggle/Mna I Streachailt* without any authorship credited.
79. Qtd. in Laurence McKeown, *Out of Time: Irish Republican Prisoners Long Kesh 1972–2000* (Belfast: Beyond the Pale, 2000) 181.

80. *Scairt Amach* also included poetry by Republican women: an untitled poem by Martina Shanahan appeared in *Scairt Amach* 4, Nollaig (Dec.) 1990: 14.
81. "Ella," *Slí na mBán*.
82. "Interview with Ella O'Dwyer," *Slí na mBán*, ed. Melissa Thompson, 1999, accessed 29 Sept. 2006 <http://www.tallgirlshorts.net/mary-mary/ella.html>
83. Darragh insists that the black clothing used by the women for uniforms "had been allowed in through the prison censor—it hadn't been smuggled in." This makes the violence of the prison administration's wing search all the more troubling, and certainly suggests that it was part of a larger attempt to crack down on protesting POWs.
84. Ibid.
85. Ibid.
86. Ibid.
87. Ibid.
88. "Alone," *Voices against Oppression* (Dublin: Sinn Féin Women's Department, 1991).
89. "From Eve," *Voices against Oppression* (Dublin: Sinn Féin Women's Department, 1991).
90. A similar tactic is evident in the name of the feminist periodical *Spare Rib*, though many of its writers would have been suspicious of Republicanism as an ideology that would merely replace British patriarchy with a united Irish patriarchy.
91. It's worth recalling here Walsh's imagery of Jesus as rebel against injustice.
92. Una Gillespie, "Women in Struggle 1969–1994," *Women in Struggle/Mna I Streachailt* Autumn 1994: 19.
93. Qtd. in McCafferty, *Armagh Women* 14.
94. Qtd. in *Mother Ireland*.
95. "Women Join Hunger Strike," *An Phoblacht/Republican News* 22 Nov. 1980: 1.
96. "Don't let them die!" [*sic*], *An Phoblacht/Republican News* 6 Dec. 1980: 16.
97. For example, O'Hearn reveals that both Bobby Sands and Danny Morrison were in favor of women in Armagh fasting again when the men in the H Blocks embarked on their second hunger strike in 1981.
98. Seamus Boyle, "Portrait of a Hunger Striker: Mairead Nugent," *An Phoblacht/Republican News* 27 Dec. 1980: 8.
99. Seamus Boyle, "Portrait of a Hunger Striker: Mary Doyle," *An Phoblacht/Republican News* 10 Jan. 1981: 12.
100. McKeown, *Out of Time* 176.
101. Republican Women Prisoners, "Conditions Document 1996" 5.
102. Ibid., 8.
103. McCafferty, *Armagh Women* 63.

104. Gayatri Chakravorty Spivak, "Can the Subaltern Speak?" *The Post-Colonial Studies Reader,* ed. Bill Ashcroft, Gareth Griffiths, and Helen Tiffin (New York: Routledge, 1995) 28.
105. Councilor Chrissy McAuley, interview, 1998.

Chapter Five "Captive Voices": Post-1981 Republican Prison Writing

1. Eoghan MacCormaic, "The Price of Freedom," *Iris* (Aug. 1984): 34–42.
2. Brian Campbell, personal interview, 1 Jul. 2003.
3. Laurence McKeown, *Out of Time: Irish Republican Prisoners Long Kesh 1972–2000* (Belfast: Beyond the Pale, 2001) 138.
4. Paulo Freire, *Pedagogy of the Oppressed* (New York: Continuum, 1993) 62. As a literary critic I cannot help but read these lines as a challenge to the excesses of New Criticism and to those critics who would attempt to bracket politics from poetry. Republican POWs tend to agree. As Brian Campbell said to me in an interview, when it came to creative writings the prisoners were very concerned about the craft of poetry, but "we weren't ignoring the world around us."
5. Freire, *Pedagogy* 54.
6. Ibid., 69.
7. McKeown, *Out of Time* 145.
8. Ibid., 138.
9. Irish Republican Prisoners of War, *Questions of History* (Dublin: Sinn Féin Education Department, 1987) 5.
10. Irish Republican Prisoners of War 76.
11. Qtd. in McKeown, *Out of Time* 146.
12. Ibid., 145.
13. McKeown, *Out of Time* 146.
14. Qtd. in McKeown, *Out of Time* 186.
15. Gerry Kelly, "Tears," *Words from a Cell* (Dublin: Sinn Féin, 1989) 36.
16. Campbell, interview.
17. Ibid.
18. Ibid.
19. Danny Morrison, *Then the Walls Came Down: A Prison Journal* (Dublin and Cork: Mercier, 1999) 224.
20. Qtd. in Morrison, *Walls* 223.
21. Morrison, *Walls* 143.
22. Ibid., 34.
23. Ibid., 38.
24. Morrison, personal interview, July 2003.
25. A "quid" is slang for one British pound sterling.
26. Morrison, *Walls* 194.

27. Morrison, interview.
28. Laurence McKeown, email to author, 9 Feb. 2007. That the guards did not consider politicized poetry "dangerous" is interesting in itself and perhaps sheds further light on the issues of poetic anonymity discussed in chapter three.
29. Morrison, interview.
30. Ibid.
31. Ibid.
32. Laurence McKeown, personal interview, 1 Jul. 2003.
33. Morrison, interview.
34. McKeown, email to author.
35. Fewer Republican women were incarcerated in the Twenty-Six Counties than in England during these years. Pamela Kane, for example, was one of only three women in Limerick Prison and the only Republican. Pamela Kane, "A Day in the Life" *An Glór Gafa/The Captive Voice* 4.1 (Spring 1992): 4. By the time of the Winter 1998 issue there were only eight women POWs, all in Maghaberry. Rosa McLaughlin, "United and Strong" *An Glór Gafa/The Captive Voice* 10.2 (Winter 1998): 19.
36. Brian Campbell, "Prison Publications," *Éirí na Gealaí*, ed. Felim Ó Hagan. (Béal Feirste: Roinn an Chultúir, Shinn Féin, Bealtaine 1991) 15.
37. Republican POWs (Long Kesh), "A Republican Way Forward," *An Glór Gafa/The Captive Voice* 5.2 (Summer 1993): 6–7.
38. Women POWs (Maghaberry), "Women and the National Struggle." *An Glór Gafa/The Captive Voice* 1.1 (Autumn 1989): 10.
39. A Wing H5, "Rás Grinn na Streachailte," *An Glór Gafa/The Captive Voice* 2.3 (Winter 1990): 18.
40. POWs C2 (Maghaberry), "Blatant Discrimination," *An Glór Gafa/The Captive Voice* 4.1 (Spring 1992): 8.
41. Women POWs (Maghaberry), "Big Pat," *An Glór Gafa/The Captive Voice* 2.2 (Summer 1990): 7.
42. *An Glór Gafa/The Captive Voice* 2.2 (Summer 1990).
43. Ibid., 26.
44. This consortium of periodicals includes the *Andersontown News*, *North Belfast News*, *South Belfast News*, and the Irish-language paper *Lá*. *Daily Ireland* was part of this group as well during its all-too-brief run.
45. Máirtín Ó Muilleoir, letter, *An Glór Gafa/The Captive Voice* 2.3 (Winter 1990): 13.
46. Ibid.
47. Ibid.
48. *An Glór Gafa/The Captive Voice* 2.3 (Winter 1990): 13.
49. Nina Wilson, letter, *An Glór Gafa/The Captive Voice* 3.2 (Summer 1991): 24.
50. Kieran McCarthy, letter, *An Glór Gafa/The Captive Voice* 3.2 (Summer 1991): 24.
51. Lucy Chisholm, letter, *An Glór Gafa/The Captive Voice* 3.2 (Summer 1991): 24.

52. Jim Hooley, letter, *An Glór Gafa/The Captive Voice* 3.2 (Summer 1991): 25.
53. *An Glór Gafa/The Captive Voice* 3.2 (Summer 1991): 25.
54. Gearóid MacLochlainn, "Aistriúcháin," *Na Scéalaithe: Cnuasach Filíochta*. (Baile Átha Cliath: Coiscéim, 1999) 67.
55. Keith Tuma, ed., preface, *Oxford Anthology of Twentieth-Century British and Irish Poetry* (New York: Oxford University Press, 2001) xxiv.
56. Gerry Bogaard, letter to the editor, *An Glór Gafa/The Captive Voice* 3.2 (Summer 1991): 25.
57. Eddie Seeley, "An Teanga," *An Glór Gafa/The Captive Voice* 3.2 (Summer 1991): 20.
58. Gearóid MacLochlainn, "800 Years," *Babylon Gaeilgeoir* (Béal Feirste: An Clochán, 1997) 86. This book contains no English translations of any of the poems contained in it.
59. In observing this I do not mean to minimize the extent to which hybridity is seen as a powerful, even necessary part of a Gaeilgeoir's life by MacLochlainn, as must be evident in his past membership in the Irish-language reggae (!) group Bréag. It is only the violence with which these outside influences are imposed on Irish culture that make them problematic: the foreign is not "by definition" harmful in the way it is in the theories of nineteenth and early twentieth-century Republicans such as Pearse. In poems such as "Cainteoir Dúchais" he contests notions of the mythic purity of the native speakers of Irish and their sycophantic devotees. Likewise, he deconstructs essentialist conceptions that consign Gaeilge and its speakers to a misty rural setting. His is an Irish-language poetry rooted firmly in the urban streets.
60. Gearóid MacLochlainn, "Rite of Passage," *Sruth Teangacha/Stream of Tongues* (Indreabhán: Cló Iar-Chonnachta, 2002) 43. There is one relatively minor alteration in the *as Gaeilge* version of the final three lines in this collection: it substitutes "céadtuiscint" (lit. "first understanding, first realization") for the original wording of the third to last line ("an chéad uair"). "Teacht i Méadaíocht," *Sruth Teangacha/Stream of Tongues* (Indreabhán: Cló Iar-Chonnachta, 2002) 42.
61. Gearóid MacLochlainn, author's notes, *Sruth Teangacha/Stream of Tongues* (Indreabhán: Cló Iar-Chonnachta, 2002) 190.
62. *An Glór Gafa/The Captive Voice* 1.1 (Autumn 1989): 3.
63. In this story the narrator is Joe, a British soldier, who is literally—if, perhaps improbably—a sympathetic character. Of the hostile nationalist women he faces on his patrol he admits "in a way I can understand them," for their children are being killed and imprisoned by British soldiers such as him. Sands fashions Joe as someone disillusioned with his role in policing the Irish, who realizes that PIRA rebels are not psychopathic sectarian killers but members of a disciplined "army." The reader also learns that Joe has a daughter who turned three the previous month—in fact, one of his last thoughts before being struck down by a bullet is of his desire to take his child to the zoo. Bobby Sands, "Come

Out, You Wee Reds," *Skylark Sing Your Lonely Song* (Dublin and Cork: Mercier, 1982) 26. I do not read this story as an exercise in sadism on Sands's part, but rather as a tragic commentary not unlike that made by Brian Friel in the disappearance—and probable murder—of the likable British soldier Yolland in the play *Translations*. Although Yolland embraces Irish culture in a way that Joe does not—Sands's character makes disparaging comments about Irish accents, for instance, and maintains a policy of shooting first and asking questions later—the basic humanity of both soldiers is clear, reminding us that not all of those who participate in colonialist enterprises do so with self-consciously malicious intent, (and indeed, some might be forced to do so because of economic necessity). By striking down these likable characters both Friel and Sands underscore some of the costs of colonial conflict, though Sands lays the blame for the death far more firmly on the British government than does Friel. Although Friel's play ponders the possibility—even necessity—of hybridity and crossings of the boundaries between British and Irish even as its characters fail to bring that change about, "'Come On, You Wee Reds" is marked by an even less optimistic atmosphere. As manifest in the schoolmaster Hugh's change of heart with regard to the teaching of English, *Translations* suggests that a pragmatism is needed in Ireland, that an acceptable level of colonialism can permit forward motion, whereas Sands's story intimates that any armed colonial presence will always elicit armed response and stagnation in violence.

64. Qtd. in "Mobilize!" *An Phoblacht/Republican News* 13 Dec. 1980: 16.
65. Ibid.
66. Ibid.
67. "Show one sign of weakness and you've dug your own grave" he reflects. Bobby Sands, *One Day in My Life* (Dublin and Cork: Mercier, 1993) 33.
68. Sands, *One Day* 48.
69. Martina Anderson and Ella O'Dwyer, "Let's Talk," *An Glór Gafa/The Captive Voice* 5.1 (Summer 1993): 21.
70. The harm caused by inflexible prison regimes is of course not limited to their effects on the prisoners. Since the time of O'Donovan Rossa and the Fenians of the mid–nineteenth century the prison struggle in Ireland repeatedly demonstrates that repressive conditions and a lack of a legitimate system of trials only breed further conflict and resistance internal and external to prison walls. As the H Blocks struggle between 1976 and 1981 shows in no uncertain terms, such inflexibility tends to prolong and escalate the conflict, not end it. As evident in the abuses of Abu Gharib—whose excesses recall the treatment of nationalist "Hooded Men" in the first days of Internment—and the progression of Guantanamo Bay from a camp structure reminiscent of the Cages of Long Kesh to its subsequent cellular compounds evocative of the H Blocks, the United States clearly has failed to learn any lessons from Ireland.

71. Brian Campbell, "Democratic Confrontation," *An Glór Gafa/The Captive Voice* 4.2 (Summer 1992): 24–25. As simplistic as Campbell's advice may seem, I cannot help but mourn the extent to which such "democratic confrontation" was absent in the United States in the run-up to the current war in Iraq, a failure on the part of both a pliant American media as well as the timorous Democratic opposition.
72. Another forceful example of such contestation of boundaries can be seen in the "fun run" to raise money for Irish-language schools that Republican POWs in Long Kesh, Maghaberry, and the United States participated in, despite their incarceration. They simply ran the equivalent distances inside their prison yards, taking great pride in their continued ability to "highlight the issue of cultural discrimination" though detained. A Wing H5, "Rás Grinn na Streachailte/Fun Run or Hard Struggle?" *An Glór Gafa/The Captive Voice* 2.3 (Winter 1990): 18.
73. Adrian Kelly, "Easter Renewed," *An Glór Gafa/The Captive Voice* 5.1 (Spring 1993): 3.
74. "The Struggle," editorial, *An Glór Gafa/The Captive Voice* 2.1 (Spring 1990): 3.
75. Ibid.
76. Ibid.
77. "Ten Years On," *An Glór Gafa/The Captive Voice* 3.2 (Summer 1991): 3–4.
78. Ibid., 4.
79. Maitiú Ó Treasaigh, "Organise [*sic*] for Changing Times—A Reply to 'Ten Years On,'" *An Glór Gafa/The Captive Voice* 3.3 (Winter 1991): 23.
80. Likewise, the leadership initiated efforts to include the POWs in important decisions. As Republicans considered the implications of the Good Friday Agreement, Sinn Féin sent high-ranking representatives such as Martin McGuinness as delegates to the H Blocks and Maghaberry. These visits are outlined in the following articles: Rosa McLaughlin, "United and Strong," *An Glór Gafa/The Captive Voice* 10.2 (Winter 1998): 19, and "Proud of the Past," *An Glór Gafa/The Captive Voice* 10.2 (Winter 1998): 17–18.
81. "H-Block Submission to Sinn Féin Peace Commission," *An Glór Gafa/The Captive Voice* 6.1 (Summer 1994): 11.
82. As I complete the final draft of this manuscript, Sinn Féin gets ready to vote on whether or not they will formally recognize the PSNI as a legitimate police force, a prospect that would have been unheard of just a matter of a few years ago.
83. "Prisoners' Address to Sinn Féin Ard Fheis," *An Glór Gafa/The Captive Voice* 6.1 (Summer 1994): 10.
84. Mairtín Óg Meehan, "Sinn Féin 90th Ard Fheis: A POW Delegate's View," *An Glór Gafa/The Captive Voice* 8.1 (Summer 1996): 25.
85. Ibid.
86. Ibid.

87. Brendi McCleneghan, "Invisible Comrades: Gays and Lesbians in the Struggle," *An Glór Gafa/The Captive Voice* 3.3 (Winter 1991): 20.
88. Ibid.
89. Ibid.
90. McKeown, *Out of Time* 186.
91. Ibid.
92. Morrison, interview.
93. Tony Gorton "Sinn Fein [*sic*] Leader Gets Warm Welcome in N.Y." *The Militant* 25 Mar. 1996.
94. Qtd. in Adam Nossiter, "Sinn Fein [*sic*] President Will March in St. Patrick's Day Parade," *New York Times* 15 Mar. Late Edition—Final Correction Appended. <http://web.lexis-nexis.com/universe/printdoc>
95. Ibid.
96. Friedman, Cindy with Brian Nunes, Bill Stosine, Jason Lin, Greg Gordon and Ron Buckmire. "Newswrap" *This Way Out*, program no. 416, distributed 18 March 1996. Accessed 1 Oct. 2006. <http://www.qrd.org/qrd/media/radio/thiswayout/summary/newswrap/1996/416–03.18.96>
97. Qtd. In Agrès Maillot, *New Sinn Féin* (New York: Routledge, 2005) 106.
98. Ibid.
99. Ger Philpott and Paul Colgan, "Sinn Fein [*sic*] in Bid to Woo Gay Voters," *The Sunday Times* 17 Feb. 2002. The Newspaper Source, 10 Jan. 2006 <http://search.ebscohost.com>
100. McKeown, *Out of Time* 187.
101. It should be noted that Gerry Kelly's poem "The Prisoners' Prisoners" raised the issue of prisoners' partners even earlier than McKeown's short story. Written in 1982 and published in 1989, this poem's protagonist feels as if she is in love with a ghost, and in turn has become wraith-like herself. This poem also suggests—though arguably with less certainty than we see in McKeown's tale—that the woman might be having an affair with someone outside: in the penultimate stanza the woman laments "I do not wish to hate myself/For seeking love/In flesh and blood." Gerry Kelly, "The Prisoners' Prisoners," *Words from a Cell* 34.
102. The anonymity of both husband and wife in "The Visit" merits comment, for it seems obvious that McKeown foregrounds through it exactly how common such tensions are in such relationships: by remaining nameless, these characters become archetypical.
103. Laurence McKeown, "The Visit," *An Glór Gafa/The Captive Voice* 2.2 (Summer 1990): 10.
104. Ibid.
105. The prison administration did not permit conjugal visits for POWs in the H Blocks at any point in their history.
106. Laurence McKeown, email to author, 22 Jan 2007.
107. "A Fighting Battle," *An Glór Gafa/The Captive Voice* 5.1 (Spring 1993): 14.

108. Jim McCann, "Love Is..." *An Glór Gafa/The Captive Voice* 5.1 (Spring 1993): 25.
109. Ibid.
110. Red Spider, "Shabby Clothes, Scruffy Runners, and Dodgy Alarms,"*An Glór Gafa/The Captive Voice* 4.3 (Winter 1992): 21.
111. Carol Cullen, "Enduring Relationships," *An Glór Gafa/The Captive Voice* 5.1 (Spring 1993): 4.
112. "A Fighting Battle" 14.
113. Ibid., 15.
114. By claiming this I certainly do not dispute that POWs also tried to spare their loved ones from worry. In his poem "On the Boards," for example, Gerry Kelly recounts his harrowing experience of the punishment cells of the H Blocks during the winter of 1976–1977. The freezing and filthy conditions are so extreme that the speaker "refused all thoughts of loved ones/In case they sensed your deep-felt fear[.]" Gerry Kelly, "on the Boards," *Words from a Cell* 21.
115. "A Fighting Battle" 15.
116. Mary McArdle and Ailish Carroll, "How Free Are the Prisoners' Partners?" *An Glór Gafa/The Captive Voice* 5.2 (Summer 1993): 10.
117. Ibid.
118. *Mother Ireland*, dir. Anne Crilly, Derry Film and Video, 1988.
119. Paddy Devenny, "An Encouraging Concept?" *An Glór Gafa/The Captive Voice* 5.3 (Winter 1993): 21.
120. Ibid.
121. Ibid.
122. "Tuso," "An Insider's View from Outside," *An Glór Gafa/The Captive Voice* 6.1 (Summer 1994): 5.
123. Christine Poland and Dáithí Adams, "Just a Prisoner's Wife," *An Glór Gafa/The Captive Voice* 11.1 (Summer 1999): 2–3.

Chapter Six Postscript: "You Look Like Jesus Christ": Images of Republican POWs in Contemporary Cinema

1. *Some Mother's Son*. dir. Terry George, perf. Helen Mirren, Fionnuala Flannigan. Castle Rock, 1996.
2. *In the Name of the Father*, dir. Jim Sheridan. perf. Daniel Day-Lewis, Emma Thompson. MCA/Universal, 1994.
3. Sheridan cowrote *Some Mother's Son* with Terry George. George himself is a Republican ex-prisoner, though he served his time in the Cages of Long Kesh rather than in the H Blocks on which *Some Mother's Son* centers. Ruth Barton, *Jim Sheridan: Framing the Nation*. (Dublin: The Liffey Press, 2002) 63–4.

4. It must be remembered that from 1971 to 1976 Internment was in effect in Northern Ireland, which meant that individuals could be arrested and detained indefinitely without charge or trial.
5. "Early Risers" is included in Adams's 1990 book *Cage Eleven*, an anthology of short stories and essays in large part written during his incarceration in the Cages of Long Kesh. The majority of these texts initially were published as articles in *Republican News*, a Belfast newspaper. Written by Adams under the pseudonym "Brownie" and smuggled out of the Cages, these articles appeared between 1975 and 1977 Gerry Adams, *Cage Eleven* (Dingle: Brandon, 1990) 3.
6. Gerry Adams, "Early Risers," *Cage Eleven* (Dingle: Brandon, 1990) 24.
7. Unlike contemporary American prisons, H Block cells did not contain their own individual toilets. Instead, prisoners were required to use chamber pots or the communal lavatories located at the end of the prison wing.
8. Laurence McKeown, *Out of Time: Irish Republican Prisoners Long Kesh 1972–2000* (Belfast: Beyond the Pale, 2001) 56–7.
9. A notable (though not widely distributed) recent release is *H3* (2002) whose screenplay was authored by two Republican ex-POWs, Brian Campbell and Dr. Laurence McKeown, both of whom served time in the H Blocks. Dr. McKeown was on the 1981 Republican hunger strike with Bobby Sands and went without food for 70 days before lapsing into a coma, at which point his family authorized medical intervention that prevented his death. (Brian Campbell, Laurence McKeown, and Felim O'Hagan, *Nor Meekly Serve My Time: The H Blocks Struggle 1976–1981* (Belfast: Beyond the Pale, 1994) 253.
10. Barton, *Jim Sheridan* 86.
11. Danny Devenny (who shared Cage Eleven with both Sands and Adams) notes that Sands began writing in Long Kesh as early as 1974, contributing to the cage news-sheet "up until his release in 1976." "Life in the cages [*sic*] of the Kesh." *An Phoblacht/Republican News*. 9 May 1981: 22. Like Adams's first writings, Sands's best-known work appeared first in *Republican News*, the Belfast newspaper that became *An Phoblacht/Republican News* in 1979.

    Sands's first seven *AP/RN* articles were credited only to "a West Belfast Republican," though after 25 November 1978 subsequent articles by Sands bore the pen-name "Marcella," Sands's sister's name. There was a long interruption in the publishing of Sands's prison literature in *An Phoblacht/Republican News* after his story "I Once Had a Life" appears on St. Patrick's Day 1979. "I Once Had a Life." *An Phoblacht/Republican News*. 17 Mar. 1979: 2. The next time Sands's work appears is during his hunger strike in a special section of *An Phoblacht/Republican News* when the paper reprints three of his stories on 21 Mar. 1981. This is the first time that Sands is publicly identified as the author of the earlier *AP/RN* writings. "The Writings of Bobby Sands." *An Phoblacht/Republican News*. 21 Mar. 1981: 6–8.

12. Sands was imprisoned in the Cages with such Republican leaders as Gerry Adams. Adams writes in his autobiography that he "got to know [Sands] better when we started to develop political lectures and other collective efforts in the cage, and he became very involved in these." *Before the Dawn: An Autobiography* (New York: William Morrow & Company Inc., 1996) 241.
13. McKeown, *Out of Time* 70.
14. Qtd. in McKeown, *Out of Time* 38.
15. Ibid.
16. Ibid., 92.
17. This historical inaccuracy may proceed from the fact that George served time in the Cages, and was perhaps more familiar with the more regimented existence in them. It is the era and area of the Long Kesh prison compound in which George was incarcerated that distinguishes him from the screenwriters of *H3* (see note 6 above), both of whom were imprisoned in the H Blocks.
18. Bobby Sands, *Skylark Sing Your Lonely Song* (Dublin and Cork: Mercier, 1982) 171.
19. Ibid., 172.
20. Such comparisons to Christ are almost categorically rejected by contemporary Republicans themselves, particularly POWs. *H3*, for example, accurately represents a number of POWs going on hunger strike with close-cropped hair: Republicans in the H Blocks ended the No-Wash Protest to focus attention on the hunger strike, and as a result many prisoners would have cut their hair short at this time. The appearance of a long-haired Bobby Sands in *H3* seems an attempt to reflect the notoriously shaggy style of the man and should not be mistaken as the employment of a Christological motif. This is a point underscored by the almost non-existent amount of time that the film devotes to dramatizing Sands's death. Unlike *Some Mother's Son*, which over the course of several minutes cuts back and forth between Sands's deathbed and a protest vigil outside a police station, *H3* gives the viewer only a split-second close-up image of Sands's face being covered with a sheet. In its brevity, *H3*'s portrayal is chillingly matter-of-fact, and more evocative of a morgue than reminiscent of Golgotha or Gethsemane.
21. Liz Curtis, *Ireland: The Propaganda War* (Belfast: Sásta, 1998) 128.
22. Martin McLoone, *Irish Film: The Emergence of a Contemporary Cinema* (London: British Film Institute, 2000) 70.
23. For instance, Sheridan's film shows unambiguously that kneecappings and other forms of policing by paramilitary groups such as the IRA do indeed receive the tacit approval of a large percentage of the Catholic/nationalist community. When IRA members threaten to shoot the cinematic Gerry Conlon and his friends in their knees for stealing, a woman calls out from a neighboring flatblock "Shoot the bastards! They're always robbing our houses!" For further evidence of the accuracy of this

portrayal, see Jeffry Sluka's research into nationalist communities' support of paramilitary policing in *Hearts and Minds, Water and Fish.*

24. McLoone, *Irish Film* 73.
25. Ibid.
26. Gerry Conlon, *In the Name of the Father* (New York: Plume, 1993) 159.
27. In making this claim it should go without saying that I am not attempting to deny IRA attacks on prison warders in other occasions such as the 1983 escape of republican POWs from the H Blocks: any number of them might be referenced, just as any number of atrocities on the part of the British Army and Loyalist paramilitaries might also be cited by Republicans. However, I find it predictable that of all the departures from historical fact contained within *In the Name of the Father*, the fictional attack on the prison officer remains least discussed by revisionist critics who claim to be interested in setting the historical record straight.

    Similarly, few of these critics seem to mind that no scenes of prison warders' abuse of Republican POWs appear in *Some Mother's Son*. The only vague reference takes place when Gerard and his comrade Frankie first are admitted to the H Blocks. The two Republicans refuse to wear the uniforms that are given to them, and the camera gives us a brief close-up of a warder's grip tightening on his baton. However, with a silent toss of the head, the guard's superior prevents any attack from taking place. Where, one might ask, are the brutal interrogations, strip searches, and beatings that Republican POWs have categorically reported as endemic to Long Kesh, and that respected human rights organizations like Amnesty International officially decried on numerous occasions?

Bibliography

A Wing H5. "Rás Grinn na Streachailte," *An Glór Gafa/The Captive Voice* 2.3 (Winter 1990): 18.

Adams, Gerry. "An Ard Fheis." *Republican News*. 18 Sept. 1976: 2.

———. "The Awakening." *Republican News*.19 Feb. 1977: 4–5.

———. *Before the Dawn: An Autobiography*. New York: William Morrow & Company Inc., 1996.

———. "Belfast: 1913 or 1976?" *Republican News*. 13 Nov. 1976: 2.

———. *Cage Eleven*. Dingle: Brandon, 1990.

———. "Cage Eleven." *Cage Eleven*. New York: Sheridan Square, 1990. 16–22.

———. "Christians for Freedom?" *Republican News*. 22 Jan. 1977: 2.

———. "Cratur." *Cage Eleven*. Dingle: Brandon, 1990. 31–35.

———. "Early Risers." *Cage Eleven*. Dingle: Brandon, 1990. 23–25

———. "Early Risers." *Republican News*. 11 Oct. 1975: 5.

———. "The Fire." *Cage Eleven*. Dingle: Brandon, 1990. 36–46.

———. "Frank Stagg." *Republican News*. 10 Jan. 1976: 4–5.

———. "Frank Stagg, 1976." *Cage Eleven*. Dingle: Brandon, 1990. 116–124.

———. *Free Ireland: Toward a Lasting Peace*. Niwot, CO: Roberts Rinehart, 1994.

———. "Inside Story." *Republican News*. 16 Aug. 1975: 6.

———. "The Moles." *Republican News*. 29 Jan. 1977: 2.

———. "The National Alternative." *Republican News*. 3 Apr. 1976: 6–7.

———. "Out There on the Motorway." *Republican News*. 23 Aug. 1975: 7.

———. "Real Poetry" (review), *Republican News*. 17 Dec. 1981: 9.

———. "The Republic: A Reality." *Republican News*. 29 Nov. 1975: 4.

———. "Screws." *Cage Eleven*. Dingle: Brandon, 1990. 26–30.

———. "Screws." *Republican News*. 10 Apr. 1976: 7–8.

———. "'Thumper' or 'Tumper.'" *Republican News*. 8 Nov. 1975: 5.

———. "A Week in the Life." *Republican News*. 29 May 1976: 3,7.

Anderson, Martina. "Interview with Martina Anderson." *Slí na mBán* ed. Melissa Thompson. Oct 1999. Accessed 29 Sept. 2006. <http://www.tallgirlshorts.net/marymary/martina.html>

Anderson, Martina, and Ella O'Dwyer. "Let's Talk." *An Glór Gafa/The Captive Voice* 5.1 (Spring 1993): 21.

Ashcroft, Bill. *Post-colonial Transformation*. New York: Routledge, 2001.

Ashcroft, Bill, Gareth Griffiths, and Helen Tiffin. *The Empire Writes Back: Theory and Practice in Post-colonial Literatures*. New York: Routledge, 1989.

Barton, Ruth. *Jim Sheridan: Framing the Nation*. Dublin: The Liffey Press, 2002.

Beard, Michael. "The Perils of the Plain Speaker." *Edebiyat* 3.1 (1978): 83–93.

Bell, J. Bower. *IRA Tactics & Targets*. Dublin: Poolbeg, 1990.

Beresford, David. *Ten Men Dead*. London: HarperCollins, 1987.

Boyle, Seamus. "Portrait of a Hunger Striker: Mairead Nugent." *An Phoblacht/Republican News*. 27 Dec. 1980: 8–10.

———. "Portrait of a Hunger Striker: Mary Doyle." *An Phoblacht/Republican News*. 10 Jan. 1981: 12–13.

Breytenbach, Breyten. *The True Confessions of an Albino Terrorist*. New York: Farrar, Straus & Giroux, 1983.

Campbell, Brian. "Democratic Confrontation." *An Glór Gafa/The Captive Voice* 4.2 (Summer 1992): 24–25.

———., ed. *H Block: A Selection of Poetry by Republican Prisoners*. Sheffield: South Yorkshire Writers, 1991.

———. Interview, Newry, Co.Down, 1 July 2003.

———. "Prison Publications." *Éirí na Gealaí*. Ed. Felim Ó Hagan. Béal Feirste: Roinn an Chultúir, Shinn Féin, Bealtaine 1991. 11–16.

Campbell, Brian, Laurence McKeown, and Felim O'Hagan. *Nor Meekly Serve My Time: The H Block Struggle 1976–1981*. Belfast: Beyond the Pale, 1994.

Cardozo-Freeman, Inez. "Slipping and Sliding: Survival Games in a Prison." *International Folklore Review* 8 (1991): 100–109.

de Certeau, Michel. *The Practice of Everyday Life*. Trans. Steven Rendall. Berkeley: University of California Press, 1984.

Challis, Jim. *The Northern Ireland Prison Service 1920–1990: A History*. Belfast: The Northern Ireland Prison Service, 1999.

Chisholm, Lucy. Letter to the editor. *An Glór Gafa/The Captive Voice* 3.2 (Summer 1991): 24.

"Conditions Document" (held in the Northern Ireland political collection of the Linen Hall Library, Belfast). Republican Women Prisoners, 1996.

Conlon, Gerry. *In the Name of the Father*. New York: Plume, 1993.

Coogan, Tim Pat. *The IRA*. Niwot, CO: Roberts Rinehart, 1994.

———. *On the Blanket*. Dublin: Ward River Press, 1980.

———. *The Troubles*. New York: Palgrave, 2002.

Coulter, Carol. *Web of Punishment*. Dublin: Attic, 1991.

Crilly, Anne. "Interview with Anne Crilly." *Slí na mBán*, ed. Melissa Thompson. Oct 1999. Accessed 29 Sept. 2006. <http://www.tallgirlshorts.net/marymary/anne. html >

Cullen, Carol. "Enduring Relationships." *An Glór Gafa/The Captive Voice* 5.1 (Spring 1993): 4.

Curtis, Liz. *Ireland: The Propaganda War*. Belfast: Sásta, 1998.

D'Arcy, Margaretta. *Tell Them Everything: A Sojourn in the Prison of Her Majesty Queen Elizabeth II at Ard Macha (Armagh)*. London: Pluto, 1981.

Darragh, Síle. Interview, conducted at the Sinn Féin offices in Belfast, 7 Jun. 2004.

Devenny, Danny. "Life in the Cages [*sic*] of the Kesh." *An Phoblacht/Republican News*. 9 May 1981: 22.

Devenny, Paddy. "An Encouraging Concept?" *An Glór Gafa/The Captive Voice* 5.3 (Winter 1993): 21.

Devlin, Anne. *Ourselves Alone*. New York: Dramatist's Play Service, 1999.

Devlin, Bobby. *An Interlude with Seagulls: Memories of a Long Kesh Internee*. 2nd edition. London: Information on Ireland, 1985.

Dillon, Martin. *The Shankill Butchers*. New York: Routledge, 1989.

Donadey, Anne. "Between Amnesia and Anamnesis: Re-membering the Fractures of Colonial History." *Studies in 20th Century Literature* 23.1 (Winter 1999): 111–116.

Dreyfus, Hubert L., and Paul Rabinow. *Michel Foucault: Beyond Structuralism and Hermenutics*. Chicago: Chicago University Press, 1982.

Driver, Felix. "Bodies in Space: Foucault's Account of Disciplinary Power." *Reassesing Foucault: Power, Medicine and the Body*. Ed. Colin Jones and Roy Porter. New York: Routledge, 1999. 113–131.

Eagleton, Terry. *The Ideology of the Aesthetic*. Cambridge, MA: Blackwell, 1990.

———. *The Illusions of Postmodernism*. Cambridge, MA: Blackwell, 1996.

Eagleton, Terry, Fredric Jameson, and Edward. W. Said. *Nationalism, Colonialism, and Literature*. Minneapolis: Minnesota University Press, 1990.

Elliott, J.E. "What's 'Post' in Post-colonial Theory?" *Borderlands: Negotiating Boundaries in Post-colonial Writing*. Ed. Monika Reif-Hulser. Amsterdam: Rodopi, 1999. 43–53.

English, Richard. *Armed Struggle: The History of the IRA*. New York: Oxford University Press, 2003.

Fairweather, Eileen, Roisin McDonough, and Melanie McFadyean. *Only the Rivers Run Free, Northern Ireland: The Women's War*. London: Pluto, 1984.

Fanon, Frantz. *The Wretched of the Earth*. Trans. Constance Farrington. New York: Grove, 1963.

Faoi Ghlas ag Gaill. Belfast: Gaeil Bhéal Feirste in Éadan H Bhloc agus Ard Mhacha, 1981.

Faul, Fr. Denis, and Fr. Raymond Murray. *The Hooded Men: British Torture in Ireland, August, October 1971*. Dungannon: Fr. Faul, 1974.

Feldman, Allen. *Formations of Violence*. Chicago: Chicago University Press, 1991.

———. "Violence and Vision: The Prosthetics and Aesthetics of Terror." *Popular Culture* 10.1 (1997): 24–60.

"A Fighting Battle." *An Glór Gafa/The Captive Voice* 5.1 (Spring 1993): 14–16.

FitzGibbon, Constantine. "Red Hand: The Ulster Colony." *Northern Ireland*. Ed. Jonathan Bartlett. New York: The H.W. Wilson Company, 1983. 8–37.

Foucault, Michel. *The Archaeology of Knowledge & the Discourse on Language*. Trans. A.M. Sheridan Smith. New York: Pantheon, 1972.

———. *Discipline and Punish*. Trans. Alan Sheridan. New York: Vintage, 1979.

———. "The Eye of Power." *Power/Knowledge: Selected Interviews and Other Writings 1972–1977*. Ed. Colin Gordon. New York: Pantheon, 1980. 146–165.

———. "Power and Strategies." *Power/Knowledge: Selected Interviews and Other Writings 1972–1977*. Ed. Colin Gordon. New York: Pantheon, 1980. 134–145.

Friedman, Cindy with Brian Nunes, Bill Stosine, Jason Lin, Greg Gordon and Ron Buckmire. "Newswrap" *This Way Out,* program no. 416, distributed 18 March 1996. Accessed 1 Oct. 2006. <http://www.qrd.org/qrd/media/radio/thiswayout/summary/newswrap/1996/416-03.18.96>

Freire, Paulo. *Pedagogy of the Oppressed*. Trans. Myra Bergman Ramos. New York: Continuum, 1993.

Fromkin, David. *The Independence of Nations*. Westport, CT: Praeger, 1981.

Fun Run Participants, A Wing, H5. "Rás Grinn na Streachailte/Fun Run or Hard Struggle?" *An Glór Gafa/The Captive Voice* 2.3 (Winter 1990): 20.

Goffman, Erving. *Asylums*. New York: Anchor, 1961.

Gorton, Tony. "Sinn Fein [*sic*] Leader Gets Warm Welcome in N.Y." *The Militant*. 25 Mar. 1996.

Greer, Herb. "Ulster: In the Empty House of the State." *Northern Ireland*. Ed. Jonathan Bartlett. New York: The H.W. Wilson Company, 1983. 37–61.

H3. Dir. Les Blair. Perf. Brendan Mackey, Dean Lennox Kelly, and Aiden Campbell. Metropolitan, 2002.

"H-Block Submission to Sinn Féin Peace Commission." *An Glór Gafa/The Captive Voice* 6.1 (Summer 1994): 11.

Haffner, Sebastian. *The Meaning of Hitler*. Trans. Ewald Osers. Cambridge, MA: Harvard University Press, 1979.

Harlow, Barbara. *Barred: Women, Writing, and Political Detention*. Hanover: Weslyan University Press, 1992.

———. "Political Detention: Countering the University." *October* 53 (Summer 1990): 41–61.

———. *Resistance Literature*. New York: Methuen, 1987.

———. "The Writing on the Wall." *Theory Rules: Art as Theory/Theory as Art*. Ed. Jody Berland, Will Straw, and David Thomas. Toronto: YYZ/Toronto University Press, 1996.

Hegel, Georg Wilhelm. *The Philosophy of Hegel*. Ed. Carl J. Friedrich. New York: Random House, 1954.

Hillen, Eileen. Interview, conducted at the Sinn Féin offices in Newry, 5 June 2004.

Hooley, Jim. Letter to the editor. *An Glór Gafa/The Captive Voice* 3.2 (Summer 1991): 25.

In the Name of the Father. Dir. Jim Sheridan. Perf. Daniel Day-Lewis and Emma Thompson. MCA/Universal, 1994.

"Irish Prison Poetry." *Seneca Review* 23 (Winter 1993): 1–2.

Jacobs, J.U. "Confession, Interrogation, and Self-interrogation in the New South African Prison Writing." *Kunapipi* 13.1–2 (1991): 115–127.

———. "Narrating the Island: Robben Island in South African Literature." *Current Writing* 4 (1992): 73–84.

Joannou, Maroula. "Gender, Militancy, and Wartime." *The Uses of Autobiography*. Ed. Julia Swindells. London: Taylor and Francis, 1995. 31–44.

Journal of Prisoners on Prisons. Special Issue: Republican Prisoners of War 7:1 (1996–1997).

Joyce, James. *A Portrait of the Artist As a Young Man*. New York: Bantam, 1992.

Kane, Pamela. "A Day in the Life." *An Glór Gafa/The Captive Voice* 4.1 (Summer 1992): 4.

Katrak, Ketu H. "Decolonizing Culture: Toward a Theory for Post-colonial Women's Texts." *The Post-colonial Studies Reader.* Ed. Bill Ashcroft, Gareth Griffiths, and Helen Tiffin. London: Routledge, 1995. 255–258.

Keena, Colm. *A Biography of Gerry Adams*. Cork: Mercier, 1990.

Kelly, Adrian. "Easter Renewed." *An Glór Gafa/The Captive Voice* 5.1 (Spring 1993): 3.

Kelly, Gerry. *Words from a Cell.* Dublin: Sinn Féin Publicity Dept., 1989.

Kennedy-Pipe, Caroline. *The Origins of the Present Troubles in Northern Ireland*. New York: Longman, 1997.

King-Irani, Laurie. "We Aren't the World." *In These Times*. 28.3 (2004).

Kojéve, Alexandre. *Introduction to the Reading of Hegel.* Trans. James H. Nichols, Jr. Ed. Allan Bloom. New York: Basic, 1969.

Kristeva, Julia. "Holbein's Dead Christ." *Fragments for a History of the Human Body*. Ed. Michel Feher with Ramona Naddaff and Nadia Tazi. New York: Zone, 1990. 238–269.

Lamming, George. "The Occasion for Speaking." *The Post-colonial Studies Reader.* Ed. Bill Ashcroft, Gareth Griffiths, and Helen Tiffin. London: Routledge, 1995. 12–17.

Lefebvre, Henri. *The Production of Space*. Trans. Donald Nicholson-Smith. Cambridge, MA: Blackwell, 1991.

Lloyd, David. *Anomalous States: Irish Writing and the Post-colonial Moment*. Durham: Duke University Press, 1993.

Lollini, Massimo. "Literature and Testimony in Gramsci's *Letters from Prison*: The Question of Subjectivity." *Canadian Review of Comparative Literature* 23.2 (1996): 519–529.

Longley, Edna. *The Living Stream*. London: Bloodaxe, 1993.

———. "From *Poetry in the Wars*." *The Field Day Anthology of Irish Writing*. Vol. 3. Ed. Seamus Deane. Derry: Field Day, 1991.

Lowry, David R. "The English System of Judicial Injustice in Northern Ireland." *Catholic League Newsletter* 7.11 (1980): 1–4.

McArdle, Mary, and Ailish Carroll. "How Free Are the Prisoners' Partners?" *An Glór Gafa/The Captive Voice* 5.2 (Summer 1993): 10–11.

McAuley, Councilor Crissy. Interview, conducted at the Belfast City Hall, 5 Aug. 1998.

McCann, Jim. *And The Gates Flew Open*. Belfast: Glandore, 1998.

———. "Love Is…" *An Glór Gafa/The Captive Voice* 5.1 (Spring 1993): 25.

McCarthy, Kieran. Letter to editor. *An Glór Gafa/The Captive Voice* 3.2 (Summer 1991): 24.

McClenaghan, Brendi. "Invisible Comrades: Gays and Lesbians in the Struggle." *An Glór Gafa*. 3.3 (Winter 1991): 20–21.

McEvoy, Kieran. *Paramilitary Imprisonment in Northern Ireland*. New York: Oxford University Press, 2001.

McGann, Jerome. J. *A Critique of Modern Textual Criticism*. Chicago: University of Chicago Press, 1983.

McGeough, Gerry. *The Ambush and Other Stories*. Jay Street Publishers, 1996.

McGowen, Randall. "Power and Humanity, or Foucault among the Historians." *Reassesing Foucault: Power, Medicine and the Body*. Ed. Colin Jones and Roy Porter. New York: Routledge, 1999. 91–111.

McIntyre, Anthony. "Provisional Republicanism: Internal Politics, Iniquities, and Modes of Repression." *Republicanism in Modern Ireland*. Ed. Fearghal McGarry. Dublin: University College Dublin Press, 2003. 178–198.

McKeown, Laurence. Email to author. 9 Feb. 2007.

———. *Out of Time: Irish Republican Prisoners Long Kesh 1972–2000*. Belfast: Beyond the Pale, 2001.

———. "The Visit." *An Glór Gafa/The Captive Voice* 2.2 (Summer 1990): 10.

McLaughlin, Rosa. "United and Strong." *An Glór Gafa/The Captive Voice* 10.2 (Winter 1998): 19.

McLoone, Martin. *Irish Film: The Emergence of a Contemporary Cinema*. London: British Film Institute, 2000.

MacCormaic, Eoghan. "The Price of Freedom." *Iris* (Aug. 1984): 34–42.

MacLochlainn, Gearóid. "800 Years." *Babylon Gaeilgeoir* Béal Feirste: An Clochán, 1997. 82–86.

———. "Aistriúcháin." *Na Scéalaithe: Cnuasach Filíochta*. Baile Átha Cliath: Coiscéim, 1999. 66–67.

———. *Babylon Gaeilgeoir*. Béal Feirste: An Clochán, 1997.

———. *Na Scéalaithe: Cnuasach Filíochta*. Baile Átha Cliath: Coiscéim, 1999.

———. *Sruth Teangacha/Stream of Tongues*. Indreabhán: Cló Iar-Chonnachta, 2002.

———. "Teacht i Méadaíocht/Rite of Passage." *Sruth Teangacha/Stream of Tongues*. Indreabhán: Cló Iar-Chonnachta, 2002. 36–43.

MacThomais, Derec. "Greetings from the Kesh." *Faoi Glas*[*sic*]. No.1 (Aug. 1975): 1, 3.

Magee, Pat. *Gangsters or Guerillas?* Belfast: Beyond the Pale, 2001.

Maillot, Agnès. *New Sinn Féin*. New York: Routledge, 2005.

Meehan, Mairtín Óg. "Sinn Féin 90th Ard Fheis: A POW Delegate's View." *An Glór Gafa/The Captive Voice* 8.1 (Summer 1996): 24–25.

Metress, Seamus. "Bobby Sands: Ethnic Culture Hero and Sociopolitical Symbol." *The Ethnic Reporter* 13.2 (Fall 1988): 3–6.

Millett, Kate. *The Politics of Cruelty*. London: Viking, 1994.

"Mobilize!" *An Phoblacht/Republican News*. 13 Dec. 1980: 16.

Morley, Dave. "Simplicity." *Faoi Glas* [*sic*]. No.1 (Aug. 1975), 3.

Morris, Norval, and David J. Rothman. *The Oxford History of Prison*. New York: Oxford University Press, 1995.

Morrison, Danny. Interview, conducted at Andersontown, Belfast, July 2003.

———. *On the Back of the Swallow*. Cork and Dublin: Mercier Press, 1994.

———. *Then the Walls Came Down: A Prison Journal*. Cork: Mercier, 1999.

Mother Ireland. Videotape. Dir. Anne Crilly. Derry Film & Video, 1988.

"A Mouse-Eye View: A Tale by an H-Block prisoner." *An Phoblacht/Republican News*. 17 Mar. 1979: 2.

Murray, Raymond. *Hard Time: Armagh Gaol, 1971–1986*. Cork: Mercier, 1998.

———. *State Violence: Northern Ireland 1969–1997*. Cork: Mercier, 1998.

Nelis, Mary. "Interview with Mary Nelis." *Slí na mBán*, ed. Melissa Thompson. Oct 1999. Accessed 29 Sept. 2006. <http://www.tallgirlshorts.net/marymary/marynelis.html >

Net, Mariana. "Representations of the Political Prison: Actual Spaces, Virtual Forms." *Spaces and Significations*. Ed. Roberta Kevelson. New York: Peter Lang, 1996. 135–150.

Níc Giolla Easpaig, Áine and Eibhlín. *Girseacha i nGéibheann*. Westport: Foilseacháin Náisiúnta Teoranta, 1987.

———. *Sisters in Cells*. Trans. Nollaig Ó Gadhra. Westport: Foilseacháin Náisiúnta Teoranta, 1987.

Nicholls, Todd R. "The First Strike for Status—and Republican Legitimacy." *The Irish News*. 6 Nov. 2000: 32–33.

Northern Ireland Prison Service Web Site (Updated Sept. 1999), 7 Jan. 2001. Available: http://www.nio.gov.uk/prisintr.htm.

Nossiter, Adam. "Sinn Fein [*sic*] President Will March in St. Patrick's Day Parade," *New York Times* 15 Mar. 1996. Late edition—final correction appended. http://web.lexis-nexis.com/universe/printdoc

O'Donovan Rossa, Jeremiah. *Irish Rebels in English Prisons*. Dingle, Co. Kerry: Brandon, 1991.

O'Dwyer, Ella. "Interview with Ella O'Dwyer." *Slí na mBán*, ed. Melissa Thompson. Oct 1999. Accessed 29 Sept. 2006. <http://www.tallgirlshorts.net/marymary/ella.html>

Off Our Knees! Videotape. Narr. Bernadette Devlin-McAliskey. '68 Committee, 1988.

O'Hagan, Felim, ed. *Éirí na Gealaí: Reflections on the Culture of Resistance in Long Kesh.* Belfast: Roinn an Chultúir, Shinn Féin, *Bealtaine* (May)1991.

O'Hearn, Denis. *Nothing but an Unfinished Song: Bobby Sands, the Hunger Striker Who Ignited a Generation.* New York: Nation, 2006.

Ó Muilleoir, Máirtín. "Letter to the Editor." *An Glór Gafa/The Captive Voice* 2.3 (Winter 1990): 13.

Ó Treasaigh, Maitiú. "Organise [*sic*] for Changing Times—A Reply to 'Ten Years On." *An Glór Gafa/The Captive Voice* 3.3 (Winter 1991): 22–23.

Ormsby, Frank, ed. *Poets from the North of Ireland* (Belfast: Blackstaff Press, 1990).

"Out of the Ashes." *An Phoblacht/Republican News.* 27 Jan. 1979: 1.

Parry, Benita. "Problems of Current Theories of Colonial Discourse." *The Post-colonial Studies Reader.* Ed. Bill Ashcroft, Gareth Griffiths, and Helen Tiffin. London: Routledge, 1995. 36–44.

Pearse, Patrick. "O'Donovan Rossa: Graveside Panegyric." *The Field Day Anthology of Irish Writing.* Ed. Seamus Deane. Derry: Field Day, 1992. 293–294.

Philpott, Ger, and Paul Colgan, "Sinn Fein [*sic*] in Bid to Woo Gay Voters," *The Sunday Times* 17 Feb. 2002. The Newspaper Source, 10 Jan. 2006. http://search.ebscohost.com

"Poems from the H Blocks." *Republican News.* 9 Sept. 1978: 10.

Poland, Christine and Dáthí Adams. "Just a Prisoner's Wife." *An Glór Gafa/The Captive Voice* 11.1 (Summer 1999): 2–3.

Portlaoise Writings. Dublin: Irish Republican Publications, July 1987.

POWs C2 (Maghaberry), "Blatant Discrimination," *An Glór Gafa/The Captive Voice* 4.1 (Spring 1992): 8–9.

Powers, William K. *Sacred Language: The Nature of Supernatural Discourse in Lakota.* Norman: Oklahoma University Press, 1986.

Price, Dolores and Marion. *Venceremos Sisters: Prison Writings of the Price Sisters.* Belfast: Cathal Brugha Cumann, n.d. [1974?]

"Prisoners' Address to Sinn Féin Ard Fheis." *An Glór Gafa/The Captive Voice* 6.1 (Summer 1994): 10.

"Proud of the Past." *An Glór Gafa/The Captive Voice* 10.2 (Winter 1998): 17–18.

Red Spider. "Shabby Clothes, Scruffy Runners, and Dodgy Alarms." *An Glór Gafa/The Captive Voice* 4.3 (Winter 1992): 21.

Remand POW and Partner. "Open Communication." *An Glór Gafa/The Captive Voice* 5.3 (Winter 1993): 20.

Republican POWs (Long Kesh). "A Republican Way Forward." *An Glór Gafa/The Captive Voice* 5.2 (Summer 1993): 6–7.

Republican Prisoners. *Jail History.* Belfast: Sinn Féin?, 1993.

Republican Prisoners of War. *Questions of History* (Dublin: AP/RN Print and Sinn Féin Education Department, 1987).

Roberts, Sheila. "South African Prison Literature." *Ariel* 16.2 (Apr. 1985): 61–73.

Said, Edward W. "Yeats and Decolonization." *Nationalism, Colonialism, and Literature*. Intro. Seamus Deane. Minneapolis: Minnesota University Press, 1990. 69–95.

Sands, Bobby. "The Agony of It All." *Republican News*. 3 Jun. 1978: 3.

———. "All God's Children." *An Phoblacht/Republican News*. 19 Sept. 1981: 9–10.

———. "The Birth of a Republican." *Republican News*. 16 Dec. 1978: 6–7.

———. "The Birth of a Republican: From a Nationalist Ghetto to the Battlefield of the H Block." *An Phoblacht/Republican News*. 4 Apr. 1981: 6–7.

———. *Bobby Sands: Irish Rebel A Self-portrait in Poetry and Polemics Issued on the 10th Anniversary of His Death*. Ed. Robert West. San Francisco: Mellen Research University Press, 1991.

———. "A Break in the Monotony." *Republican News*. 20 Jan. 1979: 2.

———. "The Captain and the Cowards." *An Phoblacht/Republican News*. 19 Sept. 1981: 8–9.

———. "Christmas on the Blanket." *Republican News*. 21 Jan. 1978: 3.

———. "'Come Out, You Wee Reds." *Skylark Sing Your Lonely Song*. Dublin and Cork: Mercier, 1982. 24–26.

———. "The Harvest Britain Has Sown [*sic*]." *Republican News*. 16 Sept. 1978: 8.

———. "'I Am Sir, Your [*sic*] Are 1066!'" *Republican News*. 1 Jul. 1978: 3.

———. "I Once Had a Life." *An Phoblacht/Republican News*. 17 Mar. 1979: 2.

———. "On the Blanket." *Republican News*. 7 Jan. 1978: 6.

———. "On the Blanket." *Republican News*. 1 Apr. 1978: 2.

———. *One Day in My Life*. Dublin and Cork: Mercier, 1983.

———. "One of Those Days That Never Ends." *Republican News*. 10 June 1978: 3.

———. *Prison Poems*. Ed. Danny Morrison. Dublin: Sinn Féin, Oct. 1981.

———. "The Rhythm of Time." [*sic*] *An Phoblacht/Republican News*. 29 Jun. 1981: 16.

———. "An Scéal." *An Phoblacht/Republican News*. 10 Dec. 1981: 10.

———. *Skylark Sing Your Lonely Song*. Dublin and Cork: Mercier, 1982.

———. "The Window of My Mind." *Republican News*. 25 Nov. 1978: 7.

———. *Writings from Prison*. Boulder: Roberts Rinehart, 1997.

———. "The Writings of Bobby Sands." *An Phoblacht/Republican News*. 21 Mar. 1981: 6–8.

———. *The Writings of Bobby Sands*. Belfast [?]: Sinn Féin [?], Mar. 1981.

———. *The Writings of Bobby Sands*. Dublin: Sinn Féin POW Department, Apr. 1981.

———. *The Writings of Bobby Sands*. Hamilton, Ontario: Irish Prisoner of War Committee, 1981.

———. *The Writings of Bobby Sands*. New York: Irish Northern Aid I.P.O.W Department, May 1981.

Sarup, Madan. *An Introductiory Guide to Post-structuralism and Post-modernism*. 2nd edition. Athens: Georgia University Press, 1993.

Scarry, Elaine. *The Body in Pain*. New York: Oxford University Press, 1985.

Schulze-Engler, Frank. "Changing Spaces: Globalization, Migration, and the Post-colonial Transition." *Borderlands: Negotiating Boundaries in Post-colonial Writing*. Ed. Monika Reif-Hulser. Amsterdam: Rodopi, 1999. 3–15.

Sedlak, Werner. "Ways of Appropriating Space in South African Prison Memoirs from Ruth First to Nelson Mandela." *Borderlands: Negotiating Boundaries in Post-colonial Writing*. Ed. Monika Reif-Hulser. Amsterdam: Rodopi, 1999. 189–204.

Seeley, Eddie. "An Teanga." *An Glór Gafa/The Captive Voice* 3.2 (Summer 1991): 20.

Shelley, Percy Bysshe, "From A Defence of Poetry," *The Norton Anthology of English Literature*. Vol. 2A. 7th edition. Ed. M.H. Abrams et al. New York: W.W. Norton, 2000. 790–802.

Sluka, Jefferey. *Hearts and Minds, Water and Fish*. New York: JAI Press, 1989.

Some Mother's Son. Dir. Terry George. Perf. Helen Mirren, Fionnuala Flanigan. Castle Rock, 1996.

Spivak, Gayatri Chakravorty. "Can the Subaltern Speak?" *The Post-colonial Studies Reader*. Ed. Bill Ashcroft, Gareth Griffiths, and Helen Tiffin. London: Routledge, 1995. 24–28.

"The Struggle." Editorial. *An Glór Gafa/The Captive Voice* 2.1 (Spring 1990): 3.

Tanselle, G. Thomas. *Textual Criticism and Scholarly Editing*. Charlottesville: University Press of Virginia, 1990.

Taylor, Peter. *Beating the Terrorists? Interrogation in Omagh, Gough and Castlereagh*. Harmondsworth: Penguin, 1980.

Tedlock, Barbara. "The Clown's Way." *Teachings from the American Earth: Indian Religion and Philosophy*. Ed. Dennis and Barbara Tedlock. New York: Liveright, 1992.

"Ten Years On." *An Glór Gafa/The Captive Voice* 3.2 (Summer 1991): 2–4.

"Thoughts from H Block by a Blanket Man's [*sic*] Brother." *Republican News*. 10 June 1978: 3.

Tobin, Michael. "Ireland's Valiant Women." *Republican News*. 31 Aug. 1974: 4.

Tompkins, Jane. "Indians." *Ways of Reading: An Anthology for Writers*. Ed. David Bartholomae and Anthony Petrosky. 3rd edition. Boston: Bedford, 1993. 584–601.

Tuma, Keith, ed. "Introduction." *The Oxford Anthology of Twentieth-Century British and Irish Verse*. New York: Oxford University Press, 2001.

"Tuso." "An Insider's View from Outside." *An Glór Gafa/The Captive Voice* 6.1 (Summer 1994): 4–5.

Walsh. Roseleen. "Imprisoned Lovers." Manuscript. 1998.

———. "Imprisoned Lovers." *Aiming Higher*... Belfast: Glandore, 1999. 32.

———. Interview, conducted at Andersontown, Belfast, 24 Jul. 1998.

———. "Interview with Martina Anderson." *Slí na mBán* ed. Melissa Thompson. 6 Oct 1999. Accessed 29 Sept. 2006. <http://www.tallgirlshorts.net/marymary/roseleen.html >

———. *Sticks and Stones*. Belfast: Glendore, 1999.

———. "To Aine." *Aiming Higher*... Belfast: Glandore, 1999. 37.

———. "To Aine." Manuscript. 1998.

———. "To My Silent Church." Manuscript. 1998.

———. "To My Silent Church." *Aiming Higher*... Belfast: Glandore, 1999. 33.

———. "To You." *Republican News*. 31 Aug. 1974: 4.

Whalen, Lachlan. "Caliban as Taig: *The Tempest* and British Colonialism in Ireland." *Proceedings of the Sixth Annual Northern Plains Conference on Earlier British Literature*. Ed. Linda Kruckenberg and W. Andrew Alexander. Wayne: Wayne State Press, 1998. 41–49.

Wilson, Nina. Letter to editor. *An Glór Gafa/The Captive Voice* 3.2 (Summer 1991): 24.

"Women Join Hunger-Strike." *An Phoblacht/Republican News*. 22 Nov. 1980: 1–2.

Women POWs. "Women and the National Struggle." *An Glór Gafa/The Captive Voice* 1.1 (Autumn 1989): 10.

Women POWs (Maghaberry). "Big Pat," *An Glór Gafa/The Captive Voice* 2.2 (Summer 1990): 7.

Wordsworth, William. "Preface to *Lyrical Ballads*." *The Norton Anthology of English Literature*. Vol. 2A. 7th edition. Ed. M.H. Abrams et al. New York: W.W. Norton, 2000. 239–251. Yeats, William Butler. *Essays and Introductions*. New York: Macmillan, 1961.

———. *Selected Poems and Three Plays*. Ed. M.L. Rosenthal. New York: Collier, 1986.

———., ed. *The Oxford Book of Modern Verse*. New York: Oxford University Press, 1937.

———. "The Tower," *Oxford Anthology of British and Irish Poetry*. Ed. Keith Tuma. New York: Oxford University Press, 2001. 43–47.

Index